HATE INC.

HATE INC.

WHY TODAY'S MEDIA
MAKES US DESPISE ONE ANOTHER

MATT TAIBBI

OR Books

New York · London

Typeset by Lapiz Digital Services.

Visit our website at www.orbooks.com

ISBN 978-1-68219-407-2 paperback
ISBN 978-1-68219-801-8 e-book

CONTENTS

Propaganda seeks to create in the public a chronic sense of crisis.

—Christopher Lasch

PREFACE: A UTOPIA OF DIVISION

I began writing *Hate Inc.* at the outset of the Donald Trump years, after watching dramatic changes in journalism during the 2015-2016 presidential election campaign. At the time, the decision by mainstream media outlets to abandon longstanding "objective" approaches in favor of a more openly adversarial take on the Donald was pitched to us in the media business as an ethical decision, a necessity for a reporting corps that needed to "do better" to save democracy.

I wasn't sure that was what was really going on, bothered by the fact that the new strategies left our business superficially polarized in terms of politics, but more unified in terms of commercial approach. Stations like Fox and MSNBC now served as perfect strategic mirrors of one another. Both networks identified core audiences and fed them constant doses of affirming content.

Essentially, news companies were commoditizing Trump, with Fox packaging simplified stories for Trump fans and stations like MSNBC packaging the same kind of content for #Resistance viewers. While smaller traditional newspapers were dying off by the thousand, old "objectivity" icons like *The New York Times* were moving to a new financial model that depended largely on recruiting and retaining digital subscribers—the *Times* would have six million by mid-2020— that incentivized a sports-like format of stoking fan bases. The press became rival cheering sections, and nuance disappeared as an unwanted product.

Whether the motivation was political or financial, the reality by late 2016 and early 2017 was that most commercial news organizations spoke exclusively to one "side" or another. The two-teams approach pushed Republicans and Democrats farther apart as they were less and less exposed to the same information.

The setup led to a four-year nightmare that unspooled like a protracted breakup, with America's two halves increasingly estranged and despising one another, ending finally in the infamous Capitol riot of January 2021. That last chapter of the Trump presidency will be the subject of countless autopsies, with questions about how Americans consume information playing a central role. After all, the "insurrection" was triggered in large part by deceptions about a stolen election. It was a news story about news, gone wrong. How did we get here?

The Capitol fiasco was the apotheosis of the *Hate Inc.* era, revealing a country driven to literal combat over frustrations accrued in separate factual universes. Senate majority leader Mitch McConnell—himself an notorious double-talker and avoider-of-truths—accurately summed us up as a country just before the fracas. We are, he said:

> Drifting apart into two separate tribes, with a separate set of facts and separate realities, with nothing in common except our hostility towards each other and mistrust for the few national institutions that we all still share.

The riot marked the end of a four-year period of transformation, in which the left-oriented and right-oriented media ecosystems switched roles. Both continued to speak exclusively to their own demographics, and used hyper-provocative language to describe the offenses of the opposite demographic. But right-wing media splintered, relying on Trump himself to serve as polarizer-in-chief. Rival media brands united and innovated striking new methods of manufacturing outrage.

In the Bush years, the conservative political universe was distinguished by unity of purpose. From Tom Delay's Congress to the Bush/Cheney White House to Rupert Murdoch's Fox News to the bulk of the country's megachurches, conservative institutions functioned as a single organism. Collectively, they produced identical rhetoric about the iniquity of everyone from Muslims to campus leftists, environmentalists, and immigrants, and until the Iraq War went south they looked poised to rule America for a generation, thanks in part to ironclad discipline of message.

By the time Trump came along, discipline was a fading memory. Trump was seldom in perfect sync either with traditional Republican media like Fox, or his own White House press office. Moments in which all three pushed the same message were rare as pearls. The disconnect between Trump and his official spokesteam often played out like an intentional slapstick routine.

For example, when Kayleigh McEnany said in July 2020 that Trump was tested multiple times per day for Covid-19, Trump himself was saying he was tested on average once every two days, and he "didn't know" if he'd ever been tested more than once in a day. When Trump actually got the disease, both Trump and his doctor were proclaiming he was "doing very well" at the exact moment his press team was saying his health situation was "very concerning." And so on.

"I might as well be a member of the public," a nameless Trump aide whispered acidly, to a reporter.

The *real* White House press office was Trump's Twitter feed, which flowed from Trump's head at all hours and often contradicted not just other conservative institutions, but itself. The feed had 88 million followers at the moment it was shut down by Twitter in January 2021, and far outpaced traditional Republican mouthpieces like Fox as a source of aggrandizing, inciting, or factually wrong statements.

Trump would say, for instance, that Joe Biden "apologized" for opposing his policy restricting travel from China, or that he'd shattered "100% of the ISIS Caliphate," or that 80 percent of the rioters in Minneapolis were from out of state (a propaganda trope that dates back to the days of the sixties race protests). In the summer of 2020, he veered into speculations about "MASSIVE FRAUD AND ABUSE" and "cheating, forgery, and theft of ballots" in the coming election, messaging that blended with a growing online movement that posited a grand conspiracy of elites, led by a corrupted Democratic Party.

Some thought the Internet would cure cancer by uniting great minds in instant transglobal communication. The actual endgame involved sites that merged porn and political thought. 4chan is bananas, an online massage parlor where white guys tell Black jokes and onanize to *Mein Kampf.* A typical 4chan post is a picture of Alexandria Ocasio-Cortez, next to a question: "Are there women who aren't nagging c—ts . . . ? Have they ever shut up? How do you make them, short of beating them or divorce?"

The conspiratorial connective tissue on a lot of these sites, ostensibly about an insider named Q with access to the White House, reporting on Trump's secret war against a cabal of child-importing pedophile elitist Democrats who may also worship Satan, was insane and hard to follow. It was also mostly beside the point. The core parts of the story were more like emotional themes, i.e. "leftist elites bent on destroying us are cheating their way to despotic rule." The specifics were increasingly interchangeable, a great fit for Trump's kaleidoscope mind.

As with porn, the customers didn't show up for the scripts. The payoff was in pure furious spewing, politics fused with forbidden impulses—rape, murder, whatever—in a gurgling mass of "Us. vs. Them" energy. The urges rising from this collective Id are often denounced as populism, a ludicrous betrayal of the term's original meaning. Whatever the real term for this "movement," Trump knew how to talk to it. We saw this from the beginning of his run.

Back in August of 2015, two Trump-supporting brothers in Boston beat up and urinated on a homeless man they believed to be an immigrant. Reportedly they said during the beating, "Trump is right, all these illegals should be deported."

Then-candidate Trump's first response was to call the incident a "shame." Then he said: "I will say, the people that are following me are very passionate. They love this country. They want this country to be great again. But they are very passionate. I will say that."

Steve and Scott Leader, the Massholes who beat up the sleeping man, ended up getting two and a half years.

It was the future Capitol riot in microcosm. Trump was expert at egging on crowds with rhetorically coy constructions: "I mean it, but I don't mean it." At one event, he might reference the QAnon saying, "calm before the storm" while being photographed with military leaders. Alternatively, he'd say "they love me very much" when asked about the Q movement, or, just like the Boston incident, "they love our country."

The bulk of the most extreme messaging about movements like "Stop the Steal" took place in the equivalent of dark pools: message boards, chats, Facebook groups, etc. Icons of Republican media like Fox were often followers to the party, beaten in the rush for ever-crazier conspiratorial explanations by outlets like

OAN and Newsmax, which were less squeamish about catering to these audiences horny for extreme culture war.

Stations like Fox improbably became sometimes-dissenters to the *Hate Inc.* formula during the Trump years, presenting points of view sure to disappoint core audiences. One of its top anchors, Chris Wallace, was a constant critic of Trump's, and the station played a huge role in what Trumpists later denounced as conspiracy by calling the Arizona presidential vote early. In fact, it was Fox's "early" call at 11:20 p.m. that triggered the first Trump tantrum that night. Meanwhile, Tucker Carlson, a much-loathed figure in blue America, was denounced in late November by Trump fans for pooh-poohing the stolen election tales, saying Trump attorney Sidney Powell had not provided evidence.

Trump, especially in his final period, pushed polarizing rhetoric to places where the commercial conservative press was not willing to follow, leading to profit-disrupting scenes of real intramural disagreement. Fox lost 6 percent of its audience in November alone as Trump urged followers to move to rival sources like OAN. The post-Trump conservative movement was rudderless, half-underground, and almost totally incoherent, united on only one question: its loathing for the cultural mainstream on the other side, which increasingly appeared as the united front conservatives used to be.

***

The blue-state media landscape once featured a broad-ish diversity of opinions. In the Bush years especially, online media created many new institutional homes for left-leaning audiences, especially for people who identified as more progressive than traditional Democrats.

The *Huffington Post, The Young Turks,* and *Daily Kos* won audience as more strident opponents of the Iraq invasion and promoters of ideas like single-payer health care. They joined existing publications like *Mother Jones* and *The Nation* to create a more labor-friendly, less militaristic counterweight to the Clintonian centrism that reigned at larger papers like *The New York Times.* In the Obama years, after the revelations of whistleblowers like Chelsea Manning and Edward Snowden, *The Intercept* appeared as yet another oppositional source, applying pressure on issues of war, privacy, and surveillance especially.

When Trump won, the distinctions between these outlets vanished almost overnight. Content increasingly was organized around furious opposition to Trump. The theme of unending crisis—not just crisis but *emergency*, a distinction expressed by news agencies via blaring chyrons screaming descriptors like BREAKING—was central to the new coverage concept. The hyper-intense tone was a deliberate strategy. A slow news day was understood as normalizing Trump's presence in the White House. It was not politically possible for nothing to be terribly wrong, even for a moment. This had to be felt in the voices of newsreaders, which meant fewer sunny asides, fewer cat-in-tree stories, fewer one-liner-laden tosses to weathermen, and—more crises.

Nearly all of institutional America joined in the howling section, from Hollywood to Wall Street to Silicon Valley to NATO and the intelligence community. Trump was described by all in tones remarkably similar to coverage of the likes of Saddam Hussein, Slobodan Milošević, and Manuel Noriega. For the first time, America's own president was in the infamous "Hitler of the month club," that union of adversaries of the American state battered in our media until the public assented to invasion or whatever policy objective was being sought against them at the time.

News in the Trump years became a narrative drama, with each day advancing a tale of worsening political emergency, driven by subplots involving familiar casts of characters, in the manner of episodic television. It worked, but news directors and editors hit a stumbling block. If you cover everything like there's no tomorrow, what happens when there is, in fact, a tomorrow?

The innovation was to use banner headlines to saturate news cycles, often to the exclusion of nearly any other news, before moving to the next controversy so quickly that mistakes, misquotes, or rhetorical let-downs were memory-holed.

The American Napoleon generated controversies at such a fantastic rate that stations like CNN and MSNBC (and Fox too) were able to keep ratings high by moving from mania to mania, hyping stories on the way up but not always following them down. The moment the narrative premise of any bombshell started to fray, the next story in line was bumped to the front.

News outlets paid off old editorial promises with new headlines: Ponzi journalism.

This technique of using the next bombshell story to push the last one down a memory-hole—call it *Bombholing*—needed a polarized audience to work.

As surveys by organizations like the Pew Center showed, the different target demographics in Trump's America increasingly did not communicate with one another. Democrats by 2020 were 91 percent of the *New York Times* audience and 95 percent of MSNBC's, while Republicans were 93 percent of Fox viewers. When outlets overreached factually, it was possible, if not likely, that the original target audience would never learn the difference.

This reduced the incentive to be careful. Audiences devoured bombshells even when aware on a subconscious level that they might not hold up to scrutiny. If a story turned out to be incorrect, that was okay. News was now more about underlying narratives audiences felt were true and important. For conservatives, Trump was saving America from a conspiracy of elites. For "liberal" audiences, Trump was trying to assume dictatorial power, and the defenders of democracy were trying to stop him.

A symbiosis developed. Where audiences once punished media companies for mistakes, now they rewarded them for serving up the pure heroin of shaky, first-draft-like blockbusters. They wanted to be in the trenches of information discovery. Audiences were choosing powerful highs over lasting ones.

Moreover, if after publication another shoe dropped in the form of mitigating information, audiences were disinterested, even angry. Those updates were betrayals of the entertainment contract, like continuity errors. Companies soon learned there was a downside to once-mandatory ethical practices. Silent edits at newspapers became common, and old standards like the italicized editor's note at the bottom of the page letting you know this or that story had been "updated" began to disappear.

The political impact of all this was that the news watcher in the Trump years became more addicted to the experience of being outraged, while retaining less about specific reasons for outrage. Audiences remembered some big stories and big themes, but stopped digesting each story on its own, rarely bothering to look back at the meaning of various manias after they'd died down.

As George Orwell understood when he created the "memory hole" concept in *1984*, an institution that can obliterate memory can control history. In the Trump era, news audiences volunteered to stop the disobedient act of remembering. They brought a pure, virginal belief to watching news, and agreed to unquestioningly accept any new versions of the past put forward.

This was *Hate Inc.* brought to its logical conclusion. Fox and MSNBC already knew how to monetize anger by setting audiences against one another. The innovation of the Trump era was companies learned they could operate on a sort of editorial margin, borrowing credibility for unproven stories from audiences themselves, who gave permission to play loose with facts by gobbling up anonymously-sourced exposes that tickled their outrage centers. Mistakes became irrelevant. In a way, they were no longer understood as mistakes.

Conservative audiences had already long ago been turned into story addicts, and were used to having the rhetorical ante constantly upped, making them susceptible to tall-tale artists like Trump and Internet fairy tales like Q.

Blue-state audiences had to be trained to think this way. Coverage of Trump was so constant and full-throated that all other topics stopped having news value. The first stories to be memory-holed were the ones that preceded Trump's entrance into politics: war crimes in Iraq, drone killings, financial inequality (destined to be re-christened a mockable fictional problem called "economic insecurity"), the failure to close Guantanamo Bay, lack of enforcement of white-collar crime, and a dozen other things.

Bombholing generated errors at a fantastic rate. There's no way to truly understand the depth of how badly this phenomenon infected media in 2016-2020 without going through each story step-by-step, but even a partial list of stories that dominated news cycles but later fell apart is instructive.

For instance, before Trump became president, *Yahoo!* cited a "well-placed Western intelligence source" in telling us that former Trump aide Carter Page was a "possible back channel" between the Trump campaign and the Kremlin. Years later it would be revealed that the "Western intelligence source" was actually ex-spy Christopher Steele, a paid researcher of the Clinton campaign, who provided the never-confirmed information to authorities. He was also the source of the "pee tape" and countless other bombshell themes.

The *Yahoo!* story itself ended up being used as part of an improper warrant application for secret FISA surveillance on Page. Writer Michael Isikoff told me he later came to understand that Steele's report was "flawed," and moreover that he didn't know at the time he wrote the report that Steele was working for Clinton.

In late October, 2016, *Slate also* told audiences of a mysterious server tied to the Russian Alfa-Bank that had been communicating with the Trump organization. Over the course of years, dozens of stories came out of this "revelation." Significantly, most were published well after the FBI determined in early 2017 that there were no links between Trump and Alfa Bank, which means many official sources stayed quiet as news they knew to be false circulated. The latter fact came out in the report of Justice Department Inspector General Michael Horowitz.

In the early Trump years, reporters were very concerned with the origin story of Trump's conspiracy with Russia. When papers like *The New York Times* were told that a Trump aide named George Papadopoulos triggered the probe after repeating a tale from a mysterious Maltese professor about the Russians having "dirt" on Hillary Clinton, Papadopoulos became front page news as the Patient Zero of the conspiracy. The first *Times* story on this figure came out in October of 2017.

Years later, Congress would release testimony from then-deputy FBI director Andrew McCabe to the effect that the Bureau concluded as early as August, 2016—over a year before the *Times* story—that evidence "didn't particularly indicate" that Papadopoulos had any links to any Russians. In fact, McCabe testified that the reason the FBI moved on to Carter Page as a target was that Papadopoulos was understood to be a dead-end (Page proved to be a similar dead-end).

Yet Papadopoulos was the predicate for the FBI's "Crossfire Hurricane" probe into Trump's relationship with Russia, the probe that became the Mueller investigation. Blue-state audiences were essentially never told that this investigation was at best grounded in erroneous information.

On the day the Horowitz report blew up the pee tape, the Carter Page story, and countless other once-hot scandals, the front page of the *New York Times* read REPORT DEBUNKS ANTI-TRUMP PLOT IN RUSSIA INQUIRY. Another headline on the same page noted that Trump possibly faced two impeachment articles, "Ukrainegate" by then being the more urgent breaking news fixation.

This showed the whole *Bombhole* formula. A series of inaccurate stories began running in 2016, introducing audiences to the idea that candidate Trump had an elaborate, secret relationship with the Kremlin. When these stories were later debunked, in the context of a report that also detailed an improper (and perhaps illegal) surveillance campaign, the press ignored that angle and quietly reported the Trump-Russia investigation had been further legitimized, while keeping the bulk of audience attention on the new bombshell topic in Ukraine.

There were more mundane screwups not directly related to Trump, like the colossal error in the *New York Times* "Caliphate" podcast. The paper of record did an entire series based upon the storytelling of a Canadian Muslim who claimed he had committed atrocities for ISIS, including crucifixions. But when Abu Huzayfah was arrested by Canadian authorities for perpetrating a hoax, the *Times* refused to take the full hit, instead claiming that their series had in part been about exploring whether or not Huzayfah's story was true. Another story involving a group of high-school-age Trump supporters from Covington, Kentucky who supposedly accosted a Native American man in Washington, was massively misreported, creating a huge swell of cultural resentment among conservatives, while mainstream audiences mostly didn't hear the story's flip side.

The extreme danger from the beginning of the Trump era was not just that the White House might be occupied by an unfit person, but that American institutions might follow him into further disrepute. This happened with institutional media, which responded to a manic, hyperbolic, unreliable president by taking on those same qualities. Their permanent crisis doubled as a political campaign to prevent Trump's "normalization" and a scheme to boost profits by addicting audiences to a never-ending narrative of moral mania.

To keep it up, elite media made the same request of audiences that Trump regularly made to his own fans, that what was said and done ten minutes ago be forgotten in a world where only the present mattered. Memory became taboo, present conflict the only allowable orientation: a utopia of division.

HATE INC.

NOTE TO READERS

Normally, an author doesn't tell you about the changes made along the way to a completed book.

In this case I have to, because this book was originally published online, in serial form, at a still-existing site for subscribers: Taibbi.Substack.Com. Those subscribers know *Hate Inc.* was originally called *The Fairway*, and that I changed my mind about the title midway through the book.

It wasn't the only change. Originally, this book was intended to be a re-thinking of the classic work of media criticism by Edward Herman and Noam Chomsky, *Manufacturing Consent*. In fact, the original title of the book was going to be *Manufacturing Discontent*.

I've carried three books with me everywhere throughout my travels over the years (I've traveled a lot in my career as a reporter, living as far away as Mongolia and Uzbekistan). Those were *Fear and Loathing: On the Campaign Trail '72* by Hunter S. Thompson, *Scoop* by Evelyn Waugh, and *Manufacturing Consent*.

Roughly speaking, the first book by Thompson is a great work of journalism, the second, *Scoop,* is the perfect parody of journalism, and *Manufacturing Consent* is an academic warning to reporters like myself, describing all the ways in which journalism can be counterproductive, serve power, and generally fail.

My original idea was to reconfigure that warning to reporters of my generation, who have far different professional and financial pressures than the ones Chomsky and Herman wrote about in the seventies and eighties.

As I was surprised to learn in the course of interviewing him for this book, Chomsky knew quite a few reporters, and this informed his work. But neither he nor Edward Herman (whose idea it was to write a media-themed book) ever worked in a newsroom, or sat down to write a lede with a deadline twenty minutes off.

I wanted to stress the personal experience I had. But when I sat down to write what I'd hoped would be something with the intellectual gravitas of *Manufacturing Consent,* I found decades of more mundane frustrations pouring out onto the page, obliterating a clinical examination.

The book quickly became more confessional than academic study. It's about the invisible pressures of the business I've been in for nearly thirty years now. Commercial media has always been sensationalistic. We were never not encouraged to aim content at your outrage center. We were always eyeball-hunting.

I know this because I was hired to do this work, over and over. My commercial niche, in fact, was the vitriolic essay that got people spitting mad, or poked fun at someone audiences hated.

I was the Triumph the Insult Comic Dog of journalism. I actually won the National Magazine Award for commentary, the highest award you can get in the magazine business, for a *Rolling Stone* article about Mike Huckabee called "My Favorite Nut Job" that called the Arkansas governor a "Christian goofball of the highest order" who resembled an "oversized Muppet." There is and was great demand in the business for "takedown artists," provided you're taking down the right people.

I never wanted to be a reporter. My heroes were comic novelists, and I believed what Hunter S. Thompson once said, that "the best fiction is truer than any journalism." The career I wanted was one producing books that did nothing but provide enjoyment, books that were like close friends you could lean on—what Raymond Chandler's books have meant to me.

But I turned out to be a terrible fiction writer, and defaulted to this work. I always had an uncomfortable relationship with the business, and at some point I made nearly all of the mistakes you'll read about in this book.

In fact, part of what started to pour out when I wrote these chapters was the self-loathing that came with knowing I'd tossed so much red meat to political audiences. Getting plaudits from liberal audiences for writing splenetic features about Mike Huckabee or Fred Thompson or Michelle Bachmann is like a comedian doing a routine in front of a bunch of potsmokers—you can't tell if the laughs are real.

More to the point, after eight years of writing about the financial services industry in the wake of the 2008 crash, I was more and more tuned into the idea that partisan politics is a bit of a con. A lot of very serious social problems (like the failure to stop mass fraud in the mortgage markets) have completely bipartisan roots, but in the press we regularly sell people on a simplified image of politics, of two parties in complete conflict about everything. If one of those sides was yours, you seldom saw it besmirched by criticism.

Did I have a part in that? There was an undeniable gravitational pull toward the *Red v. Blue* narrative, and I wrote mainly for Blue audiences. But at the reporting level, once you got into the weeds of almost any serious issue it always seemed a lot more complicated: military contracting corruption, money laundering, campaign finance fraud, financial deregulation, torture, drone assassination, you name it.

I started to believe we keep people away from the complexities of these issues, by creating distinct audiences of party zealots who drink in more and more intense legends about one another. We started to turn the ongoing narrative of the news into something like a religious contract, in which the idea was not just to make you mad, but to keep you mad, whipped up in a state of devotional anger. Even in what conservatives would call the "liberal" media, we used blunt signals to create audience solidarity. We started to employ anti-intellectualism on a scale I'd never seen before, and it ran through much of the available content.

Once, a reporter could work his or her whole life without really being a known quantity to audiences. The rare exception was someone like Thompson, who made his darkest inner dialogues part of the story. As his *Rolling Stone* colleague Tim Crouse noted in the campaign diary *The Boys on the Bus,* Thompson was alone among reporters in not having to explain to his spouse what the trail was like when he got home. She already knew from reading his articles. Even his most private asides were in print.

But everybody else in the business got to keep his or her personal character private to a degree. Insofar as you picked a team, your team was "the press," an entity separate from either party, with its own power and own institutional concerns.

A generation ago, you would never have seen members of the media arguing for enhanced censorship powers and media regulation, as we've seen in the last year or so, in the controversy surrounding "fake news." You also wouldn't have seen so many members of the press so openly invested in political outcomes.

Ironically, the kind of open devotion Thompson made famous in *Campaign Trail: '72*—when he pined for George McGovern and crisscrossed the country arguing for his election to the White House, like Kafka's Land Surveyor searching for redemption in the corridors of *The Castle*—has now become standard in both "left" and "right" media.

The difference is Thompson was pining for a poetic idealist vision of a better world that (as it turned out) never had a chance of becoming reality. Meanwhile the bulk of reporters today are soldiers for one or the other group of long-entrenched political interests in Washington. They're not just not idealists, they're anti-idealists.

They even have a word to describe the crime of idealism, calling it "purity" or "purity-testing." The current party line on my side of the media wall is that "purists" helped elect Donald Trump by undercutting the campaign of Hillary Clinton, and such people are frowned upon as enemies and deviationists. We've even made a cottage industry out of Soviet-style words for deviationism, terms like "false-balancer," "horseshoe theorist," "neo-Naderite," and the Soviet classic, "whataboutist."

My dirty little secret is that I've never particularly cared about politics. My personal religion is neither right nor left but absurdist. I think the world is basically ridiculous and terrible, but also beautiful. We try our best, or sometimes we don't, but either way, we typically fail in the end.

Humanity to me is the Three Stooges, and gets funnier the more it attempts to deny it. I don't think this all the time, but it's a guiding principle. I vote, and am involved in small ways with a few activist causes, but I try not to take the circus so seriously that it distracts from the more important business of being a dad, a husband, etc.

Under torture I would say one party is better than the other, and I will even give money or volunteer if asked, but this is different from energetic advocacy. I doubt this is an uncommon view. Covering campaigns, you meet a lot of people who care more about their cats than elections (they are never quoted in campaign stories, of course). Most people don't vote, which I've found is most often an expression of disgust or sarcastic indifference toward the range of political choices offered. I don't go that far, but I do try to keep enough distance from politics to keep it in perspective.

Again, this attitude, which allowed me to write with enthusiasm about the candidacy of Barack Obama but critically of his failure to enforce laws governing Wall Street crime, was once considered proper and healthy for a journalist. Today, it doesn't fit within either of the currently allowed categories of thought in commercial media.

Worse, while the foibles of the press once mostly seemed amusing (I still chuckle with envy at *New York Times* columnist Thomas Friedman writing a smash bestseller called *The World Is Flat* based upon the faulty premise that a flat world is more interconnected than a round one) I began a few years ago to be conscious of the business drifting toward something truly villainous.

In 2016 especially, news reporters began to consciously divide and radicalize audiences. The cover was that we were merely "calling out" our divisive new president, Donald Trump. But from where I sat, the press was now working in collaboration with Trump, acting in his simplistic mirror image, creating a caricatured oppositional demographic and feeding it content. As Trump rode to the White House, we rode to massive profits. The only losers were the American people, who were now more steeped in hate than ever.

I struggled with this as a citizen, but like all reporters I had the additional problem of having to maintain a public byline while working through it. My initial instinct was to hide, and maybe get myself assigned to cover something like the oil and gas beat until it all blew over. An attentive reader will notice I've spent the last few years trying to cover a variety of cross-partisan topics, from drones to the attempted audit of the Department of Defense, a thirty-year-old story.

In the end, though, it hasn't worked, and one of the ways I've tried to work through the confusion has been writing this book. This has forced me to look back at history to see if the change in industry approach has been as dramatic as it seemed in real time. Had I imagined it?

I learned many things I never knew about the business, and interviewed colleagues with fascinating stories of their own about the changes. It turns out a lot of us are quietly struggling with the same issues. In different ways, we've been unsure of how to toe the line between traditional notions of distance and the new pressures to serve up mountains of highly politicized, vituperative content.

I have, of course, worried this book will not make sense to either of our two reigning brands of political partisan. Democrats may react with more anger than Republicans. The Appendix explaining Rachel Maddow's presence on the cover may do little to alleviate this. Comparing MSNBC to Fox in any way will be deemed unforgivable.

But it's not a hot take. The subject here is the phasing out of independent journalism, replacing it with deeply politicized programming on both "sides." Which "side" is better is immaterial: neither approach is journalism.

Fox may have more noxious politics, but MSNBC has become the same kind of consumer product, a political safe space for viewers in ironclad alignment with a political party. If you tune in now, you won't see any content critical of Democrats, which is exactly the intellectual weakness we used to see and denounce in Fox viewers. There will come a time, guaranteed, when Americans pine for a powerful, neither-party-aligned news network to help make sense of things.

Conservatives meanwhile will probably hate the book for a variety of reasons, beginning with my natural antipathy for Republican politics, which is fine. To people of both persuasions, I would say, this book is intended to help start a conversation about how much of our disdain for each other is real, and how much of it is a product of the media machine.

I despair at the blame-a-thon of modern political media and wonder all the time if I didn't help construct this new attitude with the flamboyant insults I put in print for years. Worse, today's media debate has left its sense of humor behind, and we now argue even minor issues as life-or-death matters, despite not even knowing each other. People who would certainly engage in courteous chats at their kids' birthday parties freely trade horrific threats on Twitter. It's insane.

We have representative democracy precisely so we can let other people do our vitriolic arguing for us. It's true that the system is corrupted by money, among other things, but I wonder why we don't take more advantage of this one social service we do actually get in America. Much of it must be our fault, i.e. the media's fault. So to conservatives and liberals both, the idea of this book is really an attempt to help you sort out how much of your anger and fear is real, and how much of the upset in your head comes from people like me, pushing your buttons for cash.

When this book comes out in physical form, readers will notice it's been written over a period of time in the style of periodical journalism. That's because it was being published, online, as I wrote each chapter. Those reading this as an e-book will find the links still work, and I hope to add a few features over time, including perhaps a parlor trick I've worked on over the years that involves marking up the deceptive claptrap on the front page of a newspaper to a stopwatch.

For now, however, this is the form of *Hate Inc.*, a book about a business that at its best informs us and makes us better citizens, but of late has become an instrument of tragedy, dividing us all and filling our lives with pessimism and mistrust. Fixing it will be difficult. But there are secrets to protecting yourself from it, and I hope you'll find some of them here.

INTRODUCTION

I grew up in the media. In seventies Massachusetts, my father took a job at a fledgling ABC affiliate called WCVB-TV. These being the glory days of local television news, my childhood ended up being a lot like the movie *Anchorman*.

I was regularly exposed to the plaid suits, terrible facial hair, and oversized microphone logos the Will Ferrell movie made famous. There are photos of my father in a yellow bow tie and muttonchops.

More seriously, Channel 5 and journalism became as intimately a part of my identity growing up as, say, baseball must have been for Barry Bonds. I was fascinated by my father's work.

He had a ritual he called the "phone attack." When he came home at night, he would pour himself a drink, light up a Camel unfiltered, and start going through a giant Rolodex, pulling names out at random. Then he would dial his clunky rotary phone and call people to chat.

As a boy watching, I learned this lesson: sources are relationships that must be managed both when you're doing a story, and also when you're not. People need to feel like you're interested in their lives for their own sake, not just when you need something from them. Also: ask people about whatever they want to talk about, not about one thing in particular.

This is an investigative principle articulated well in another goofy movie comedy, *The Zero Effect*. As Holmesian detective Daryl Zero says:

When you go looking for something specific, your chances of finding it are very bad. Because of all the things in the world, you're only looking for one of them.

When you go looking for anything at all, your chances of finding it are very good.

There's a lesson in this for modern journalists who've been raised to eschew talking in favor of searching for links (a type of "research" in which you're really just confirming a point you've already decided to make). My father taught me reporting is not just about talking, but being willing to be surprised by what people say.

I thought I understood this and many other things about the journalism business at a young age. I even knew everything that "off the record" entails—really knew, as if it were a religious tenet—before I hit junior high. I thought I was an expert.

Then I read *Manufacturing Consent*.

The book came out in 1988 and I read it a year later, when I was nineteen. It blew my mind.

Along with the documentary *Hearts and Minds* (about the atrocities of the Vietnam War) and books like *Soul on Ice, In the Belly of the Beast,* and *The Autobiography of Malcolm X, Manufacturing Consent* taught me that some level of deception was baked into almost everything I'd ever been taught about modern American life.

I knew nothing about either of the authors, academics named Edward Herman and Noam Chomsky. It seemed odd that a book purporting to say so much about journalism could be written by non-journalists. Who were these people? And how could they claim to know anything about this business?

This was the middle of the George H. W. Bush presidency, still the rah-rah *Top Gun* eighties. Political earnestness was extremely uncool. America was awesome and hating on America was sad. Noam Chomsky was painted to me as the very definition of uncool, a leaden, hectoring bore.

But this wasn't what I found on the page. *Manufacturing Consent* is a dazzling book. True, like a lot of co-written books, and especially academic books, it's written in slow, grinding prose. But for its time, it was intellectually flamboyant, wild even.

The ideas in it radiated defiance. Once the authors in the first chapter laid out their famed propaganda model, they cut through the deceptions of the American state like a buzz saw.

The book's central idea was that censorship in the United States was not overt, but covert. The stage-managing of public opinion was "normally not accomplished by crude intervention" but by the keeping of "dissent and inconvenient information" outside permitted mental parameters: "within bounds and at the margins."

The key to this deception is that Americans, every day, see vigorous debate going on in the press. This deceives them into thinking propaganda is absent. *Manufacturing Consent* explains that the debate you're watching is choreographed. The range of argument has been artificially narrowed long before you get to hear it.

This careful sham is accomplished through the constant, arduous policing of a whole range of internal pressure points within the media business. It's a subtle, highly idiosyncratic process that you can stare at for a lifetime and nonetheless not see.

American news companies at the time didn't (and still don't) forbid the writing of unpatriotic stories. There are no editors who come blundering in, red pen in hand, wiping out politically dangerous reports, in the clumsy manner of Soviet Commissars.

Instead, in a process that is almost 100 percent unconscious, news companies simply avoid promoting dissenting voices. People who are questioners by nature, prodders, pains in the ass—all good qualities in reporting, incidentally—get weeded out by bosses, especially in the bigger companies. Advancement is meanwhile strongly encouraged among the credulous, the intellectually unadventurous, and the obedient.

As I would later discover in my own career, there are a lot of C-minus brains in the journalism business. A kind of groupthink is developed that permeates the upper levels of media organizations, and they send unconscious signals down the ranks.

Young reporters learn early on what is and is not permitted behavior. They learn to recognize, almost more by smell than reason, what is and is not a "good story."

Chomsky and Herman described this policing mechanism using the term "flak." Flak was defined as "negative responses to a media statement or program."

They gave examples in which corporate-funded think tanks like The Media Institute or the anti-communist Freedom House would deluge media organizations that ran the wrong kinds of stories with "letters, telegrams, phone calls, petitions, lawsuits" and other kinds of pressure.

What was the wrong kind of story? Here we learned of another part of the propaganda model, the concept of *worthy and unworthy victims*. Herman and Chomsky defined the premise as follows:

> *A propaganda system will consistently portray people abused in enemy states as worthy victims, whereas those treated with equal or greater severity by its own government or clients will be unworthy.*

Under this theory, a Polish priest murdered by communists in the Reagan years was a "worthy" victim, while rightist death squads in U.S.-backed El Salvador killing whole messes of priests and nuns around the same time was a less "worthy" story.

What Herman and Chomsky described was a system of informal social control, in which the propaganda aims of the state were constantly reinforced among audiences, using a quantity-over-quality approach.

Here and there you might see a dissenting voice, but the overwhelming institutional power of the media (and the infrastructure of think-tanks and politicians behind the private firms) carried audiences along safely down the middle of a surprisingly narrow political and intellectual canal.

One of their examples was Vietnam, where the American media was complicit in a broad self-abnegating effort to blame itself for "losing the war."

An absurd legend that survives today is that CBS anchor Walter Cronkite, after a two-week trip to Vietnam in 1968, was key in undermining the war effort.

Cronkite's famous "Vietnam editorial" derided "the optimists who have been wrong in the past," and villainously imparted that the military's rosy predictions of imminent victory were false. The more noble course, he implied, was to face reality, realize "we did the best we could" to defend democracy, and go home.

The Cronkite editorial sparked a "debate" that continues to the present.

On the right, it is said that we should have kept fighting in Vietnam, in spite of those meddling commies in the media.

The progressive take is that Cronkite was right, and we should have realized the war wasn't "winnable" years earlier. Doing so would have saved countless American lives, this thinking goes.

These two positions still define the edges of what you might call the "fairway" of American thought.

The uglier truth, that we committed genocide on a fairly massive scale across Indochina—ultimately killing at least a million innocent civilians by air in three countries—is pre-excluded from the history of that period.

Instead of painful national reconciliation surrounding episodes like Vietnam, Cambodia, Laos, the CIA-backed anti-communist massacres in places like Indonesia, or even the more recent horrors in Middle Eastern arenas like Afghanistan, Iraq, Syria, and Yemen, we mostly ignore narrative-ruining news about civilian deaths or other outrages.

A media that currently applauds itself for calling out the lies of Donald Trump (and they are lies) still uses shameful government-concocted euphemisms like "collateral damage." Our new "Democracy Dies in Darkness" churlishness has yet to reach the Pentagon, and probably never will.

In the War on Terror period, the press accepted blame for having lost the most recent big war and agreed to stop showing pictures of the coffins coming home (to say nothing of actual scenes of war deaths).

We also volunteered to reduce or play down stories about torture ("enhanced interrogation"), kidnapping ("rendition"), or assassination ("lethal action," or the "distribution matrix").

Even now, if these stories are covered, they're rarely presented in an alarmist tone. In fact, many "civilian casualties" stories are couched in language that focuses on how the untimely release of news of "collateral damage" may hinder the effort to win whatever war we're in at the time.

"After reports of civilian deaths, U.S. military struggles to defend air operations in war against militants," is a typical American newspaper headline.

Can you guess either the year or the war from that story? It could be 1968, or 2008. Or 2018.

As *Manufacturing Consent* predicted—with a nod to Orwell, maybe—the scripts in societies like ours rarely change.[1]

When it came time for me to enter the journalism business myself, I discovered that the Chomsky/Herman diagnosis was mostly right. Moreover, the academics proved prescient about future media deceptions like the Iraq War. Their model predicted that hideous episode in Technicolor.

But neither Herman nor Chomsky could have known, when they published their book in 1988, that the media business was going through profound change.

As it turned out, *Manufacturing Consent* was published just ahead of three massive revolutions. When I met and interviewed Chomsky for this book (see Appendix 2), we discussed these developments. They included:

1. The explosion of conservative talk radio and Fox-style news products. Using point of view rather than "objectivity" as commercial strategies, these stations presaged an atomization of the news landscape under which each consumer had an outlet somewhere to match his or her political beliefs. This was a major departure from the three-network pseudo-monopoly that dominated the *Manufacturing Consent* period, under which the country debated a commonly held set of facts.

2. The introduction of twenty-four-hour cable news stations, which shifted the emphasis of the news business. Reporters were suddenly trained to value breaking news, immediacy, and visual potential over import. Network "crashes"—relentless day-night coverage extravaganzas of a single hot story like the *Kursk* disaster or a baby thrown down a well, a type of journalism one TV producer I knew nicknamed "Shoveling Coal For Satan"—became the first examples of binge-watching. The relentless *now now now* grind of the twenty-four-hour cycle created in consumers a new kind of anxiety and addictive dependency, a need to know what was happening not just once or twice a day but every minute. This format would have significant consequences in the 2016 election in particular.

3. The development of the Internet, which was only just getting off the ground in 1988. It was thought it would significantly democratize the press landscape. But print and broadcast media soon began to be

---

1 In fact that piece is from the *Washington Post* in 2017, and it describes our "air campaign in Syria and Iraq."

distributed by just a handful of digital platforms. By the late 2000s and early 2010s, that distribution system had been massively concentrated. This created the potential for a direct control mechanism over the press that never existed in the *Manufacturing Consent* era. Moreover the development of social media would amplify the "flak" factor a thousandfold, accelerating conformity and groupthink in ways that would have been unimaginable in 1988.

Maybe the biggest difference involved an obvious historical change: the collapse of the Soviet Union.

One of the pillars of the "propaganda model" in the original *Manufacturing Consent* was that the media used anti-communism as an organizing religion.

The ongoing Cold War narrative helped the press use anti-communism as a club to batter heretical thinkers, who as luck would have it were often socialists. They even used it as a club to police people who weren't socialists (I would see this years later, when Howard Dean was asked a dozen times a day if he was "too left" to be a viable candidate).

But the fall of the Berlin Wall and the dissolution of the Soviet empire took a little wind out of the anti-communist religion. Chomsky and Herman addressed this in their 2002 update of *Manufacturing Consent,* in which they wrote:

> The force of anti-communist ideology has possibly weakened with the collapse of the Soviet Union and the virtual disappearance of socialist movements across the globe, but this is easily offset by the greater ideological force of the belief in the "miracle of the market..."

The collapse of the Soviets, and the weakening of anti-communism as an organizing principle, led to other changes in the media. *Manufacturing Consent* was in significant part a book about how that unseen system of informal controls allowed the press to organize the entire population behind support of particular objectives, many of them foreign policy objectives.

But the collapse of the Wall, coupled with those new commercial strategies being deployed by networks like Fox, created a new dynamic in the press.

Media companies used to seek out the broadest possible audiences. The dull third-person voice used in traditional major daily newspapers is not there for any moral or ethical reason, but because it was once believed that it most ably fulfilled the commercial aim of snatching as many readers/viewers as possible. The press is a business above all, and boring third-person language was once advanced marketing.

But in the years after *Manufacturing Consent* was published the new behemoths like Fox turned the old business model on its head. What Australian tabloid-merchant Rupert Murdoch did in employing political slant as a commercial strategy had ramifications the American public to this day poorly understands.

The news business for decades emphasized "objective" presentation, which was really less an issue of politics than of tone.

The idea was to make the recitation of news rhetorically watered down and unthreatening enough to rope in the whole spectrum of potential news consumers. The old-school anchorperson was a monotone mannequin designed to look and sound like a safe date for your daughter: *Good evening, I'm Dan Rather, and my frontal lobes have been removed. Today in Libya...*

Murdoch smashed this framework. He gave news consumers broadcasts that were pointed, opinionated, and nasty. He struck gold with *The O'Reilly Factor,* hosted by a yammering, red-faced repository of white suburban rage named Bill O'Reilly (another Boston TV vet).

The next hit was *Hannity & Colmes,* a format that played as a parody of old news. In this show, the "liberal" Colmes was the quivering, asexual, "safe date" prototype from the old broadcast era, and Sean Hannity was a thuggish Joey Buttafuoco in makeup whose job was to make Colmes look like the spineless dope he was.

This was theater, not news, and it was not designed to seize the whole audience in the way that other debate shows like CNN's *Crossfire* were.

The premise of *Crossfire* was an honest fight, two prominent pundits duking it out over issues, and may the best man (they were usually men) win.

The prototypical *Crossfire* setup involved a bombastic winger like Pat Buchanan versus an effete liberal like *New Republic* editor Michael Kinsley. On some days the conservative would be allowed to win, on some days the liberal would score a victory. It looked like a real argument.

But *Crossfire* was really just a formalized version of the artificial poles of allowable debate that Chomsky and Herman described. As some of its participants (like Jeff Cohen, a pioneering media critic who briefly played the "liberal" on the show, about whom we'll hear more later) came to realize, *Crossfire* became a propagandistic setup, a stage trick in which the "left" side of the argument was gradually pushed toward the right over the years. It was propaganda, but in slow motion.

Hannity & Colmes dispensed with the pretense. This was the intellectual version of Vince McMahon's pro wrestling spectacles, which were booming at the time. In the Fox debate shows, Sean Hannity was the heel, and Colmes was the good guy, or babyface. As any good wrestling fan knows, most American audiences want to see babyface stomped.

The job of Colmes was to get pinned over and over again, and he did it well. Meanwhile rightist anger merchants like Hannity and O'Reilly (and, on the radio, Rush Limbaugh) were rapidly hoovering up audiences that were frustrated, white, and often elderly. Fox chief Roger Ailes once boasted, "I created a network for people 55 to dead." (Ailes is now dead himself.)

This was a new model for the media. Instead of targeting the broad mean, they were now narrowly hunting demographics. The explosion of cable television meant there were hundreds of channels, each of which had its own mission.

Just as *Manufacturing Consent* came out, all the major cable channels were setting off on similar whale hunts, sailing into the high demographic seas in search of audiences to capture. Lifetime was "television for women," while the Discovery Channel did well with men. BET went after black viewers. Young people were MTV's target audience.

This all seems obvious now, but this "siloing" effect that spread across other channels soon became a very important new factor in news coverage. Fox for a long time cornered the market on conservative viewers. Almost automatically, competitors like CNN and MSNBC became home to people who viewed themselves as liberals, beginning a sifting process that would later accelerate.

A new dynamic entered the job of reporting. For generations, news directors had only to remember a few ideological imperatives. One, ably and voluminously described by Chomsky and Herman, was, "America rules: pay no attention to those napalmed bodies." We covered the worthy victims, ignored the unworthy ones, and that was most of the job, politically.

The rest of the news? As one TV producer put it to me in the nineties, "The entire effect we're after is, 'Isn't that weird?'"

Did you hear about that guy in Michigan who refused to mow his lawn even when the town ordered him to? Weird! And how about that drive-thru condom store that opened in Cranston, Rhode Island? What a trip! And, hey, what happened in the O.J. trial today? That Kato Kaelin is really a doof! And I love that lawyer who wears a suede jacket! He looks like a cowboy!

TV execs learned Americans would be happy if you just fed them a nonstop succession of *National Enquirer*–style factoids (this is formalized today in meme culture). The *New York Times* deciding to cover the O.J. freak show full-time broke the seal on the open commercialization of dumb news that among other things led to a future where Donald Trump could be a viable presidential candidate.

In the old days, the news was a mix of this toothless trivia and cheery dispatches from the front lines of Pax Americana. The whole fam could sit and watch it without getting upset (by necessity: an important principle in pre-Internet broadcasting is that nothing on the air, including the news, could be as intense or as creative as the commercials). The news once designed to be consumed by the whole house, by loving Mom, by your crazy right-wing uncle, by your earnest college-student cousin who just came home wearing a Che T-shirt.

But once we started to be organized into demographic silos, the networks found another way to seduce these audiences: they sold intramural conflict.

The Roger Ailes types captured the attention of the crazy right-wing uncle and got him watching one channel full of news tailored for him, filling the airwaves with stories, for instance, about immigration or minorities committing crimes. Different networks eventually rose to market themselves to the kid in the Che T-shirt. If you got them in different rooms watching different channels, you could get both viewers literally addicted to hating one another.

There was a political element to this, but also not. It was commerce, initially. And reporters stuck in this world soon began to realize that the nature of their jobs had changed.

Whereas once the task was to report the facts as honestly as we could—down the middle of the "fairway" of acceptable thought, of course—the new task was mostly about making sure your viewer came back the next day.

We sold anger, and we did it mainly by feeding audiences what they wanted to hear. Mostly, this involved cranking out stories about people our viewers loved to hate.

Selling siloed anger was a more sophisticated take on the WWE programming pioneered in *Hannity & Colmes*. The modern news consumer tuned into
news that confirmed his or her prejudices about whatever or whoever the villain of the day happened to be: foreigners, minorities, terrorists, the Clintons,
Republicans, even corporations.

The system was ingeniously designed so that the news dropped down the
respective silos didn't interfere with the occasional need to "manufacture" the
consent of the whole population. If we needed to, we could still herd the whole
country into the pen again and get them backing the flag, as was the case with
the Iraq War effort.

But mostly, we sold conflict. We began in the early nineties to systematically pry families apart, set group against group, and more and more make news
consumption a bubble-like, "safe space" stimulation of the vitriolic reflex, a consumer version of "Two Minutes Hate."

How did this serve the needs of the elite interests that were once promoting
unity? That wasn't easy for me to see, in my first decades in the business. For a
long time, I thought it was a flaw in the Chomsky/Herman model. It looked like
we were mostly selling pointless division.

But it now seems there was a reason, even for that.

The news media is in crisis. Polls show that a wide majority of the population
no longer has confidence in the press. Chomsky himself despairs at this, noting in
my discussion with him (at the end of this book) that *Manufacturing Consent* had
the unintended consequence of convincing readers not to trust the media.

There are many ways of mistrusting something, but people who came away
from *Manufacturing Consent* with the idea that the media peddles lies misread
the book. Papers like the *New York Times,* for the most part, do not traffic in outright deceptions.

The overwhelming majority of commercial news reporting is factual (with
one conspicuous exception I'll get into later on), and the individual reporters who
work in the business tend to be quite stubborn in their adherence to fact as a
matter of principle. (Sadly, in the time it's taken to write this book, even this has
begun to change some). Still, people should trust most reporters, especially local
reporters, who tend to have real beats (like statehouses or courts), have few of

the insular prejudices of the national media, and don't deserve the elitist tag. The context in which reporters operate is most often the problem.

Now, more than ever, most journalists work for giant nihilistic corporations whose editorial decisions are skewed by a toxic mix of political and financial considerations. Without understanding how those pressures work, it's very difficult for a casual news consumer to gain an accurate picture of the world.

This book is intended as an insider's guide to those distortions.

The technology underpinning the modern news business is sophisticated and works according to a two-step process. First, it creates content that reinforces your pre-existing opinions, and, after analysis of your consumer habits, sends it to you.

Then it matches *you* to advertisers who have a product they're trying to sell to your demographic. This is how companies like Facebook and Google make their money: telling advertisers where their likely customers are on the web.

The news, basically, is bait to lure you into a pen where you can be sold sneakers or bath soaps or prostatitis cures or whatever else studies say people of your age, gender, race, class, and political persuasion tend to buy.

Imagine your Internet surfing habit as being like walking down a street. A man shouts: "Did you hear what those damned liberals did today? Come down this alley."

You hate liberals, so you go down the alley. On your way to the story, there's a storefront selling mart carts and gold investments (there's a crash coming—*this billionaire* even says so!).

Maybe you buy the gold, maybe you don't. But at the end of the alley, there's a red-faced screamer telling a story that may even be true, about a college in Massachusetts where administrators took down a statue of John Adams because it made a Hispanic immigrant "uncomfortable." Boy, does that make you pissed!

They picked that story just for you to hear. It is like the parable of Kafka's gatekeeper, guarding a door to the truth that was built just for you.

Across the street, down the MSNBC alley, there's an opposite story, and set of storefronts, built specifically for someone else to hear.

People need to start understanding the news not as "the news," but as just such an individualized consumer experience—anger just for you.

This is not reporting. It's a marketing process designed to create rhetorical addictions and shut any non-consumerist doors in your mind. This creates more than just pockets of political rancor. It creates masses of media consumers who've been trained to see in only one direction, as if they had been pulled through history on a railroad track, with heads fastened in blinders, looking only one way.

As it turns out, there is a utility in keeping us divided. As people, the more separate we are, the more politically impotent we become.

This is the second stage of the mass media deception originally described in *Manufacturing Consent*.

First, we're taught to stay within certain bounds, intellectually. Then, we're all herded into separate demographic pens, located along different patches of real estate on the spectrum of permissible thought.

Once safely captured, we're trained to consume the news the way sports fans do. We root for our team, and hate all the rest.

Hatred is the partner of ignorance, and we in the media have become experts in selling both.

I looked back at thirty years of deceptive episodes—from Iraq to the financial crisis of 2008 to the 2016 election of Donald Trump—and found that we in the press have increasingly used intramural hatreds to obscure larger, more damning truths. Fake controversies of increasing absurdity have been deployed over and over to keep our audiences from seeing larger problems.

We manufactured fake dissent, to prevent real dissent.

1. THE BEAUTY CONTEST: PRESS COVERAGE OF THE 2016 ELECTION

Why do they hate us?

We in the press always screw up this question.

Many of the biggest journalistic fiascoes in recent history involved failed attempts at introspection. Whether on behalf of the country or ourselves, when we look in the mirror, we inevitably report back things that aren't there.

We fumbled "Why do they hate us?" badly after 9/11, when *us* was guiltless America and *they* were Muslims in the corrupt Middle Eastern petro-states we supported.

We made a joke of it during the Occupy protests, when "Why are they so angry?" somehow became a common news feature assignment after a fraud-ridden financial services sector put millions in foreclosure and vaporized as much as 40 percent of the world's wealth.

More recently, we've cycled through a series of unconvincing responses to *Why do they hate us?*—themed stories like Brexit, the Bernie Sanders primary run of 2016, and the election of Donald Trump.

We've botched them all, for reasons that range from incompetence to willful blindness. The Trump story in particular was an industry-wide failure that exposed many of our greatest weaknesses (I was part of the problem, too) and remains a serious concern heading into 2020.

But the story that flummoxes us most has to do with our own business.

Everyone hates the media. Nobody in the media seems to understand why.

An oft-cited Gallup poll taken just after the 2016 election showed just 20 percent of Americans expressed "a great deal" or "quite a lot" of confidence in newspapers.

An 80 percent no-confidence vote would be cause for concern in most professions. Reporters, however, have been unimpressed with the numbers.

Some of this surely has to do with the fact that the media business, at least at the higher end, has been experiencing record profits since Donald Trump tabbed us the "enemy of the people." In the "Democracy Dies in Darkness" era, many in the press wear their public repudiation like badges of honor, evidence that they're on the right journalistic track.

Few seem troubled by the obvious symbiosis between Trump's bottom-feeding, scandal-a-minute act and the massive boom in profits suddenly animating our once-dying industry (even print journalism, a business that pre-Trump seemed destined to go the way of 8-track tapes, has seen a bump in the Trump years).

We certainly didn't worry about it early in 2015, when the unseemly amount of attention paid to Trump-as-ratings-phenomenon gave the insurgent candidate billions in free publicity and helped secure his nomination.

Later, as Trump cruised toward the nomination, media execs couldn't hide their excitement. Since-disgraced CBS jackass Les Moonves blurted out that Trump "may not be good for America, but it's damn good for CBS," adding, "the money's rolling in."

Comments like these triggered an avalanche of anti-press complaints, this time not from flyover country (where hatred of the "elite" press was already considered a given) but from urban, left-leaning intellectuals, aka the media's home crowd.

An example was Ralph Nader, who focused on the entire system of commercial media. Nader said that campaign coverage had devolved into a profit bonanza in which media firms "cash in and give candidates a free ride."

The former third-party candidate also noted that the constant attention paid to people like Trump excluded other voices, including "leading citizens who could criticize the process." (Like, presumably, Ralph Nader, although he had a point).

I remember watching Nader's comments with interest, having just returned from covering Trump's nomination-sealing win in the Indiana primary. Trump had beaten Ted Cruz, a politician who tried his damnedest to be as cruel and reactionary from a policy standpoint as Trump, but was out of his league when it came to manipulating sensationalist campaign media coverage.

Cruz was routed in Indiana after Trump took the highly creative step of accusing Cruz's father of helping assassinate John F. Kennedy. The *correct* response for Cruz in that media climate would probably have been to counter-accuse Trump of eating Christian babies, or maybe buggering Lenin's corpse (the Democrats would later catch on and try a version of this). But Cruz didn't get it and actually denied the JFK charges, which of course had the practical effect of just making us think about them more. "Garbage," he told reporters.

Worse, Cruz's wife Heidi was asked by a *Yahoo!* reporter if her husband was the Zodiac Killer, a popular Internet meme at the time. She, too, made the mistake of answering in earnest, providing more headlines. "I've been married to him for 15 years and I know pretty well who he is, so it doesn't bother me," was her answer.

I was at the miserable Cruz "victory" party in Indianapolis on the night of May 3, 2016, when the returns came in. A lot of reporters present were joking about Heidi's answer. Many noted that it was a "non-denial denial" and "exactly what the wife of the real Zodiac would say" (this hot take later made it into a lot of real news reports, including, embarrassingly, my own).

The pretense that the presidential campaign was anything but an insane, absurdist reality show was almost completely gone by that point. Reporters were openly enjoying the ridiculousness of it all. Many of us tasked with its daily updates had given into the campaign's grotesque commercialism several election cycles before Trump even arrived on the scene.

To digress briefly: the campaign process, for a generation, has been too long by at least a year. With each cycle, it grew even more unnecessarily protracted, and increasingly eschewed real policy discussions. By the seventies and eighties, when the nomination process left the smoke-filled room and became a more public affair, it became a kind of elite beauty contest in which Washington journalists assumed the role of judges.

Pre-Trump, the two-year saga was really a series of tests whose purpose was to produce obedient major-party mannequins worthy of "Miss Republican

Orthodoxy" or "Miss Democrat Orthodoxy" sashes. There were both political and commercial elements to this dynamic.

We routinely flunked candidates in our version of the swimsuit competition. Dennis Kucinich was hounded for his "elfin" appearance, and others, like Bobby Jindal, were dismissed with sleazy code terms like, "He doesn't look presidential."

Myriad class/race/gender biases were veiled just in this one "presidential" descriptor, in addition to flat out high school–style shallowness celebrating looks, height, even jockiness. To reassure us on this last point, candidates learned to "relax" by shooting baskets or tossing footballs around us in highly scripted episodes that went sideways with unsurprising frequency. Marco Rubio boinking an Iowan child in the face with a terrible spiral is the most recent viral classic of the genre.

Other tests, like the "most nuanced" competition (awarded to the candidate most adept at advocating the appearance of policy action instead of the real thing) helped produce the likes of John Kerry as a nominee. Kerry himself then *lost* to George W. Bush when the press flunked him by another asinine standard, the now-infamous "likability" test.

Heading into the 2016 race, pundits openly celebrated all of this. We were proud of the dumbed-down barriers to political power we'd created. We bragged incessantly about how the "candidate you'd most want to have a beer with" had practically become a formal part of the process. We even made Barack Obama submit to this horseshit. "The president has been polishing his 'regular guy' credentials by talking a lot about beer," explained NPR (NPR!) in 2012.

By the last election, outlets like the *Daily Beast* cheerfully described the "beer standard" as the key to winning the "likability Olympics."

It was therefore stunning to watch the universal lack of insight when the anti-candidate who rampaged through our idiotic campaign carnival in 2016 was not only a reality star, but also a beauty contest aficionado. Trump was a demon from hell sent to punish all of these reporting sins.

He was like Tony Clifton snuck into the *Miss Universe* pageant, doing a farts-only version of "Stairway to Heaven" as the musical portion. He pissed on "nuance" and spent his campaign flouting our phony "presidential" standard.

So long as we thought he couldn't actually win, most of us in the press were hugely entertained, even flattered. Floating on soaring ratings and click numbers, we cheerfully reported all of his antics. Yet very few picked up on the fact that the joke was on us, that Trump was winning votes precisely by running against our sham beauty contest.

As soon as it became clear Trump was going to secure the nomination, however, a new kind of criticism of the media began to appear. This one was of the *When a Stranger Calls* variety: it came from inside the house, i.e. from within our own ranks.

High priests of conventional wisdom like Nicholas Kristof of the *New York Times* began running pieces in early 2016 with titles like, "My Shared Shame: The Media Helped Make Trump." Kristof talked a bit about the commercial dynamics of the business, and he did cop to the "mother lode" of ratings Trump provided. But in the end, his key conclusion read:

> It's not that we shouldn't have covered Trump's craziness, but that we should have aggressively provided context in the form of fact checks and robust examination of policy proposals.

Around the same time that Kristof's much-discussed column came out, Obama gave a speech at Syracuse in honor of Robin Toner, the first black woman to be a national *Times* correspondent. Though the speech didn't mention Trump by name, it was clearly about Trump, and the media's role in bringing about his success.

It was obvious that Obama had deeply held feelings about the subject. This made sense given Trump's role in pushing the vicious birther campaign. Trump was one of the few figures capable of inspiring Obama to break character.

Obama, like Kristof, touched on the profit motive. He went much deeper than Kristof in his assessment of the media's structural problems, however, essentially saying that it was our intentional, profit-motivated indulgence of stupidity and mindless conflict that had brought us to this dark place. I personally was surprised he didn't lead with a diatribe about how Washington reporters are so dumb, you can get them to call you a "regular guy" just by publishing a beer recipe on the White House website.

But he stuck to hounding us for valuing profit over substance. "The choice between what cuts into your bottom lines and what harms us as a society is an important one," he scolded.

Ultimately Obama landed near to Kristof in this critique: "A job well done is about more than just handing someone a microphone. It is to probe and to question, and to dig deeper, and to demand more."

Some pundits rejected the notion that Trump was the media's fault. The *Guardian* around this time even did a "fact check" about this nebulous question (how does one "fact check" such a premise?). The paper concluded that there were "reasons to raise doubt" about our culpability in causing the Trump phenomenon, with the observation that Trump voters don't pay attention to our fact-checks anyway as one of the reasons listed.

But by the summer of 2016, it became accepted belief among our ranks that "the media" had created Trump. Reform became the watchword of the day. It was eye-opening to see how quickly my colleagues ran from their own "likability" cliché once it began to look like it might be a factor in the increasingly infamous race. This was despite the fact that virtually every poll showed that Trump was actually significantly *more* disliked than his Democratic opponent.

Characteristically, there was no remorse over the fact that we had overemphasized the likability factor for a generation, helping ruin the candidacies of wonky dullards like Mike Dukakis, Al Gore, John Kerry, and even Mitt Romney in the process. ("Professorial" was one of our negative code words for too policy-centric candidates).

Instead, it was now determined that "likability" was only a problem in this particular race, because (pick one) it wasn't actually true about Hillary, or it was sexist, or because we reporters just mistake dedication, seriousness, and workaholism for a lack of charisma. People actually liked Hillary, or if they didn't they were wrong not to, or we were wrong to report that fact—or something.

"How much do voters have to like their politicians?" wondered *Time*, the same magazine that had put a giant black-and-white photo of Hillary over the headline LOVE HER HATE HER (check one) in 2006, back when this sort of analysis was not considered world-imperiling stupidity.

The *Atlantic* in 2012 had reinforced the cult of likability with a long piece explaining Obama's dominance over Romney by writing, "In every instance [since 1984] the candidate seen as more likable won the election." In 2016, the same outlet trashed likability as a moral wrong, saying we shouldn't want a leader on our level, but one "demonstrably above us."

Beyond such changes, reporters on the trail began to sound sheepish notes, as if chastened by public displeasure. They began to talk about recasting their whole approach to Trump, and soon, we did.

Under the new formulation, *One Million Hours of Trump* became *One Million Hours of Trump (is bad!)*. Conveniently for our sales reps, the new dictum centered around the idea that we not only should *not* reduce the volume of TrumpMania, but rather we must, if anything, increase it, because we now had an enhanced "responsibility" to "call him out."

We would hear a lot about "responsibility" in the coming years from the same people who *still* remind us every four years (and even, sometimes, in between) that Mike Dukakis is an all-time loser because he allowed himself to be photographed in a tank.

Later in the summer, in a seminal op-ed in the *New York Times,* writer Jim Rutenberg argued that we reporters had an obligation as citizens to ward off the historical threat Trump posed.

Because Trump was a demagogue who played "to the nation's worst racist and nationalistic tendencies," you had to "throw out the textbook American journalism has been using for the better part of the past half-century" and "approach [Trump] in a way you've never approached anything in your career."

Rutenberg argued that journalists had to cast ourselves free of the moorings of "objectivity," and redefine fairness, fact, and truth. We should now be "true to the facts… in a way that will stand up to history's judgment."

The Rutenberg column never explained why changing to a factual approach was necessary, if the Trump fact pattern was as bad as it was (and it was). Bad candidates and bad politicians looked bad even under the old "objectivity" standard, the old language, the old headlines. What were we changing and why?

Rutenberg said we had to grit our teeth and give up "balance, that idealistic form of journalism with a capital 'J' we've been trained to always strive for." Why? Because "now that he is the Republican nominee for president, the imbalance is cutting against [Trump]." An increased effort to scrutinize this candidate, call out his shit, etc., would hurt him at the polls, the theory went.

In reality, this column helped plant the seeds of the infamous symbiosis of today. What Rutenberg really meant by giving up "balance" wasn't going after Trump more—we were already calling him every name in the book—but de-emphasizing scrutiny of the other side.

Announcing this gave Trump an opening to blast the press even more as being biased against him, validating his paranoid politics. Conversely, the posture rallied the core audiences of papers like the *Times,* at least for a while. A year after Rutenberg's column, the paper was reveling in a so-called "Trump bump" in subscriptions, with the fourth quarter of 2016, when the *Times* had the honor of giving horrified audiences the bad news about Trump's election, being its best year since it launched a digital pay model.

By the summer of 2018, however, the "Trump bump" was gone and the paper was seeing most of its digital growth in crosswords and cooking. However, it still had the honor of having ditched its long-standing and hard-won reputation for objectivity in pursuit of a few quarters of growth.

One additional bizarre Trump-inspired change to reporting that took place in 2016 involved polls: we increasingly ignored data favorable to Trump and pushed surveys suggesting a Clinton landslide. The *Times* ran a piece in October pronouncing the race essentially over, telling us to expect a "sweeping victory at every level" for Clinton. The papers all throughout the race were full of confident predictions and demographic analyses with titles like, "Relax, Trump Can't Win" and "Donald Trump's Six Stages of Doom."

These stories were a crucial poker tell. The ostensible reason for our new adversarial posture was to advocate against Trump. But underreporting the seriousness of the Trump threat didn't help Democrats at all. If anything, the opposite was true. Defanged data reporting dulled attention to correctable weaknesses in the Clinton support base and, who knows, perhaps even motivated a voter or a thousand to stay home out of unconcern.

On the other hand, such reports got lots of clicks from blue-state voters, thanks to the same dynamic that inspires sports fans to read rosy predictions even when their teams suck. The vibe was closer to fanboy homerism (which incidentally is completely defensible in an entertainment genre like sportswriting) than to "advocacy reporting."

Trump's victory came as a complete shock to millions in large part because of this quirk in the sub-genre of data reporting, whose whole purpose was to be a buffer against conventional wisdom and groupthink.

Election Day, 2016 was a historic blow to American journalism. It was as if we'd invaded Iraq and discovered there were no WMDs in the same few hours. Almost immediately, new conventional wisdom coalesced to explain the coverage failures in ways that incentivized future mistakes.

Chomsky and Herman wrote about how the elite reaction to America's military loss in Vietnam was to create a revisionist history that not only steered us away from the reality of American crimes and policy failures, but set the stage for future invasions and occupations. The post-Vietnam story blamed an "excess of democracy" for the loss, especially in the media: loserific criticism of our prospects for victory undermined the popular resolve to keep fighting a winnable war.

So the press sheepishly abandoned a lot of its "excessively democratic" practices. We stopped showing deaths in battle, coffins coming home, etc. If you did any war zone reporting, you had to be "embedded" as part of an American unit, a practice that gave most war reporting a *Stars and Stripes* flavor. Even I submitted to these conditions.

In the same way, conventional wisdom after the 2016 vote steered attention away from the generation of press practices that had degraded the presidential campaign process to the point where the election of someone like Trump could even be possible.

Any real assessment of what happened would have focused on the fact that the campaign press had been so pompous for so long in telling voters what "presidential" meant, and in dictating fealty to crass stupidities like "nuance" and "the beer standard," that voters entering 2016 were willing to cheer any pol with the insight to tell us to fuck off. The subtext of all of this was that our rants about beer and "likability" and so on, were only the Washington press corps' *idea* of what was important to a voter in flyover country.

Given that most actual voters were sunk in debt, working multiple jobs, uninsured, saddled with ruined credit scores, and often battling alcohol and opiate addiction and other problems, it was a horrific aristocratic insult to tell people each election cycle that what *really* mattered to them was what candidate looked most convincing carrying a rifle on a duck hunt. But we were so out of touch, we doubled down on these insults every four years.

That this was a huge part of Trump's appeal was obvious. But it was left out of electoral post-mortems.

Instead, the legend became that we hadn't been obnoxious *enough* during the election season. What America really needed, the press barons decided, was a more directly didactic approach to who was and was not an appropriate political choice.

The same pundit class that had raised us on moronic messaging, like *Newsweek's* "Fighting the Wimp Factor" cover of George H. W. Bush, created a new legend about how the Trump-era press corps had learned its lesson, and would be returning to its more natural role as serious-minded opponents of dumb populism.

For example, we weren't going to screw around with words like "misstatement" anymore. The new Press Corps 2.0 would put the word "lie" in headlines. Go ahead and see if we wouldn't. We were tough now.

No less a figure than Dan Rather sounded the "lie" bugle as we entered the era of—gulp—*President* Trump. Rather's take was in response to a *Meet the Press* segment in which *Times* executive editor Dean Bacquet and *Wall Street Journal* editor Gerard Baker harrumphed at length as they debated this use of the "lie."

Eventually there was a great collective patting of backs when most of the major papers and networks decided to approve the forbidden word. And despite the fact that the entire journalism business had just been forced to eat cauldrons of shit after nearly two years of misreads and smug dismissals of Trump's chances had exploded, Space Shuttle–style, on Election Day, papers and news networks everywhere were suddenly congratulating themselves on their new #Resistance, fight-the-power posture. (Incidentally, what were we doing before Trump? *Not* challenging power?) The *Washington Post,* for fuck's sake, actually ran a *Behind the Music*–type feature about how it settled on its new "Democracy Dies in Darkness" slogan.

Around the same time that Bacquet and Baker were holding their televised discussion about journalism's future, I was interviewing Bernie Sanders about the lessons of the 2016 race. He didn't use this language, but one of the big takeaways for Sanders from his run was that nobody out there gave a shit about *Meet the Press*.

What politics passes for now is somebody goes on *Meet the Press* and they do well: "Oh, this guy is brilliant, wonderful." No one cares about *Meet the Press*.

Sanders spoke of the divide between the public and elite institutions, of which the press was now clearly considered one.

"It's not just the weakness of the Democratic Party and their dependency on the upper middle class, the wealthy, and living in a bubble," he said. "It is a media where people turn on the television, they do not see a reflection of their lives. When they do, it is a caricature. Some idiot."

When Sanders won the New Hampshire primary, Stephen Colbert invited him on the show—and had him drink beer and eat peanuts. "If you like boiled peanuts, it'll certainly give you a leg up in South Carolina," Colbert said.

Yuk, yuk.

Trump's election kicked off a lengthy period of personal despair for me, but not for the reasons you'd guess.

2016 was the fourth presidential election campaign I'd covered for *Rolling Stone*. Across all those races I'd been forced into a highly unusual position. The other "kids in the class" were constantly finking on me for various reasons. On my first-ever day on the trail for the magazine in 2004, an unnamed reporter called Howard Kurtz at the *Washington Post* to complain—this really happened—because I'd broken an unwritten rule by taking video of the press section without permission. I was also "spoken to" by a Kerry press aide, who relayed the complaints of other unnamed reporters.

Later, when colleagues on that same trip went after Kerry for reacting after Matt Drudge published an unsubstantiated rumor that Kerry had a mistress, I made the mistake of asking other reporters on the plane why we were giving this story life without first doing any work to see if it was true. Reporters took in the treacherous fact that I was doing a story on *us* with varying degrees of fury.

"This," one reporter said to me, waving a hand across the press seats in the Kerry campaign plane, "is a fucking *no-fly zone*, dude."

After that incident, the Kerry campaign (which had been victim to the Drudge bumrush) acquiesced to demands from other trail reporters, and had me sent to the back of the plane with the techies and documentarian Alexandra Pelosi. This should have struck me as a vivid demonstration of the unnatural relationship between campaigns and press corps, and of the group policing instinct that also led campaign reporters to school candidates in various unwritten political rules about "nuance" and "likability." But at the time I just thought being stuck in the back of the plane was funny.

I didn't agree with the core idea that reporters weren't "part of the campaign story" and therefore should be exempt from all questions. But in subsequent elections I gave in to the argument that we couldn't do our jobs without having a "safe work space," and stopped hassling colleagues.

In 2008 and beyond, though, I kept getting in the soup. Because my print schedule was so different from everyone else's—I only had to file once every few weeks or months—I spent a lot of time twiddling my thumbs in filing rooms. Hour after hour, I watched colleagues slave away three or four times a day to send out the Urgent News that Fred Thompson or Mike Huckabee or whoever had just given the same speech he'd given fifty times in a row.

To pass the time I'd often read (in Iowa, I was hissed at by a campaign staffer for turning the pages of a *Sports Illustrated* too loudly) or else I'd do even dumber things (a Rubik's cube earned me a rebuke in Houston). I finally learned that the only safe activity during filing hours was to do nothing. So I sat there, hour after hour, primary after primary, just thinking about what we were doing.

By 2012 I had a theory of the presidential campaign as a complex commercial process. On the plane, two businesses were going on in tandem. The candidates were raising money, which mostly entailed taking cash from big companies in exchange for policy promises. In the back, reporters were gunning for hits and ratings.

The candidate who most quickly found the middle ground between these two dynamics would become the nominee. Any candidate who was both good at raising money and deemed a suitable lead actor for the media's campaign reality show—who was "likable" and "nuanced" but also not too "left" or "weak on defense" or espousing of "fringe" politics like Nader or Ron Paul—would be allowed to move on to the general.

Journalists and candidates were not just political partners, but business partners. There was a massive sales aspect to the job that led reporters to take liberties with the truth more or less constantly. Politicians, even at their own expense, were often willing to help them there.

In 2012, there was consternation among campaign reporters early on that it was going to be hard to "sell" the Obama-Romney general as suspenseful, since we all got the feeling that Obama would win easily. This was not because of polls, but largely because of the same kinds of non-quantitative clues we would ignore in 2016: Obama's events were uproarious and huge, whereas Romney struggled to pack halls even in his home state, and seemed to be every Republican's third choice.

I went on CNN in the middle of that race and said aloud that reporters were pushing polls showing a close race just to rescue ratings. Despite the fact that many were saying this behind the scenes, I was the only one dumb enough to say it out loud. Noted Democratic consultant James Carville quickly came out to address the fact that he'd heard the same talk in private, and admonished everyone to remember that "complacency is dangerous" and Obama could lose.

Before long, we saw the remarkable phenomenon of Democrat-leaning pundits everywhere praising the absurdly maladroit Romney as a contender. The *Independent* called Obama "limp" (about the worst comment you get from a campaign reporter) and expressed shock that Obama wasn't fighting harder against Romney, because anyone who has "seen him play pick-up basketball" knows "how competitive [Obama] is." (You see how all of this idiocy ties together; as if one can actually glean anything from watching a politician play basketball!).

Meanwhile Carville praised Romney's nonexistent debating skills, saying he "came in with a chainsaw." Another high priest of conventional wisdom, CNN's self-described "centrist" David Gergen, declared, "We've got a horse race."

We didn't, of course. Obama won with relative ease. But even if Romney had somehow found an advantage and won, the Gergens of the world wouldn't have shed a tear: having a tax-slashing, leveraged buyout artist in the White House—a Mormon Gordon Gekko—would have been okay with most of these clowns.

It was the ultimate demonstration of the *Manufacturing Consent* principle of a concocted, artificially narrowed public debate. We were meant to understand that the distance between Romney and Obama was vast, that much was at stake, and that the outcome was in doubt.

In reality everyone knew the outcome, and the people bleating the loudest about "dangerous complacency" would have shrugged at seeing a banker-supported private equity titan replace Barack Obama, who by then was in his fourth year of letting Wall Street toadies like Tim Geithner and Citigroup execs like Jack Lew lead his post-crash economic policy.

After 2012 I believed any candidate smart enough to run against all this insanity would do well. In early 2016, when I saw that Trump was doing exactly this, I had a flash of insight that he was going to be president. In the first feature I wrote about Trump, I talked about how he was looking "unstoppable," and explained:

> It turns out we let our electoral process devolve into something so fake and dysfunctional that any half-bright con man with the stones to try it could walk right through the front door and tear it to shreds on the first go.

And Trump is no half-bright con man, either. He's way better than average.

This was not something I was happy about, but I understood it. The most devastating part of Trump's campaign is that we'd spent decades giving him the ammunition he would need to punch his way to the top. When Trump talked about conspiracies of elites, he was not 100 percent wrong, and this was not going to change.

During the Republican primary, he spoke at length about things that by tradition we rarely discussed on the trail, like the financial backers who often traveled with the candidates. "Do you think Jeb Bush is going to make drug prices competitive?" Trump asked. "He's got Woody Johnson as his head of fund-raising." Johnson was the head of Johnson & Johnson, a major drugmaker.

Johnson and a slew of other Big Pharma execs had been in the room during the Republican debate the night before. Johnson & Johnson was of particular interest because it owns Janssen Pharmaceuticals, which among other things makes Fentanyl, the drug reportedly responsible for just under half of the 70,200 overdose deaths in 2017.

Trump didn't mention this—in fact he crudely blamed New Hampshire's drug problems on dealers "across the southern border"—but he was giving voters a peek into the kingmaking process. No major candidate that I could remember had talked about the donors being in the room during debates.

I knew Trump would use the same tactics against Clinton that he'd used against Bush, and wrote:

> Trump will surely argue that the Clintons are the other half of the dissolute-conspiracy story he's been selling, representing a workers' party that abandoned workers and turned the presidency into a vast cash-for-access enterprise, avoiding scrutiny by making Washington into Hollywood East and turning labor leaders and journalists alike into starstruck courtiers.
>
> As with everything else, Trump personalizes this, making his stories of buying Hillary's presence at his wedding a part of his stump speech. A race against Hillary Clinton in the general, if it happens, will be a pitch right in Trump's wheelhouse.

Later, Trump did in fact make it a point to describe Clinton and Jeb Bush as basically the same politician, only Clinton had even "less energy." In the general, he relentlessly pounded NAFTA and the TPP to hammer home the idea that he was the friend of the worker (this, from the same person who said auto workers were overpaid and threatened to move auto factories to union-hostile states). He hammered Clinton for her real ties to banks like Goldman Sachs, in the same way he'd hammered Bush for his real ties to corporate donors.

It all worked. Were there other factors? Were racism and sexism huge themes that Trump exploited, perhaps more than any other? Of course. But he also explicitly ran against *us,* the flying backroom deal that was the campaign.

He ran against the unseen policing that for generations had carefully kept the presidency between mainstream Republican and mainstream Democratic poles. Whether it was intentional or not, it was highly effective. And the horror of the genteel press corps was, for Trump's voters, a major selling point.

The reaction by my colleagues was not to concede any of this, but to publish story after story trying to punch holes in the few true things Trump said. Progressive outlets suddenly started telling us that NAFTA wasn't so bad. We heard that taking speech money from banks was legitimate because politicians are people too and need to make money. Moreover the same warnings we'd heard from people like Carville four years before about "complacency" were now absent. Carville himself came out in September 2016 and declared the race all but over, saying Republicans "continue to make a bad bet" on "non-college whites." This was the same political consultant who'd put Bill Clinton in the White House targeting... non-college whites.

In the summer of 2016, I lost my nerve. I let pollsters talk me into the impossibility of a Trump win. Like a lot of journalists, I started ignoring what I was seeing at rallies. It was a huge, inexcusable mistake. Once Trump was president, I realized that I'd fallen for the con in my own business, which preached that all races are exciting and close—unless one of the candidates is somehow politically unacceptable.

I thought the failure of the press in 2016 would lead to a prolonged period of introspection and re-evaluation. Instead, we created an environment in which reporters are more committed than ever to the elite policing behaviors that won us Trump in the first place.

To me the 2016 campaign was just a particularly dramatic demonstration of the "siloing" phenomenon, in which media content—not just news, but all content, entertainment included—is tailored for the consumption of highly individualized demographics.

The same news that for decades hadn't shown poverty on TV unless it was shirtless and being subdued by cops had discovered the ultimate cash cow in Trump, a billionaire who turned the presidential election into a pro wrestling–style ratings magnet. When it got caught clucking over how rich Trump was making them, big media was faced with a choice: cover him less, or find a way to justify covering him more.

We chose door number two. The rhetorical trick we employed was an openly adversarial stance, supposedly a bold new step. The papers will tell you this was an ethical/political choice. Perhaps it was, in some cases. But as much as anything else, it was a business decision. Most outlets, whether they admitted it or not, basically chose to double down with half the news audience, rather than concede all of it.

Trump won because the media can't resist a hot-selling story. When this quirk turned out to have disastrous consequences, we invented a new approach to selling Trump that just seemed less irresponsible. In this new environment there would only be two acceptable takes in the press: pro-Trump and anti-Trump.

Both takes would sell extremely well, in respective venues. But this formalized our descent into a sportslike coverage paradigm, which had been building for decades.

Two data points stood out after 2016. One involved those polls that showed confidence in the media dipping to all-time lows. The other involved unprecedented ratings. People believed us less, but watched us more.

We are now eating into the profits of the entertainment business. Completing a decades-long slide, the news has become a show, and not just in campaign years, but always.

What went wrong? When did this start?

2. THE TEN RULES OF HATE

Pick up any major newspaper, or turn on any network television news broadcast. The political orientation won't matter. It could be Fox or MSNBC, the *Washington Post* or the *Washington Times*. You'll find virtually every story checks certain boxes.

Call them the ten rules of hate. After generations of doing the opposite, when unity and conformity were more profitable, now the primary product the news media sells is division.

We also sell content that's just plain stupid, what that TV producer friend of mine calls the *Isn't This Weird?* effect. But the easiest media product to make is called *This Bad Thing That Just Happened Is Someone Else's Fault*. It has a virtually limitless market.

I know this because I've created a lot of that content. Over the years I became increasingly uneasy about feeding readers' hate reflexes. I tried to get around this by only picking stories about things that were genuinely outrageous, but eventually you start to feel the tail wagging the dog. In recent years I started to hear from other reporters who'd begun doing the same thing. You'll hear from some of them below.

The problem we all have is the commercial structure of the business. To make money, we've had to train audiences to consume news in a certain way. We need you anxious, pre-pissed, addicted to conflict. Moreover we need you to bring a series of assumptions every time you open a paper or turn on your phone, TV, or car radio. Without them, most of what we produce will seem illogical and offensive.

The trick is to constantly narrow your mental horizons and keep you geeked up on impotent anger. It's a twist on *Manufacturing Consent*'s description of an artificially narrowed debate.

The Herman/Chomsky thesis in the mid-1980s highlighted how the press "manufactured" public unity by making sure the population was only exposed to a narrow range of political ideas, stretching from Republican to Democrat (with the Democrat usually more like an Eisenhower Republican). So long as you stayed on that little median strip, you accepted a broad range of underlying principles that never popped up in the sanitized, Nerfball version of debate that op-ed pages exhibited.

The difference now: we encourage full-fledged division on that strip. We've discovered we can sell hate, and the more vituperative the rhetoric, the better. This also serves larger political purposes.

So long as the public is busy hating each other and not aiming its ire at the more complex financial and political processes going on off-camera, there's very little danger of anything like a popular uprising.

That's not why we do what we do. But it *is* why we're allowed to operate this way. It boggles my mind that people think they're practicing real political advocacy by watching major corporate TV, be it Fox or MSNBC or CNN. Does anyone seriously believe that powerful people would allow truly dangerous ideas to be broadcast on TV? The news today is a reality show where you're part of the cast: *America vs. America,* on every channel.

The trick here is getting audiences to think they're punching up, when they're actually punching sideways, at other media consumers just like themselves, who just happen to be in a different silo. Hate is a great blinding mechanism. Once you've been in the business long enough, you become immersed in its nuances. If you can get people to accept a sequence of simple, powerful ideas, they're yours forever. The Ten Rules of Hate:

1. THERE ARE ONLY TWO IDEAS

There are only two baskets of allowable opinion: Republican and Democrat, liberal and conservative, left or right. This is drilled into us at a young age. By the time we hit college, most of us, roughly speaking, will have chosen the political identity we'll stick with for the rest of our lives. It's the Boolean version of politics, pure binary thought: blue or red, true or false, zero or one.

Open up a *New York Times* op-ed page if you want to see the contours. The spectrum of ideas is narrow. There is no Paul Goodman preaching revolutionary pacifism. There's no Thoreau, denouncing the spiritual bankruptcy of our work-centric lives, urging us to reconnect with nature. There are no Twains telling us that to "lodge all power in one party and keep it there is to ensure bad government." There are no Bierces or Swifts helping us laugh at the rich and powerful and pompous.

There is, however, always a Bret Stephens or a Ross Douthat representing the red side, along with the standard lineup of Paul Krugmans and Nick Kristofs repping the blue side. The *Washington Post* has George Will and Max Boot. "Intellectual diversity" in a major news outlet means "someone from both parties."

You will connect with one or the other. It doesn't matter which one.

2. THE TWO IDEAS ARE IN PERMANENT CONFLICT

It was a joke in the seventies, with *Saturday Night Live's* "Point/Counterpoint." The *Saturday Night Live* news show pitted Dan Aykroyd and Jane Curtain against each other, viciously railing over issues no sane person could possibly care about. "Jane, you ignorant slut!" seethed Aykroyd, in a "debate" about actor Lee Marvin's palimony case. The skit was hilarious precisely because normal human beings don't dress up in suits and ties to yell insults at each other over issues that have nothing to do with their actual lives.

This joke became a formal part of the news landscape not long after. It began with shows like *The McLaughlin Group* on PBS, then continued more famously with *Crossfire* on CNN.

Crossfire solidified the idea that politics is a fight, and that Democrats and Republicans not only must never come to an agreement about things, but must debate to the end in a sports-like forum.

Some of the early *Crossfire* shows on CNN with Pat Buchanan ("from the right") and Tom Braden ("from the left") were confused duds in terms of format. There were actually episodes where the "left" and "right" positions were weirdly in agreement, almost as though human beings could share commonsense reactions to certain things.

Take, for instance, the show when both Braden and Buchanan blasted Pan Am Airlines for not warning passengers of terrorist threats before the Lockerbie disaster.

But the show quickly settled on the never-agree format that would make it a hit. Buchanan and Braden would duke it out to the end, often over cultural issues. An episode in which they debated the propriety of a Dan Rather interview with then–vice president George H. W. Bush shows Buchanan in a preview of early anti-press populism.

A dynamic of the show perfectly predicted by *Manufacturing Consent* was that the "from the left" actor usually spent most of the episode sniveling and begging for compromise, while the "from the right" actor was always attacking. This sent a message to audiences that lefties were, basically, weenies.

Journalist Jeff Cohen, who would end up cast in a later version of the show, and who wrote a terrific book about the experience called *Cable News Confidential,* described it this way: "The libs were like boxers who didn't know how to punch."

Future debate shows like *Hannity & Colmes* and one I've been on, *Real Time with Bill Maher*, also depended on the theater of conservatives endlessly battling with liberals.

Much in the way that TV shows like *M*A*S*H,* which habituated viewers to the Orwellian idea that Americans were always at war far away with some Asiatic enemy somewhere (this was why the director of the *M*A*S*H* movie, Robert Altman, hated the popular TV show), *Crossfire* trained us to see our world not just as a binary political landscape, but also as one permanently steeped in conflict.

Cohen was cast as the "liberal" opposite the likes of Buchanan and comedian Ben Stein (and Cohen writes humorously about the rattling discovery that Stein's nasal delivery turns out to be his actual voice). He was soon so weighed down by the cross-sniping format that he set as his goal trying to "say something unconventional, to stretch the limits of debate," at least once per episode.

Even that turned out to be extremely difficult. The shows are not designed to expand mental horizons. They're about two things: reinforcing the notion that the world is split in half (what Cohen calls the "two and only two" message), and the spectacle of combat.

"These TV debates are not about ideas or solutions or ideology, but simply partisan sniping and talking-point recitation," Cohen says now. "I enjoy a genuine right-left philosophical debate, when it's between serious analysts or journalists—as opposed to Democrat vs. Republican BS artists, and party hacks."

In his book, Cohen referenced an old joke: *What do pro wrestling and the U.S. Senate have in common? Both are dominated by overweight white guys pretending to hurt each other.* He said, "The intellectual level of cable news is one step above pro wrestling."

Cohen wrote that over a decade ago. Today the news is *at* the level of pro wrestling. This is one reason we have a WWE performer in the White House. It's the ultimate synthesis of politics and entertainment, and the core of it all is the ritual of conflict. Without conflict, there's no product.

Once you accept the "two, and two only" idea, we basically have you. The only trick from there is preventing narrative-upsetting ideas from getting onscreen too often. Hence:

3. HATE PEOPLE, NOT INSTITUTIONS

Trump is not just the perfect media product; he's a brilliant propaganda mechanism. Though most of our problems are systemic, most of our public debates are referendums on personality. Not many people can be neutral on the subject of Trump, so we wave him at you all day long.

Meanwhile, a vast universe of systemic issues is ignored. We've been steadily narrowing that field of view for decades, particularly in investigative reporting.

In the late nineties there was a series of high-level efforts by journalists to take on major corporate interests. One of them, the *60 Minutes* download of Big Tobacco whistleblower Jeffrey Wigand, was made into a feature film called *The Insider,* starring Al Pacino and Russell Crowe.

A second involved the *Cincinnati Enquirer*, which did a sweeping investigation of anti-labor practices at the Chiquita Banana company (which included paying millions to designated terrorist organizations and death squads in Colombia and other countries). A third effort involved married TV reporters Steve Wilson and Jane Akre at WTVT-TV in Tampa, a Fox affiliate. They prepared a huge exposé on Monsanto and its use of Bovine Growth Hormone.

All three big-swing exposés ended in actual or threatened litigation, and disaster. *60 Minutes* famously screwed over their source, Wigand, out of fear of being sued by tobacco firm Brown & Williamson, a moment that was an Alamo for press credibility. From that moment, sources could never be sure if they were making a deal with reporters, or reporters' lawyers.

The Chiquita reporters were denounced for using a voice-mail code given to them by a source to access Chiquita communications. This is an offense that seems to pale in comparison to helping death squads intimidate workers, but it won the headlines in the end. The paper ended up paying $10 million to Chiquita.

In *Manufacturing Consent,* Chomsky and Herman noted that in the aftermath of our loss in Vietnam, we regularly debated the morality of war journalism, but more rarely discussed the apparently less important subjects like invasion, occupation, bombing civilians, and so on. We still regularly examine the behaviors of investigative journalists as a source of potential overreach. It's the same species of overhyped controversy as tort reform. Chiquita was a story about the very worst kind of corporate misbehavior, but in the cultural memory it's become a story about dicey journalism.

In a headline years later, the *New Yorker* described the story as the "Chiquita Phone-Hacking Scandal," as opposed to, say, the "Chiquita buys AK-47s for death squads" scandal.

Akre/Wilson were bluntly told by their new masters at Fox, "We paid $3 billion for this station, we'll decide what the news is," and were then fired. After losing wrongful termination and whistleblower suits when they protested being let go for doing their jobs, Akre and Wilson were counter-sued for damages.

"We ended up paying them for the privilege of having our story killed," recalls a seething Akre.

In the years after *Manufacturing Consent* came out, big corporate conglomerates bought up most major media outlets. Station directors and publishers without reporting backgrounds suddenly became common. Now when you went to your boss to press for an important story, you were often talking to someone who looked back at you the way an auto executive might at an engineer pushing production of a car with a super-cool optional exploding-tire feature. As in, why the hell would we *try* to get sued?

The biggest outlets learned there's no percentage in doing big exposés against large, litigious companies. Not only will they sue, but they're also certain to pull ads as punishment (this was a big consideration in the Monsanto case, as Fox had 22 stations that could all have used NutraSweet ads). Why make trouble?

News audiences had also been trained by then not to value this kind of work the way they once had. It was easy enough to sell something else instead—better weather graphics, celebrity news, faster delivery, etc. Papers and stations that had their own correspondents abroad or in Washington increasingly shuttered those offices and relied on the wires. Nobody much cared.

The message to reporters working in big corporate news organizations was that long-form investigative reports targeting big commercial interests weren't forbidden exactly, just not something your boss was likely to gush over.

"I don't know if it was my case or just common sense, but there are some things you just know," says Akre. "Like if you want to work in TV in Florida, you're not going to do exposés on Disney."

"Consumer reporting" instead increasingly focused on softer targets.

"What you get instead is an exposé about some little Vietnamese restaurant. Because they won't fight back, obviously," says Akre. She drops her voice as she imitates a consumer-report VO: "You know, it's *'We'll take you... Behind the restaurant door...'*"

Akre, who was asked by her boss if she was sure a Monsanto exposé was the "hill" she wanted to "die on," never worked in TV again.

The reason these tales are important is that, when media companies aren't doing the right stories, they start self-sorting for the wrong ones. You could call this the *Worthy and Unworthy Targets* principle.

Worthy targets are small-time crooks, restaurant owners with rats, actors, athletes, reality stars, and other minor miscreants. In the nineties, to this list of worthy subjects, we added two more: "Either of the two approved political parties."

Akre was present for the birth of this innovation. She worked at early Fox stations that had the look, but not yet the politics. "Chandelier earrings, shoulder pads, giant blown-out hair," she laughs, describing the costume of female anchors at a Miami affiliate where she'd worked in the early nineties. "They had the outrageousness, but not yet the slant."

It was after the Monsanto episode that Fox struck gold with the Lewinsky story and the Clinton impeachment. Roger Ailes, the new CEO who'd helped kill the Monsanto piece, was learning to cash in by terrifying elderly audiences with images of evil hippie power couple Bill and Hillary Clinton.

Hillary denigrated *baking cookies* while letting her husband run around with his pants around his ankles. Thanks in large part to Lewinsky and the Starr probe—stories that Fox rode to riches as white hat/black hat soap dramas—the network went from launch to top of the cable market in less than six years.

Fox nailed the formula of the modern news story. Forget just doing a cable variety show with conservatives and liberals engaged in ritualized fighting. Why not make the whole news landscape a rooting section?

It would be a while before other networks embraced Fox-style open political slant (and when they did, they did it in a different way). But Ailes quickly had a lot of imitators when it came to the blame game, because:

4. EVERYTHING IS SOMEONE ELSE'S FAULT

Here's how we create political news content. Something happens, it doesn't matter what. Donald Trump nominates Brett Kavanaugh. A hurricane hits Puerto Rico. The financial markets collapse. Bill Clinton is impeached for perjury over a sex act. A massive humanitarian crisis hits Syria. Whatever it is, our task is to turn it into content, quickly running it through a flow chart:

BAD THING HAPPENS
Can it be blamed on one or the other party?
YES (we do the story)
NO (we don't do the story—see rule #5)

The overwhelming majority of "controversial news stories" involves simple partisan narratives cleaved quickly into hot-button talking points. Go any deeper and you zoom off the flow chart.

We like *easy* stories. This is another reason Trump has been such a savior to the news business, no matter how much Brian Stetler wants to deny it. Every narrative involving Trump is perfect: easy enough for the most uneducated audiences to digest (it has to be, because Trump usually has to understand it), and pre-packaged in crude binary format.

"Trump lied about 3,000 deaths in the Puerto Rico hurricane" is a story you can put in almost any big-city newspaper. If your audience is conservative, you can go with the flipped version, about how the media is out to screw the Donald: "No, it was Democrats who lied about the numbers!"

And what about Donald Trump's border policies separating families? Aren't they inhumane, literally concentration camps?

Concentration camps on our border? Yes, say some outlets.

But Trump says it was Obama's policy! No way, says Politifact, a fact-checking site preferred by liberal audiences. Well, sort of, says Obama's former Homeland Security Chief Jeh Johnson, who went on Fox and "freely admitted" the Obama administration did jail families and separate children in what he called a "controversial" policy.

If you weren't watching Fox but MSNBC, which ran "horrifying" details of new DHS reports of "just plain inhumane" conduct, you'd be right back where you probably started if you belonged to their target demographic: outraged by a brutal Trump policy.

In the days when we had a public interest standard that mandated companies using the public airwaves produce at least some non-sociopathic, non-commercial content, or when we had a Fairness Doctrine that required that reporters seek out credible representatives of different viewpoints, all of this back and forth would typically be weighed in one story.

Part of the reporter's job was to put aside the fault question and just describe the factual picture. The thornier the issue, the harder that job was. Immigration is a classic example of a story where blame for widespread misery and suffering is almost always diffuse and systemic, and very difficult to lay on any one politician or party.

Trump's "zero tolerance" gambit stands out because part of the intent of the policy seems to have been to dial up the inhumane aspects of enforcement bureaucracy to send a message. Moreover it comes from a president who's used lines like "they're bringing rapists" to rally anti-immigrant sentiment for political reasons.

But it is true that immigrant children were routinely separated from their parents long before Trump. Moreover the entire enforcement system is, and long has been, draconian and inhumane in a way that would shock most non-immigrants.

Also, it's not as if this problem was entirely created by American border officials. The numbers are lower today, but we've had years where nearly seventy thousand unaccompanied children tried to cross the southern border. Is there a *good* way to handle that? Administrations of both parties have had differing levels of failure dealing with this, but it's almost never looked good.

The best news stories take issues and find a way to make readers think hard about them, especially inviting them to consider how they themselves contribute to the problem. You want people thinking, "I voted for *what*?" Most problems are systemic, bipartisan, and bureaucratic, and most of us, by voting or not voting, paying taxes or not, own a little bit of most disasters.

But we veer you away from that mental alley, and instead feed you stories about how someone else did the bad thing, because:

5. NOTHING IS EVERYONE'S FAULT

If both parties have an equal or near-equal hand in causing a social problem, we typically don't cover it. Or better to say: a reporter or two might cover it, but it's never picked up. It doesn't take over a news cycle, doesn't become a thing.

The bloated military budget? Mass surveillance? American support for dictatorial regimes like the cannibalistic Mbasogo family in Equatorial Guinea, the United Arab Emirates, or Saudi Arabia? Our culpability in proxy-nation atrocities in places like Yemen or Palestine? The drone assassination program? Rendition? Torture? The drug war? Absence of access to generic or reimported drugs?

Nah. We just don't do these stories. At least, we don't do them anywhere near in proportion to their social impact. They're hard to sell. And the ability to market a story is everything.

Nomi Prins used to be a banker for Goldman Sachs. She left the industry prior to the 2008 crash and became an important resource for all Americans in the years that followed, helping explain what banks were doing, and why, from an inside perspective.

In recent years she became increasingly alarmed by central banking policies around the world. In Europe and the United States, she zeroed in on programs like Quantitative Easing that overworked the money-producing powers of the state and pumped giant sums of invented cash into the finance sector. She called this a "massive, unprecedented, coordinated effort to provide liquidity to [the] banking systems on a grand scale."

These policies are a kind of permanent welfare mechanism for the financial sector, and have had a dramatic impact around the world. They've accelerated an already serious financial inequality problem and addicted the banking sector to an unsustainable subsidy.

There's only one problem, at least in terms of editors. You can't sell this story as any one party's fault.

"It is a purely bipartisan situation that things are as fucked up as they are," laughs Prins.

The central banking policies have been supported by what we think of as the entire range of allowable political thought in America, i.e. from Bush-era Republicans who signed off on the original bank bailouts through the Obama Democrats who followed.

Prins's recent book on the topic, *Collusion*, describes a classic systemic problem, one that ought to have deep interest to "both" camps. For liberals, it's a story about an obscene subsidy of the very rich, while for conservatives, it's a profound story about the corruption of capitalism.

But TV bookers have struggled to figure out how to market Prins. She tells a story of a TV host who, in a troubled voice, quizzed her off air.

"He was like, 'I can't tell if you're progressive or conservative.' And I thought, that's good, isn't it?"

In the Trump era, Prins has faced an even steeper uphill climb. Not only did she write a book called *Collusion* that isn't about *that* collusion, she's writing about a topic that really has no direct Trump angle. Although her book does explicitly talk about how central banking problems contributed to political unrest that led to both Brexit and Trump, that topic is not a popular one on lefty media.

Prins figures she's ended up appearing more on Fox, which now sells Fed criticism in the "conspiracy of elites" vein that Trump used to great effect in 2016. Traditional left-leaning media has been less interested, with the exception of Ali Velshi on MSNBC, who happens to have some expertise and understanding of these issues.

When Velshi interviewed Prins, he made sure to tell viewers that her critique was different from the "secret society" conspiracism right-wingers often toss the Fed's way. He asked her why viewers should care about the issue. She talked about how banks take Fed largesse and use it to buy back their own stock and feed asset bubbles, creating danger and accelerating inequality.

All important—but no partisan angle, not really. The one partisan take you could point to is Trump taking credit for a soaring stock market when a lot of it is central bank dope in the economy's veins. But the larger problem is a constant one reaching back a decade or more.

Nonetheless (and I'm sure it wasn't Velshi doing this), the taglines during the Prins interview were almost all about Trump:

> TRUMP SET TO REMAKE FED TO REFLECT POLICIES
> TRUMP LIKELY TO LEAVE LASTING FINGERPRINTS ON FED
> AUTHOR: TRUMP'S FED MOVES COULD LEAVE GLOBE DEVASTATED

"If it's not either for or against Trump, you don't get airtime," Prins says. "You kind of have to pick one side."

This is the WWE-ization of news, incidentally encouraged by Trump, who has striven from the beginning to inject himself into the headlines. The problem is that this has paid off tremendously for him, and for commercial media across the political spectrum. But it hasn't been so good for us.

The notion of a crisis caused by a bipartisan confluence of powerful interests doesn't fit into the way we cover news today. It would be hard to do a story saying conservative higher-education profiteers like the DeVos family are gorging themselves on non-dischargeable, over-available federal student debt of the type congressional Democrats pushed for decades. This might be the truth, but it cannot be marketed, because it doesn't compute, not for modern news audiences. It upsets the format:

6. ROOT, DON'T THINK

By the early 2000s, TV stations had learned to cover politics exactly as they covered sports, a proven profitable format. The presidential election especially was reconfigured into a sports coverage saga. It was perfect: eighteen months of scheduled contests, a preseason (straw polls), regular season (primaries), and playoffs (the general), stadium events, a sub-genre of data reporting (it's not an accident that sabermetrics guru Nate Silver fit so seamlessly into political coverage).

TV news stations baldly copied visual "live variety" sports formats for coverage of primary elections, debates, election night, and soon enough, Sunday "discussion" shows like *Meet the Press*. If you've noticed, the sets bear an eerie resemblance to NFL pre-game shows. There's a reason for that.

"Panels are typically two conservative advocates versus two mainstream reporters/analysts who are obviously moderate libs but not allowed to admit it or strongly advocate much of anything," is how Cohen, formerly of *Crossfire*, puts it. Chuck Todd is Chris Berman is James Brown is Wolf Blitzer. The professional talker stands on one side of the panel and tosses to the various energetic advocates for and against the team's chances (Ana Navarro is Terry Bradshaw is Steve Mariucci is Van Jones), then they mediate the blather when everyone agrees and it all breaks down into conventional wisdom.

By the election of 2016, virtually all the sports graphic ideas had been stolen. There were "countdown to kickoff" clocks for votes, "percent chance of victory" trackers, "our experts pick" charts, a "magic number" for delegate counts, and a hundred different graphic doodads helping us keep score in the game. John King fiddling with his maps with Wolf Blitzer on the "magic wall" has become as much a part of our election mindscape as watching ex-athletes like David Carr or Jalen Rose chart football or hoops plays with civilians like Zach Lowe or Rachel Nichols.

You could wallpaper the Grand Canyon with debate-coverage boxing clichés. Try this in the 2020 cycle. See how often you read/hear one or more of these words in a debate story: "spar," "parry," "jab," "knockout," "knockdown," "glass jaw," "uppercut," "low blow," "counterpunch," "rope-a-dope," "rabbit punch," "sucker punch," "in the ring," "TKO," or any of about a dozen other terms. It will be shocking if future debates don't have weigh-in ceremonies.

Actually, they already *do* have weigh-in ceremonies for debate shows. Consider a super-loathsome special event reuniting *Crossfire* grads Paul Begala and Tucker Carlson at the Conservative Political Action Conference, in which an announcer introduces the two:

Weighing in with years of experience as a commentator for CNN, standing tall beside Bill and Hillary Clinton, Paul 'Big Government' Begala!

(Begala here actually entered the "ring" with a triumphant raised-hands pose, as in, yes, call me "Big Government" Begala)

In the right corner... standing tall as the founder of the Daily Caller... Tucker "Cut it all" Carlson!

(Carlson enters, and the two men sit at seats with boxing gloves draped over them)

This nonsense has all had the effect of depoliticizing elections and turning them into blunt contests of tactics, fundraising, and rhetorical technique (CNN even pioneered the use of real-time dial surveys of focus groups, to help "keep political score" in debates). It also hardened the winner-take-all vision of politics for audiences.

By 2016 we'd raised a generation of viewers who had no conception of politics as an activity that might or should involve compromise. Your team either won or lost, and you felt devastated or vindicated accordingly. We were training rooters instead of readers. Since our own politicians are typically very disappointing, we particularly root for the other side to lose. Being an American in the 1 percent era is like being a Jets fan whose only conceivable pleasure is rooting against the Patriots. We're haters, but what else is there?

The famous appearance of Jon Stewart on *Crossfire* in 2004 unmasked the conceit of all of this. The comedian blasted Carlson (from the right!) and Begala (from the left!) for "partisan hackery" and nailed them with a simple request: stop fighting and say something nice about an opposing-party politician.

Carlson was clever enough to say, "I like John Kerry, I care about John Kerry," which made him sound human-ish—until he spent the rest of the segment trying to hound Stewart into admitting he was a "butt boy" for Kerry.

(A central fixation of the right-wing media universe Carlson occupies involves forcing every coastal intellectual to admit he or she is in the tank for the Dems. But he was wrong about Stewart. The uniqueness of the *Daily Show,* what made it funny, was that it ridiculed both parties. The Bush administration just happened to be more absurd than the Democrats at the time).

Meanwhile, when Stewart turned to Begala and asked him to say something nice about George W. Bush, Begala could only say, "He'll be unemployed soon."

Audiences today will cheer that, but it was a lousy answer. In the show format—"emphasis on show," as Cohen says—Begala, a former Clinton advisor, wasn't allowed to break character. Even I could probably think of something nice to say about George W. Bush, his family, his voters, something. But in this business, everyone is on a side, and we're always fighting, never looking for common ground. It ruins everyone's suspension of disbelief if we do.

7. NO SWITCHING TEAMS

That symbolic moment when Paul Begala and Tucker Carlson were unable to find something nice to say about each other has since spilled into all news coverage. The concept of "balance," which used to be considered a virtue, has been twisted all the way around to mean a taboo trade practice, a form of dishonesty.

Roger Ailes at Fox started this. He made the whole concept of "balance" an inside joke among right-wing media. It's the reason the preposterous slogan, "Fair and Balanced," was so effective, both for recruiting conservative viewers and infuriating liberals.

Ailes used to say: "The news is like a ship. If you take hands off the wheel, it pulls hard to the left." Translation: you needed to pull hard the other way to achieve "balance" overall.

"Fair and balanced," in other words, was a rip on the idea that standard, dull, third-person *New York Times*–style media was *already* balanced. Twenty years before it would become a popular rallying cry on the other side, Roger Ailes was essentially using an argument about "false balance" to market Fox.

In recent years, but especially during the 2016 election, an array of Soviet-sounding terms started appearing to describe a new brand of thoughtcrime. Reporters had always taken lots of criticism from right-wing audiences for showing bias. In the last election, those same criticisms started to come from college-educated, liberal-leaning audiences.

They started to throw around terms like "false balance," "false equivalency," and "both-sideism."

In late 2016, *New York Times* public editor Liz Spayd started to get lots of angry mail about "false balance." Mainly, they were accusations that the *Times* over-covered Hillary Clinton's emails and legitimized Clinton Foundation stories. There was enough of this that she felt a need to respond to charges in the paper.

"The problem with false balance doctrine is that it masquerades as rational thinking," she said, adding: "What the critics really want is for journalists to apply their own moral and ideological judgments to the candidates."

She added a hypothetical:

Suppose journalists deem Clinton's use of private email servers a minor offense compared with Trump inciting Russia to influence an American election by hacking into computers—remember that? Is the next step for a paternalistic media to barely cover Clinton's email so that the public isn't confused about what's more important? Should her email saga be covered at all? It's a slippery slope.

Spayd probably had no idea that the "slippery slope" argument was also on its way to being delegitimized as well, but that's another topic.

While Spayd was pushing back on the "false balance" controversy, the *Times* was embracing a significant change internally. The Jim Rutenberg editorial calling for reporters in the Trump age to rethink old "norms of objectivity" was a significant step. He wrote his piece in August, right as Spayd was beginning to engage readers on the balance issue.

Rutenberg argued we should re-imagine "objectivity" in a way that would "stand up to history's judgment." This was basically code for accepting the argument about making political judgments about impact before running stories, even newsworthy ones. Was it a major step for the *Times*? I know I thought so, and a few other reporters did. So did Spayd.

"I thought it was," she says. "And didn't they put it on the front?"

They did: the Rutenberg clarion call about "norms of objectivity" ran on their page A1, the choicest real estate in American media. This said a lot about what the paper was thinking.

After Trump won, Spayd made what many considered the unforgivable offense of going on Tucker Carlson's TV show. Carlson opened by brandishing the day-after *Times* headline about Trump's win:

DEMOCRATS, STUDENTS, AND FOREIGN ALLIES
FACE THE REALITY OF A TRUMP PRESIDENCY

The *Times* of course is not obligated to celebrate a Trump presidency, but this headline was a major stylistic departure. It was less reporting than audience signaling, a blunt list of demographics: "THE SANE AMONG US BRACE FOR TRUMP PRESIDENCY."

Spayd pushed back when Carlson called this "advocacy," and said it was something more subtle and maybe worse: an "unrecognized point of view that comes from... being in New York in a certain circle, and seeing the world in a certain way."

In a classic example of the always-attacking style of TV conservatives, Carlson didn't accept the olive branch Spayd was trying to offer. Instead, he just kept pounding away.

He quizzed her on reporters' political bias. Spayd had protested that the paper's reporters tried hard to be fair and professional, but Carlson scoffed. "I would believe you," he said, "except that I know for a fact it isn't true."

He then read off a series of horrified anti-Trump tweets written by *Times* line reporters. Liam Stack's "The electoral college was meant to stop men like Trump from taking office" was an example. "Are you kidding me?" Carlson snapped.

Spayd nodded and said, "Yeah, I think it's outrageous." This was a line that would be much howled over, because it gave pro-Trump types and people like Carlson a talking point, another unforgivable offense.

But Spayd's point was not that having political views is bad, or that too many reporters are liberals. Rather, she was saying a reporter airing personal political views in public was unseemly, at least according to that's paper's venerable standards.

She noted we all have personal political beliefs, but "they ought to be personal," and "when you sign up to be a journalist, that's what you ought to be."

I watched the Carlson interview of Spayd after colleagues insisted I click to "see how awful" she was. I did and was shocked. I thought reporters misunderstood. Spayd was taking a view that ten years ago would have been completely uncontroversial. It was very old-school *Times,* and in a way, very pro-reporter.

In the age before social media, most reporters didn't have to expose their political opinions to the world. Today everyone is effectively an op-ed writer. Spayd's take was, this isn't necessarily a good idea, and exposes both reporters and papers like the *Times* to accusations of bias in ways we never had to worry about before.

Spayd today recalls that summer with dismay. She was no fan of candidate Donald Trump, but felt she couldn't say so in her position. She also knew that opening a discussion about "false balance" was dangerous.

"I knew I was poking the bear," she says now. "I figured the bear would probably poke back."

But she did it because she felt it was important to argue a general principle, "trying to hold on to that value." By "that value," she meant the very old *Times* principle of reporters at least pretending to keep their own views separate from the topics they covered. In the new environment, however, arguing this was only understood as doing something for the other side.

"It's just a way of disguising the argument, to say, 'Oh, she's a Republican,'" she says.

Not only did the *Times* end up firing Spayd, they eliminated her position. Even journalists of long experience cheered her dismissal in terms that were remarkably harsh. *Gizmodo* called her "incompetent," the *Daily Beast* said she was "failed," while *Slate* went with "failing." Spayd, wrote *Vox*, was "so bad at her job that the elimination of her role might be seen as an improvement."

This is another feature of the new media environment: conventional wisdom is now capable of doing full U-turns virtually overnight. Spayd was taking heat essentially for defending an approach that less than a year before had been industry standard: "objectivity."

The neutral-sounding third-person tone we used to understand as "objectivity" was itself primarily a commercial strategy.

In the early days of mass media, the big press enterprises operated in artificially scarce markets. Limited numbers of FCC licenses for broadcasters and the gigantic expense of maintaining and building distribution networks for newspapers meant most media outlets were only taking on a competitor or two. Big daily newspapers had gravy trains of captive local advertisers. TV and radio shows could charge fortunes for scarce ad time.

What this meant for journalism was a stress on inoffensiveness. Radio broadcaster Lowell Thomas, who at one point was the primary source of news for over 10 percent of the country, once said that his first radio sponsor, the *Literary Digest,* insisted that he report everything "down the middle."

Thomas became famous for his opening line: "Good morning, *everybody.*" The appeal to an "everybody" audience became the template for commercial success. (Contrast this with Roger Ailes once bragging about making a network for people "55 to dead," or even the *Times* headline aimed at Democrats, students, and foreigners.) Their normal voice was even, unemotional, and "above the fray," in a way that was often easy to lampoon.

But the fact that "objectivity" was less about principle than profit, stylistically silly, and easily manipulated into masking all sorts of awful political realities (historically, from racism to American military atrocities abroad), didn't mean it was worthless.

"Objectivity," above all, was great protection for reporters. Having no obvious political bent was a prerequisite for taking on politicians. If you announced yourself as an ally of one party or another, you lost your credibility with audiences.

"Balance" didn't mean having to quote science-deniers. It was mainly a way for journalists to stay out of unspoken political alliances. Once you jump in that pit, it's not so easy to get out.

Two years ago, unnerved by a lot of the same comments about "false balance," I wrote: "The model going forward will likely involve Republican media covering Democratic corruption and Democratic media covering Republican corruption."

This is more or less where we are now, and nobody seems to think this is bad or dysfunctional. This is despite the fact that in this format (especially given the individuated distribution mechanisms of the Internet, like the Facebook news feed) the average person will no longer even see—ever—derogatory reporting about his or her own "side."

Being out of touch with what the other side is thinking is now no longer seen as a fault. It's a requirement, because:

8. THE OTHER SIDE IS LITERALLY HITLER

Shortly after 9/11, Fox began a long streak at the top of the cable ratings. Beginning in the first quarter of 2002, the company was number one for over fifteen years straight.

A crucial part of its success was its reaction to 9/11. Post-attack America was afraid and in need of someone to blame. Fox and its minions were more than happy to comply. They began using language about liberals that was extreme even by their standards.

Their fellow Americans, leading conservative thinkfluencers told them, were not just lily-livered suckups who pretended to be enlightened. They were actively in cahoots with al-Qaeda. Murderers. Traitors. Not wrong, but evil.

Fox promoted Sean Hannity as their perfect vision of conservative manhood. The rectum-faced blowhard was celebrated for his fake daily victories over the intellectual Washington Generals act that was Alan Colmes.

Unlike Rush Limbaugh, who, in his early days, was a serviceably witty top-40 disc jockey in Pittsburgh, Hannity was charmless. He was not literate like William Safire or Bill Buckley, nor was he an entertainingly unstable wreck like Glenn Beck, nor could he talk volubly about Marx and other thinkers like Michael Savage, a person who clearly has read more than three or four books.

Hannity wouldn't know the difference between Marcuse and a cucumber, the Frankfurt School and a frankfurter. He won fake arguments, preened, and spewed constant aggression. After 9/11, one of his signature lines of attack was that liberals were in league with terrorists.

He wrote a book called *Deliver Us from Evil: Defeating Terrorism, Despotism and Liberalism* that came out in 2004. It was a paint-by-numbers hate-your-neighbor manual, whose blunt cover was just Hannity's coiffed head floating under the Statue of Liberty's armpit.

The main argument was that liberals, by refusing to accept the existence of terrorist evil, were themselves part of the nexus of wrongdoing. They were insufficiently stoked about the capture and hanging of Saddam Hussein and, let's face it, wimps. He held off for two whole pages before bringing up Neville Chamberlain.

Many others chimed in. Ann Coulter's redundant classic was *Treason: Liberal Treachery from the Cold War to the War on Terrorism*. Savage's windy effort, *The Enemy Within: Saving America from the Liberal Assault on Our Schools, Faith, and Military*, contributed the key word "enemy." He would later go with *Liberalism Is a Mental Disorder*.

If you're keeping score at home, Americans were being told they were surrounded by millions of people who were in league with homicidal terrorists, plotting to overthrow free enterprise and install a dictatorship of political correctness. Liberals were also clinically insane.

Glenn Beck would take Hannity's Neville Chamberlain thread and run lap after lap with it, pioneering the "Your neighbor is literally Hitler" movement. Beck was awesome at this. Al Gore was Hitler. Obama was constantly Hitler.

The National Endowment of the Arts was Hitler! ("It's propaganda... you should look up the name 'Goebbels.'"). ACORN was Hitler. The bailouts were Hitler (well, they actually were a little bit Hitler). Comedian Lewis Black had a hilarious *Daily Show* freakout when Beck compared even the Peace Corps to the SS!

As Black put it, it was "Six degrees of Kevin Bacon, except there's just one degree, and Kevin Bacon is Hitler!"

Beck was a mixed-metaphor enthusiast who was capable of calling a target both fascist and communist, Hitler *and* Stalin, in the same telecast. But his money gimmick was Hitler. It won him a huge audience, until it also ruined him.

His Fox show was canceled in 2011 after he said Barack Obama had a "deep-seated hatred for white people." Within two years he was apologizing for being divisive—but still carrying around a napkin that supposedly contained Hitler's bloodstains.

There's nowhere to go from Hitler. It's a rhetorical dead end. Argument is over at that point. If you go there, you're now absolving your audiences of all moral restraint, because who wouldn't kill Hitler?

You can draw a straight line from these rhetorical escalations in right-wing media to the lunacies of the Trump era. If you can believe the Peace Corps is the SS, then why doubt Muslims in Jersey City were cheering 9/11, or question the logic of an anti-rape wall across the Rio Grande? Stupid is stupid.

When Donald Trump ran for office, he posed serious problems for anyone conscious of Godwin's Law. As Chomsky points out, Trump's campaign was a familiar authoritarian pitch: "Go after the elites, even while you're supported by the major elites."

His stump speeches hit a lot of notes to which history professors quickly perked up. He preached that modern life was a failure of decadence (this from a man whose personal life was a monument to tacky consumption). He told of a once-proud society in ruin, surrounded by mongrel assassins. "They kill us," he said in his opening speech. "They're laughing at us, at our stupidity... They're killing us."

A strong hand was needed to help our return to national values. He attacked left and right ideologies. Democracy was undemocratic, an aristocratic trick, rigged. In a debate with Hillary Clinton, he threatened to jail his opponent, a stunt that would have impressed Mobutu.

Anyone with an education saw the parallels. But Trump was legally winning elections, and he was bolstered by the fact that his riffs on corrupt elites rang true with audiences.

The financial bailouts had been an extraordinary betrayal of the population by the political class, which is why Trump scored when he painted Ted Cruz and Hillary Clinton as creatures of Goldman Sachs. *Citizens United* meant political bribery on a grand scale was legal, and this theme helped Trump knock out Jeb Bush and Ted Cruz and Marco Rubio.

He ripped the Koch Brothers, and denounced his primary opponents as sock-puppet fronts for corporate PACs. Then he did the same to Hillary Clinton. These clowns are just fronts for someone else's money, Trump told voters. With me, I *am* the money.

Trump, like all great con artists, depended upon true details to sell lies.

The major challenge for reporters in covering Trump was to explain his rise. There were a million reasons, beginning with the billions in free coverage he received. He certainly played on racial panic and feelings of lost status. This was a dominant theme of his announcement speech, how low we'd sunk, how we never win anymore, etc.

The failures of decades of policy, with little real wage growth since the Nixon era, were surely also a factor.

It was complicated. You couldn't say it wasn't. There were 4Chan crazies and elderly church ladies alike in the Trump coalition. Trump was a vote for anyone with a grudge, and in America, there is a spectacularly wide spectrum of grudges.

I met one voter in Wisconsin who said the following: "I usually don't vote, but I'm going Trump because fuck everything."

Sometime in the spring or summer of 2016 I started to notice blowback every time I mentioned the economy in connection with Trump voters. Very quickly (it's amazing how fast these trends gain traction in the social media age) the use of the term "economic insecurity" became a meme-worthy offense on social media.

Greg Sargent of the *Washington Post* posted quotes of Trump voters saying "Build a wall, kill them all," "Trump that bitch!" and "Kill her!" above the punch line: "Can't you just feel the economic insecurity and desire for disruption? "

All of this roughly coincided with Clinton saying in September that "half of Trump's supporters" were "racist, sexist, homophobic, xenophobic, Islamophobic, you name it," what she deemed a "basket of deplorables."

Most outsiders recognized this as a political mistake on par with Romney's 47 percent gaffe. According to the book *Shattered: Inside Hillary Clinton's Doomed Campaign* by Jonathan Allen and Amie Parnes, it was Clinton's "first unforced error of the fall," or so her staffers were said to have thought.

But the "unforced error" soon became gospel in the press. *Saturday Night Live's* "Racists For Trump" skit from earlier in the year, which showed Trumpers in swastika armbands and Klan hoods and so on, became the go-to, exclusive explanation for Trump's rise.

The conventional wisdom was that Trump *was* Hitler, effectively, even before he got elected. "Is Donald Trump a fascist?" was the *Times* book review headline shortly before the vote (several authors said "yes").

After Trump was elected, a whole new line of rhetoric was unveiled in connection with Russiagate. It became common, encouraged even, to use words like "traitor" and "treason" in headlines.

After the fiasco of Charlottesville, when Trump couldn't bring himself to denounce open racists and said instead that "both sides" were at fault, the terms "white supremacist" and "white nationalist" became common to describe Trump's tenure.

It was one thing to apply the terms to Trump, who deserves all of these epithets and then some. But his voters? Did it really make sense to caricaturize sixty million people as *racist, white nationalist traitor-Nazis*?

The supposed sequels to Charlottesville (one rally in Boston, another one a year later in Washington) were jokes: maybe a dozen mental health cases surrounded by thousands of furious anti-racist protesters, trailed by packs of reporters.

But scary photos of the loons became fodder for the new party line, which is that we could turn off the thinking mechanism and move to pure combat. Charles Taylor of the *Boston Globe*, in a column under a scary photo of a man waving a swastika, summed it up when he scoffed:

> Those bent on understanding Trump supporters—as if there is something deep to understand—wonder how his working-class acolytes can vote against their own economic interests. What they refuse to see is that all Trump supporters, from the working class to the upper class, have voted their chief interest: maintaining American identity as white, Christian, and heterosexual.

Before you can argue the justice of this point, realize what it means. If we're now saying all Trump supporters are mainly bent on upholding the supremacy of white, Christian, heterosexuals, that's miles beyond even Hillary Clinton's take of just half of Trump supporters being unredeemable scum.

It's a sweeping, debate-ending dictum. There is *us* and *them*, and they are Hitler.

When I first started to hear this talk among reporters during 2016, I thought it was just clickbait. *Of course* race was a dominant factor in Trump's rise. Virtually all Republican politicians from the Goldwater days on (and all Southern Democrats before) made race a central part of their pitches.

The appeals were usually somewhat coded, but whether it was Goldwater blasting urban "marauders" or Reagan's "welfare queens," or Willie Horton, or Jesse Helms and his "white hands," the messages weren't exactly subtle.

Trump blew past those parameters, of course, and his lunatic inability to renounce the KKK or Nazis surely dragged us all into new depths.

But racism as the sole explanation for Trump's rise was suspicious for a few reasons. Chief of which being that it completely absolved either political party (both the Republican and Democratic party establishments were rejected in 2016, in some cases for overlapping reasons) of having helped create the preconditions for Trump.

Trump doesn't happen in a country where things are going well. People give in to their baser instincts when they lose faith in the future. The pessimism and anger necessary for this situation has been building for a generation, and not all on one side.

A significant number of Trump voters voted for Obama eight years ago. A lot of those were in rust-belt states that proved critical to his election. What happened there? Trump also polled 2–1 among veterans, despite his own horrific record of deferments and his insulting of every vet from John McCain to Humayun Khan.

Was it possible that his rhetoric about ending "our current policy of regime change" resonated with recently returned vets? The data said yes. It may not have been decisive, but it likely was one of many factors. It was also common sense, because this was one of his main themes on the campaign trail—Trump clearly smelled those veteran votes.

The Trump phenomenon was also about a political and media taboo: class. When the liberal arts grads who mostly populate the media think about class, we tend to think in terms of the heroic worker, or whatever Marx-inspired cliché they taught us in college.

Because of this, most pundits scoff at class, because when they look at Trump crowds, they don't see *Norma Rae* or *Matewan*. Instead, they see *Married with Children,* a bunch of tacky mall-goers who gobble up crap movies and, incidentally, hate the noble political press. Our take on Trump voters was closer to Orwell than Marx: "In reality very little was known about the proles. It was not necessary to know much."

Beyond the utility that calling everything racism had for both party establishments, it was good for that other sector, the news media.

If all Trump supporters are Hitler, and all liberals are also Hitler, this brings *Crossfire* to its natural conclusion. The *America vs. America* show is now *Hitler vs. Hitler*! Think of the ratings! The new show leaves out 100 million people who didn't vote at all (a group that by itself is nearly as big as both the Clinton and Trump electorates combined), but this is part of the propaganda.

Non-voters are the single biggest factor in American political life, and their swelling numbers are, just like the Trump phenomenon, a profound indictment of our system. But they don't exist on TV, because they suspend our disbelief in the *Hitler vs. Hitler* show.

We don't want you thinking about anything complicated: not non-voters, not war fatigue, not the collapse of the manufacturing sector, not Fed policy, none of that. None of what happened in 2016 is your fault: it's all the pure evil of white nationalism. For conservatives, it's the opposite: don't believe anything in the *New York Times*, don't think about the impact of upper-class tax cuts and deregulation, just stay in your lane. Remember, you are surrounded by determined enemies, out to destroy tradition, the nuclear family, increase your taxes, take your job and your gun, and remove your president by any means, legal or illegal.

It's a fight for all the marbles. Politics today is about one side against the other side, and there's only one take allowed: pure aggression.

9. IN THE FIGHT AGAINST HITLER, EVERYTHING IS PERMITTED

Cohen's take on *Crossfire* was right. The early staged TV battles depended on a propaganda trick for their success. The networks didn't want to encourage constructive political activism, so the "fight" always involved a ferocious, deregulation-mad, race-baiting winger pounding the crap out of a spineless, backpedaling centrist masquerading as a "leftist."

Cohen's Fairness and Accuracy in Reporting (FAIR) did a "field guide to TV's lukewarm liberals" that explained how this works. Michael Kinsley, probably the most famous voice "from the left," once described himself as a "wishy-washy moderate" and added, "There is no way... that I'm as far left as Pat Buchanan is right."

Cokie Roberts played the "liberal" on *The Week*, but her main liberal credentials were that she was a woman who'd been on NPR. Her advice to Bill Clinton after the midterm losses of 1994: "Move to the right, which is the advice that somebody should have given him a long time ago."

Crossfire even once hired corporate lobbyist Bob Beckel, who called Gulf War protesters "punks," for playing the "from the left" role.

If your only experience of life was watching these shows, you might conclude that the chief problem of American politics is one of tactics. Why does Paul Begala let Tucker Carlson just pound away at him like that? Why is he such a *wuss*?

When you watched these shows, you were always looking at an aggressor and a conciliator. "From the right" always looked more confident because it was representing a "real" political agenda.

When Tucker Carlson denounced unions, he meant it. When Paul Begala blathered that unions were "All-American, essential for democracy," he looked like he was spouting pat gibberish, because he was. He had worked for the administration that passed NAFTA and pioneered the Democrats' move away from union money and union infrastructure, toward big-business cash to support campaigns.

After years of this phony debate, along came Trump, who could easily have been a *Crossfire* actor (although the nineties version of "very pro-choice" Trump probably would have played "on the left").

The modern Trump is pretty much exactly Buchanan, right down to the race views and the appropriation of trade issues, only he's better at playing the heel. For most of liberal America, the election played out like an old *Crossfire* episode.

Trump pounded away at Clinton, and refused to take back even the most shameless behaviors. Meanwhile Clinton tried to observe decorum, apologized for her "unforced errors" like the "deplorables" comment, and was unrewarded for her efforts.

Years ago, when Jon Stewart went on *Crossfire*, he did what most liberal TV watchers had been waiting for someone to do for ages: he called Carlson a dick. Hugely satisfying! Great TV!

But that's all it was: great TV. The solution wasn't to create more satisfying entertainment. The solution was to have better politics. Or more real politics. Something that was not a staged fight.

Begala's problem wasn't that he was a weenie and insufficiently aggressive: it was that he didn't stand for anything. This was Stewart's larger point about how the phony combat was "hurting America." It wasn't educational, it wasn't political in any meaningful way.

After Trump won, though, another consensus formed. Liberal America had to be less polite. Samantha Bee was a pioneer, calling Ivanka Trump a "feckless cunt." Creaky old Robert De Niro (He was tough! He once played a boxer!) won the Internet when he said "Fuck Trump!" at an awards show.

When a restaurant owner in DC refused to serve Sarah Huckabee Sanders in the wake of the Trump-immigration mess, and cadaverous Trump aide Stephen Miller was called a "fascist" by a protester at a Mexican restaurant, this quickly triggered a farcical media debate about "civility."

Politicians were asked to chime in. Maxine Waters was one of the first to endorse the "yes, you may bother assholes at restaurants" idea. Hillary Clinton, who once insisted, "when they go low, we go high," had had enough and co-signed.

Clinton said, "You cannot be civil with a political party that wants to destroy what you care about." She added, "Civility can start again" when Democrats re-take the White House.

Before long it was a media trope that civility was actually a regressive thing, a balm to fascism. Incivility was a requirement, a show of solidarity. "Fuck civility" was the *Guardian's* take. "Trump officials don't get to eat dinner in peace— not while kids are in cages."

Before long, it was typical for once-staid media figures and elected officials alike to swear like sea captains in public. *Harper's Bazaar* didn't just call Trump's claims about Obama's border policies wrong: they were "bullshit." Even the headline read "bullshit"! In *Harper's Bazaar*!

By the time the Kavanaugh debate rolled around, the floor of the U.S. Senate sounded like the set of *Goodfellas*. Senator Mazie Hirono, on Senator Chuck Grassley: "That is such bullshit I can hardly stand it."

Senator Lindsey Graham, to Senator Bob Menendez: "What y'all have done is bullshit." (That was on TV). Menendez, tweeting on the FBI investigation of Kavanaugh: "It's a bullshit investigation."

Watching all of this had me weirded out, among other things because I was infamous for my own use of bad language in print and had been trying for years to weed it out of my work. I thought: *Now* this is okay?

Then I realized the trend toward nastier language was based on a faulty syllogism:

Civility got us nowhere.
The uncivil Donald Trump won.
Therefore, we must be uncivil to win.

Actually, none of those three things have anything to do with one another. Democratic voters were nowhere after 2016 for a lot of reasons, and very few of them had anything to do with being insufficiently rude.

Trump was uncivil, and did win, but about the last thing in the world any sane person would advise is following his example.

During the race, I kept trying to imagine how someone like Martin Luther King would have responded to Trump. I don't think the answer would have been, "We need to start saying *fuck* more."

Does Stephen Miller have the right to enjoy an enchilada in peace? I have no idea. Probably not. Is this a question of earth-shattering importance? Also probably not.

The incivility movement is not about politics. It's about money and audience. In a hyper-competitive media environment where a billion pieces of content per day are created on platforms like Facebook, one has to work in overdrive to win eyeballs.

Which headline is the Hawaiian Democrat going to click on first:

"Ballast Discharge Measure Won't Protect Hawaii's Coastal Waters"?

Or:

"11 Times Marie Hirono Had Zero Fucks to Give"?

Scatological blather scores shares and retweets, and now that there's no ideological or commercial requirement to avoid pissing off the whole audience—no more "Good morning, everybody"—there's no disincentive to using the strongest language.

That's why this stuff is coming out in factory-level amounts on both sides now. It's why Samantha Bee, at this very moment, is searching the Internet for a word worse than "cunt," and why ostensibly devout Christians will love it in 2020 when Donald Trump calls his Democratic opponent a cocksucker or a whore, just as I watched them cheer in New Hampshire when he called Ted Cruz a pussy.

Meanness and vulgarity build political solidarity, but also audience solidarity. Breaking barriers together builds conspiratorial closeness. In the Trump age, it helps political and media objectives align.

The problem is, there's no natural floor to this behavior. Just as cable TV will eventually become seven hundred separate twenty-four-hour porn channels, news and commentary will eventually escalate to boxing-style, expletive-laden, pre-fight tirades, and the open incitement of violence.

If the other side is literally Hitler, this eventually has to happen. It would be illogical to argue anything else. What began as *America vs. America* will eventually move to *Traitor vs. Traitor,* and the show does not work if those contestants are not eventually offended to the point of wanting to kill one another.

10. FEEL SUPERIOR

Hunter Pauli is a young writer based in Montana. He started as an intern at the *Montana Standard,* which at the time was doing hardcore local investigative work, often on environmental issues. Pauli got into this line of work because "punching up seems like the only worthwhile thing to do in journalism."

When the *Standard*'s crime beat opened, Pauli took the job and found that he was being asked to pump out an endless stream of stories about poor people doing stupid things.

Pauli soon found himself feeling uneasy. He was in one of the worst gigs in journalism: a local crime beat. His job mostly consisted of getting details from a public official like a police spokesperson, who would give him the state's version of low-rent arrests.

Few think about this, but the press routinely puts the names and personal information of people arrested in newspapers, on TV, and, worst of all, online, where the stories live forever.

Yet these people have not been convicted of crimes. They have merely been arrested or charged.

"I was getting third-hand info from someone like a public information officer, and we were routinely publishing stories without getting the point of view of the person it affected most," Pauli recalls. "In this kind of crime reporting we typically don't even take the most basic steps... [such as] seeking confirmation from a secondary source."

"I wasn't out there covering murders every single day," Pauli recalls. "There just wasn't a lot of crime. Maybe someone goes running down the street naked because they can't afford their meds, or shoplifts from a Wal-Mart because they're broke..."

Sometimes, there would be nights when nothing at all would happen.

"So I'd tell my editor, 'Hey, nothing happened.' And he'd say, 'Just find something.' Because he can't afford for there to be nothing."

Pauli began to feel conflicted, particularly about putting information about people's arrests online, which would prevent them from getting jobs in the future, as well as affect them in all sorts of ways. He tried to pitch his paper on more important subjects, like abnormally high rates of lead in the blood of children born in Butte. But it was a no go.

"I had three sure-fire investigations in a row spiked," says Pauli.

Things came to a head after he ran a story about a guy who escaped from custody after a mental-health evaluation. Police called the man "Dickface" because of an unfortunately-shaped tattoo.

The "Dickface" story went viral, and Pauli began to think about leaving the job. He began self-editing, leaving out stories about people shoplifting from Walmart "despite how frequently it happened and how much readers loved laughing about it."

Looking back, he explains: "There are people in the world worth laughing at. They're called politicians. But these people?"

Pauli ended up quitting journalism, writing about his decision in the *Guardian*.

What's remarkable about Pauli's story is how rare it is. Pauli happened to be in one of the worst corners of the game, covering crime, which is a genre primarily concerned with needlessly stoking class/racial fears on the one hand, while making people feel superior on the other.

But the core dynamic of his job was not much different from what most of us do. We're mainly in the business of stroking audiences. We want them coming back. Anger is part of the rhetorical promise, but so are feelings of righteousness and superiority.

It's why we love terrible people like Casey Anthony or O.J. as news subjects a lot more than we'd *like* someone who spends his or her days working in a pediatric oncology ward. Showing genuinely heroic or selfless people on TV would make most audiences feel inferior. Therefore, we don't.

It's the same premise as reality shows. The most popular programs aren't about geniuses and paragons of virtue, but instead about terrible parents, morons, people too fat to notice they're pregnant, people willing to be filmed getting ass tucks, spoiled rich people, and other folks we can deem freaks.

Why use the most advanced communications technology in history to teach people basic geography, or how World Bank structural adjustment lending works, when we can instead show people idiots drinking donkey semen for money?

Your media experience is designed to nurture and protect your ego. So we show you the biggest losers we can find. It's the underlying principle of almost every successful entertainment product we've had, from *COPS* to *Freakshow* to, literally, *The Biggest Loser*. We're probably just a few years way from a show called *What Would You Suck For a Dollar?"*

This dynamic was confined to the entertainment arena for a while, but it became part of political coverage long ago.

As far back as 1984, the Republican Party was urging people to vote Reagan because Walter Mondale was a "born loser." On the flip side, the name "George McGovern" became so synonymous with "loser" that it birthed an entirely new brand of "Third Way" politics, invented by the Democratic Leadership Council and people like Chuck Robb, Al From, Sam Nunn, and Bill Clinton. The chief principle of this new politics was that it had a chance of winning.

The media started following along. We invented the "Wimp Factor" for George H. W. Bush and saddled Dan Quayle with the "bimbo" tag. This was propaganda, of course, as the idea was that politicians could only not be losers by bombing someone. But we were also telling audiences that a loser was someone who didn't attack.

In the early nineties, the *Weekly Standard* wrote that Republicans wanted Quayle to "dispel his bimbo image" by "showing some teeth, Spiro Agnew style."

Agnew is one of the biggest disgraces in the history of American politics, a blowhard with no discernible ideas beyond the promiscuous use of every conceivable form of political corruption—yet in the American consciousness, he's not a loser. He's an aggressor.

Presidential campaign coverage as far back as the early 2000s was basically *Heathers* on an airplane. We developed lots of words for "loser," and spent countless hours developing new methods of telling audiences which candidates were in that category.

Dennis Kucinich, who was constantly ridiculed in the press plane for both his shortness and his earnestness, was dubbed the "lovable loser of the left." The contravening kind of story was usually about the abject dumbness of Republicans. I actually won an award for such an effort, an article about Mike Huckabee called "My Favorite Nut Job."

Pauli is right: politicians should be fair game. But the obsession with winners and losers runs so deep in the press that it has become the central value of the business.

It's not an accident that Trump won the presidency on "winning" and spent much of his political career calling people "losers"—from Cher to Richard Belzer to Graydon Carter to Rosie O'Donnell to George Will to Michelle Malkin.

Trump sells the vicarious experience of being a "winner" compared to other schlubs. His lack of empathy is often cited as evidence of narcissistic sociopathy, and maybe it is, but it's a chicken-and-egg question. Was he always like this? Or did he become *more* this way because among other weaknesses, he's addicted to the worst kind of political media?

When you look back at the generation of *Heathers*-style coverage, the evolution toward Trump starts to make sense. We can excuse almost anything in America except losing. And we love a freak show.

Trump was the best of both worlds, as far as the press was concerned: an Agnew-style attacker on the one hand, and a lurid and disgusting monster-freak for audiences to look down on on the other. There is no better commercial situation for the American media than a president about whom a porn star can write, "*I had sex with that,* I'd say to myself. *Eech.*"

Leo Tolstoy, in a novella called *The Kreutzer Sonata,* described a character who visited a PT Barnum circus in Paris. The character went into a tent promising a rare "water-dog," and paid a franc to see an ordinary canine wrapped in sealskin.

When he came out, the man remembered, Barnum used him to sell more tickets to the crowd:

> 'Ask the gentleman if it is not worth seeing! Come in, come in! It only costs a franc!'
> And in my confusion I did not dare to answer that there was nothing curious to be seen, and it was upon my false shame that the Barnum must have counted.

We count on your shame in the same way. We know you know the news we show you is demeaning, disgusting, pointless, and not really intended to inform.

But we assume you'll be too embarrassed to admit you spend hours every day poring over content specifically designed to reenforce your point of view. In fact, you'll consume twice as much, rather than admit you don't like to be challenged. Like Tolstoy's weak hero, you'll pay to hide your shame.

It took a while for news reporters to figure out how to deliver the same superiority vibe you can get from reading local crime blotters or watching bearded-lady acts like *Fear Factor, Who's Your Daddy?*, and *The Swan*. The idea behind most political coverage is to get you to turn on the TV and within minutes have you tsk-tsking and saying, "What idiots!" And, from there, it's a short hop to, "Fuck those commie-loving tree-huggers!" or "Fuck the Hitler-loving freaks!"

We can't get you there unless you follow all the rules. Accept a binary world and pick a side. Embrace the reality of being surrounded by evil stupidity. Feel indignant, righteous, and smart. Hate losers, love winners. Don't challenge yourself. And during the commercials, do some shopping.

Congratulations, you're the perfect news consumer.

3. THE CHURCH OF AVERAGENESS

Have you noticed that the most famous people in media—the people with the most influential slots in top newspapers, prime-time shows of their own, voices first heard by senators and CEOs and other key decision-makers—tend not to be all that bright?

Don't get me wrong: they're not dumb. The people who rise to positions of high influence in this business are usually at least literate, and quick-minded enough not to drown on live television.

But, as is curiously also the case with high-level politicians, top on-air personalities and print editorialists are never geniuses. They almost never say or write surprising things. They don't dazzle or amaze.

You'd trust the average newspaper editorialist to be able to assemble an IKEA product, but not much beyond that. If we were smarter, we'd be in another business, removing brain tumors, designing wind turbines, etc.

Even the age of the intellectual *poseur* is vanishing. There are no more William Safires or Bill Buckleys who make sure to remind you every few weeks or so they like to read *The Iliad* and listen to Bach and expect you to know that Hilaire Belloc walked from Paris to Rome.

The last of this breed is probably George Will of the *Washington Post*, who writes about baseball to convince intellectuals he's ordinary and writes about Byron to convince ordinary people he's intellectual. Will was once the patron saint of conservatives who felt a need to rationalize meanness as smartness. When Trump successfully ridiculed such people as phonies, Will lost his demographic niche.

Now he has been forced to try to rebrand himself as a kind of Democrat, using the same goofball Dennis Miller-isms he once used as a GOP attack dog, only in reverse (Trump, he wrote more recently, is a "Vesuvius of mendacities").

It might work. People like David Frum and Bill Kristol have undergone similar rebrandings, although they've also hurled themselves at the ankles of Democratic Party orthodoxy far more enthusiastically than Will has. He'll probably need to do the same to hang in there.

All of this is similar, in a less deadly way, to something George Orwell wrote about in *1984*.

The book contains a character named Syme, a philologist coworker of protagonist Winston Smith. Winston is terrified of Syme, because Syme is smart, which means he's capable of detecting Winston's secret thoughtcrime.

But Syme's intelligence is of a particular, limited kind. He is fantastic at the job of dystopian propaganda, a master of the hideous intricacies of "Newspeak" and an ardent supporter of Big Brother: "In an intellectual way," Orwell wrote, "he was venomously orthodox."

Unlike Winston, who spent his days terrified of being found out as a secret human, Syme radiated confidence. He believed deeply in The Party, so why would they ever snatch on him?

But in Airstrip One, being too smart in any way was an offense. Syme, Winston knew, would sooner or later be vaporized. The crime would not be the wrong politics, but simply having too functional a brain.

There's an element of this with the press. The people in this business who are clever or original in any way—even in negative ways—almost always meet their comeuppances. They find themselves replaced by duller, meaner, more muddle-headed versions of themselves.

This is how you know there is a step down coming from Rush Limbaugh, a former top-40 deejay who occasionally seems like he cares more about nailing impersonations of people like Bill Clinton and John McCain than he does about the underlying vicious message.

Limbaugh is a Syme. He helped invent the modern right wing, and intellectually is about as venomous as they come. But that's his problem: his schtick comes from his head, whereas this business likes people who think with their stomachs and gallbladders. It prefers herd animals to true hunters.

Rush is still a titan of afternoon radio, even after losing many of his part-nerships because he called Georgetown student Samantha Flake a "slut." But his incessant bragging about his brilliance, his goofball chest-thumping about being "America's anchorman" who is "literally indestructible," a man of "zero mis-takes"—all of those stylistic curlicues will be his undoing, because being capable of even quasi-irony is a strong predictor of trouble in this business.

Alex Jones was the obvious next devolutionary step after Rush. Jones is another fat-faced bully with broadcast skills, only significantly dumber and less self-aware. But even if he hadn't been zapped by Silicon Valley, Jones would likely have flamed out, being too unstable and egotistical in the wrong ways.

Sean Hannity is the better version of the template. He has no belief system, not even a negative one; he forms his opinions the way a cuttlefish changes colors, by unconsciously absorbing his professional surroundings. His ability to move from unquestioningly supporting George Bush to unquestioningly supporting Donald Trump (who hates Bush) is what makes him a superstar.

Thirty years from now, Hannity will be getting a tin medal from whomever is Reichsmarschall of the ex–United States by that point, which will identify him, not Rush, as "America's anchorman."

The kind of person who becomes a media institution, and spends retire-ment accepting awards and honorary doctorates, is the person who doesn't have private thoughts or interests. We want that person's mind full of brand names and framed pictures with ex-presidents. We want the person who can con-fess to *Parade* magazine that Cinnabon fumes "have a hold over me like crack cocaine would over an addict" because "I'm blissfully in love with food courts" (that's Brian Williams).

It's not an accident that people like Dave Chappelle and Jon Stewart, when you do see them in public today, look like Gulag escapees—beards, glassy eyes, speaking in cryptic self-help aphorisms, seemingly desperate to get the fuck away somewhere. Having a sense of humor or a conscience or both in a high-profile media job is a quick way to end up wandering New York or some distant farm, Vincent Gigante–style, in a bathrobe and stubble.

In a nation of three hundred million people, the handful of men and women we pick to be our leading opinion merchants are almost universally terrible writ-ers. They don't inspire, challenge, lyricize, or make us laugh. Why would media companies steeped in money go so far out of their way to hire the most mediocre performers they can find? What's the value-add?

John Kenneth Galbraith, who invented the term "conventional wisdom," stressed that the two most important qualities in the brand of non-thought he was describing were acceptability and predictability. Just as FBI profilers can guess the perpetrator of crimes by looking at victimology, you can reverse-engineer your way to popular op-ed stances just by looking at audiences and determining what points of view are most likely to please them.

Writers like *New York Times* columnist Thomas Friedman and cohort David Brooks are perfect examples. Friedman, whose target audience is upscale New Yorkers and international businesspeople, has been writing the same "Capitalism, surprisingly, works!" column for thirty years.

In 2002, *Slate* ran a story about why Friedman was the most important columnist in the world. "He's effective not because he sounds like a historian, but because he sounds like an advertisement. Friedman has no ideas that can't be expressed in a catchphrase," author David Plotz wrote, in a piece that was genuinely intended to be complimentary.

Brooks meanwhile wrote an entire book called *Bobos in Paradise* about how rich New Yorkers had achieved the apex of consumer taste. This was like Francis Fukuyama's *The End of History*, except the Brooks version was *The End of the History of Buying Tasteful Furniture*.

Lineups full of themes like this are designed to make sure that readers—particularly upper-class readers—are never surprised or offended when they click on an op-ed page. Humor is discouraged because humor is inherently iconoclastic and trains audiences to think even powerful people are ridiculous (or at least as ridiculous as everyone else, which of course is a taboo thought).

Within all of this is the solution to the oft-contemplated mystery of why columnists are never fired for being wrong. It's not true—you can be fired for being wrong. You just can't be fired for being wrong in concert. If you go back and look, you'll find many of America's highest-profile media figures are not only wrong very frequently, but absurdly so. Their saving grace is that the wrong things they express are the same wrong things everyone else is expressing.

The editorial opinions you're exposed to most often are not individual points of view, but aggregated distillations of conventional wisdom. There is no punishment, ever, for going too far in pushing this form of market-tested non-thought. The most powerful example of this was the Iraq War (see The Scarlet Letter Club). But there are so many other examples.

Today, one almost looks back fondly at Nicholas Kristof and Rush Limbaugh beating the Iraq War drum together. Those were the days! At least the upper media ranks all agreed on something once, even if it was a murderous, unforgivable mistake.

Such cuddly rhetorical cooperation between pseudo-left and genuine-right poles of commercial media seems impossible now, when the two camps of our ongoing cultural war don't seem to intersect at all.

Except they do. From bombing Syria (remember Van Jones declaring that Trump "became president in that moment"?) to rolling back the already-weak Dodd-Frank bill, there are still huge areas of political overlap between even Trump Republicans and "mainstream" Democrats.

A classic example of how we in the press commoditize division—even in clear and important areas of bipartisan cooperation—involves the passage of this year's $716 billion military appropriations bill.

It was a huge bill. The year one increase in Trump's defense budget that passed with overwhelming Democratic cooperation—*85–10* in the Senate—was $82 billion, higher than the Iraq War appropriations for either 2003 or 2004.

The two-year increase of $165 billion eclipsed the peak of annual Iraq War spending and is also higher than the entire military budget for either China or Russia.

Yet what was the story about the defense bill? "Trump signs defense bill, but snubs the senator the legislation is named after—John McCain," was the *Washington Post* headline.

This was before McCain's death. The *Post* assigned three reporters to this story—three!—and ripped Trump for having "name-checked" four other members of Congress, but not McCain—whom Trump, they wrote, "frequently disparages." They quoted a mortified John Kerry, who seethed: "Disgraceful."

This story was picked up by the *New York Times,* the *Los Angeles Times, ABC, The Hill, CNN, CBS,* the *AP,* and others. Cindy McCain even tweeted about it.

To recap: Democrats and Republicans spent a year writing themselves a pork-packed Christmas list on the scale of the Iraq invasion, full of monster expenditures, including money for dangerous new forms of nukes. Yet the headline when Trump signed the freaking thing was that he forgot to mention the senator whose name was attached to the legislation.

This is the trick. The schism *is* the conventional wisdom. Making the culture war the center of everyone's universe is job one.

A better way to think about it is that there are two sets of conventional wisdom: one for one "side," one for the other. Think about media iniquity in pairs. For every hack on one side, there's an opposite hack on the other side. One may be worse than the other, but their mirroring takes on big issues cumulatively create a consistent message.

Take, for instance, the *Why Do They Hate Us?* question, about why the public mistrusts the press.

The highest priest of the "Liberal Bias" question is Emmy-winning former CBS producer Bernard Goldberg. Goldberg crafted the modern conservative take on liberal media, beginning with a 1996 editorial in the *Wall Street Journal* entitled "Networks Need a Reality Check."

Most of the modern tenets of the liberal-bias religion are found in that early editorial, which he elucidated at greater length with a subsequent smash-hit number one bestselling book, *Bias*.

If one could surgically remove its obnoxious thesis, and re-cast it as a lurid tell-all about egomaniacal network TV personalities, *Bias* would actually be a funny book. With a few tweaks, you could re-write it as *The Unbearable Full-of-Shitness of Dan Rather* and you'd have the raw material for a great comic movie, or a long-running series in the *Larry Sanders* vein.

Unfortunately, he went another way. The basic plot of *Bias* traces how Goldberg, who says he voted for McGovern twice and never voted Republican in his life, began over the years to be troubled by the liberal slant of his own CBS network.

His Road to Damascus moment supposedly came when a Florida neighbor—a "good ol' boy" building contractor named Jerry Kelley who sounds like an early prototype for Joe the Plumber—called Goldberg to complain about a CBS story.

Kelley had watched a Dan Rather/CBS "Reality Check" piece about presidential candidate Steve Forbes and his flat tax proposal. The story, done by reporter Eric Enberg, quoted three experts who basically thought the flat tax was stupid.

Enberg himself used words like "wacky" to describe the idea, and closed by quoting an unnamed economist who suggested we test the idea "in Albania." With a smirk, he added: "Eric Enberg, CBS News, Washington."

Seeing this piece, Kelley calls Goldberg to complain, and says, "You got too many snippy wise guys doin' the news." Goldberg actually wrote doin', underscoring the regular-guy-ness of Kelley, who Goldberg said had "saved my family" by rebuilding Goldberg's house after Hurricane Andrew.

Goldberg probably didn't know it, or maybe he did, but he was doing the very thing he would later accuse "liberal media" of doing, i.e. cartoonizing the little guy. *Bias* furthered the cliché of the hardworking, salt-of-the-earth "silent majority" American fella (it's always a fella) who gets ridiculed by the cruel snobbishness of upper-class media jerks.

Goldberg, a lifelong TV producer who'd been in the business since 1972 and knew the mechanics of journalism inside and out, was right that the "Reality Check" piece was a hatchet job, and that Enberg was plainly making fun of his subject.

But Enberg wasn't making fun of little guys like Jerry Kelley. He was making fun of congenital billionaire Steve Forbes, one of the world's biggest assholes, a lecturing nasal weirdo whose face is frozen in a creepy pinched-cheek smile, as if even the inside of his mouth was stuffed with dollars.

In the pre-Trump era, Forbes would have led every *Top Talentless Rich Douchebags with the Temerity to Run For President* listicle. His flat tax proposal was a transparent ploy to make the Jerry Kelleys of the world pay proportionally more tax, and the Steve Forbeses pay less.

Goldberg left this part out. That it's the only important part of the story is unfortunate, because he got everything else right.

Goldberg captures the fact that the news business is full of pompous jackasses. When Goldberg told his co-worker/boss Rather that he was going to write a *Wall Street Journal* editorial accusing the business of being slanted in a liberal direction, Rather exploded. "I'm getting viscerally angry about this," he said, and proceeded to remind Goldberg that as a young man, he had enlisted in the Marines not once, but twice!

Goldberg went on to recount an episode when the Murrah building was blown up in Oklahoma City while Rather was on vacation. Anchor Dan was summoned back to work, but in the meantime, someone had to do the news, and that someone happened to be Connie Chung.

While 168 bodies were still sizzling, Rather showed up at CBS and was "so incensed that Connie was on air first" that he spent hours calling media buddies and ranting off the record about what a second-rate journalist Chung was.

This is all basically Genesis 1:1 of the "liberal bias" religion. Goldberg tells a true story about the upper ranks of network news being full of people who run editorials disguised as news more or less constantly, and are, like Rather, often so far up their own asses that they'll start screaming their regular-person credentials at you at the slightest hint of criticism.

This story casts Dan Rather as the obnoxious "elite" and makes humble contractor Jerry "Doin' the News" Kelley the working-class victim. But it's all in service of selling the politics of the ultimate aristocrat, Steve Forbes, a man who probably didn't blow his own nose until he was at least thirty.

In that one unholy trinity you have the outlines of modern conservatism's whole argument, which casts the press and Hollywood as "elites," while their corporate overlords are kept off-camera.

The "liberal media" argument Bernard Goldberg founded almost always focuses on the individual political leanings of people high up in media organizations. The numbers there are actually pretty hard to ignore. Even the *Washington Post* recently ran stats showing only 7 percent of reporters currently identify as Republicans.

Goldberg, whose path to journalism was similar to my father's—he went to Rutgers in the sixties—regularly comments on the upper-crust schools his colleagues favor. So, for instance, onetime CBS executive vice president Jon Klein is "an Ivy Leaguer, he went to Brown."

It's regularly part of his quips about political hypocrisy. "They love affirmative action schools, as long as their own kids get into Ivy League schools," he snaps.

The news business is absolutely different in a class sense than it once was, particularly at the national level. These days it's almost exclusively the preserve of graduates from expensive colleges, when it was once a job for working-class types who started as paper-kids or printers. And being graduates of universities, most people in the business start with a pretty uniform political worldview, at least from a partisan standpoint.

Conservapedia cites this stat, culled from a George Washington University study: "The ratio of Yale faculty donations in the 2004 presidential election between Kerry and Bush was 150:3. The ratio at Princeton was 114:1, and at Harvard, 406:13."

That sounds about right. Goldberg is correct that the national press is a cultural and political bubble in this sense, and has been for a while.

The story he tells about *New Yorker* film critic Pauline Kael disbelieving that McGovern could lose to Nixon because "I don't know a single person who voted for him!" might as well have been about Trump, because the same dynamic is still true.

What he leaves out is that all these college-educated Democrats work for giant bloodless corporations who dictate coverage on a much broader level that actually drifts to the extreme in a different direction.

Goldberg hyper-focuses on how culture-war issues are treated in the hands of the Rathers of the world, but he gets even that wrong. Take this sentence, for instance, about the *New York Times* and its invidious failure to cover his first "liberal bias" editorial:

> The world's most important newspaper, which would make room on page one for a story about the economy of Upper Volta or about the election of a lesbian dogcatcher in Azerbaijan or about affirmative action in Fiji, didn't think a story about media bias, leveled by a network news correspondent, was worth even a few paragraphs.

Actually, Bernard, we basically don't cover Africa at all. Also, Upper Volta was renamed Burkina Faso about fifteen years before you wrote *Bias*. I'm not sure exactly where things stand today, but by 2007, the only American news network to have a bureau in Africa was ABC. So that's one TV office for a few billion people.

Studies consistently show (and everyone in the business knows this) that you need to kill third-worlders in massive numbers to earn anything like the coverage we'd devote to one dead American, particularly an upper-class American.

One of the ugliest stats ever recorded about the press in this country that almost, but not quite, validates Goldberg's thesis involves CNN coverage of Congo between 2004 and 2008. At the time, about fifty thousand Congolese a month were dying from war, genocide, and associated problems like disease. It's one of the major humanitarian disasters of the last hundred years, rivaling World War II for deaths.

But of the forty-four Africa segments on *Anderson Cooper 360* during that four-year period, only sixteen did not involve either Angelina Jolie or the plight of gorillas.

Forget about lesbians in third-world counties—we don't cover people in third-world countries period.

Goldberg consistently tells his audiences that "liberal bias" is the big uncovered story. It is, he says, "the one topic that had pretty much been out of bounds on network news."

You can't smoke enough crack to make that sentence seem remotely true. Liberal bias is the "one topic" network news doesn't cover? There are so many massive stories that the national press ignores on a daily basis.

We don't cover child labor, debt slavery, human rights atrocities (particularly by U.S. client nations), white-collar crime, environmental crises involving nuclear or agricultural waste, military contracting corruption (the Pentagon by now cannot account for over six trillion dollars in spending), corporate tax evasion and dozens of other topics.

How about process stories? Does the average American know how the World Bank operates? Have audiences heard terms like "structural adjustment"? Who out there knows what the Overseas Private Investment Corporation is? How central banks work? How a bill gets passed through Congress? How and where military forces are deployed?

Does the average American know we have special forces deployed in 149 nations right now (that's 75 percent of the world, and that the number has expanded in the Trump years)? That we have ongoing combat operations in eight nations?

These sweeping coverage omissions reflect the real biases of news companies. The so-called "liberals" at the infantry level of the business staffing the foxholes of day-to-day news broadcasts are rarely concerned with the important stories we're not asked to cover, which are usually institutional and complex in nature.

Goldberg's "liberal bias" schtick was a significant development on the road to Trump. He took an ugly truth about the demographics of the news business and used it to make an argument that "the elites" are journalists, not their bosses or their advertisers.

Trump took this argument and ran with it on the trail in 2016. It's been at the core of his rhetoric ever since.

Ironically, Goldberg—far too late—tried to argue with Bill O'Reilly a few years ago that while "liberal media" bias may be a problem, Fox isn't any better. (It's actually about a hundred times worse, but give Goldberg credit for trying). "Liberal news organizations are going to play down liberal screw-ups," he said, "but Fox News is gonna play down conservative screw-ups."

Naturally, O'Reilly balked at this simple observation, leading to the following exchange:

> **Goldberg:** So Fox isn't the conservative network, is that what you're trying to tell us?
> **O'Reilly:** I never bought that, that Fox is the conservative network... I buy that Fox gives traditional conservatives a voice that they don't have on the other network.

Bill O'Reilly being unable to even cop to Fox being a "conservative network" says pretty much everything you need to know about how deep the derangement, or maybe the cynical spin, is over there.

The flip side of the *Bias* con—why it works, despite its pretty transparent stupidity—is that most working journalists are too self-serious to admit the true part of it. We constantly validate right-wing caricatures of us as humorless upper-class snobs.

Here's the argument espoused by most working reporters on the *Why Do They Hate Us?* debate:

1. Most of the distrust of the media is found among conservatives. Statistician/poll guru Nate Silver, a onetime baseball stats nerd who has somehow become the High Data Mullah of All Things since he began writing about politics, summed it up in simple terms. "Republicans hate the media a lot, and Democrats hate the media a little."

2. Those discontented Republican voters, the thinking goes, are really upset because they just can't deal with reality. This is because, as comedian Stephen Colbert and enlightened press figures like Paul Krugman of the *New York Times* alike have been quick to point out, reality has "a well-known liberal bias."

3. Therefore, ordinary people don't really hate us. They just hate reality.

This is a version of a depressingly common journalistic trope: "People just suck." It's the line we reach for when we run out of real explanations for things.

They hate us for our freedom, the George W. Bush-ism that went mostly unchallenged for years as an explanation for Islamic hostility to America's Middle Eastern ambitions, is a classic example of the genre. Various versions of the same explanation (spinoffs of Clinton's "deplorable" observation) have become go-to explanations for the Trump phenomenon.

But we see this answer most often applied to the question of our own unpopularity. Since Goldberg first went public and more so since Trump's election, there have been repeat expeditions into flyover country, in search of the elusive source of the liberal bias religion.

Take Margaret Sullivan of the *Washington Post*, who in late 2017 decided to tackle the issue. Sullivan was tired of the despicable abuse she was getting from MAGA-type readers,[1] and decided to answer an angry, Trump-supporting letter-writer named Daniel Hastings.

Hastings challenged Sullivan to leave her DC/LA/New York media bubble and "Take a visit to the heart of the country. Go to a diner or a flea market. Strike up some conversations. Come back and report without malice or deceit..."

Sullivan was offended at first. After all, she said, she'd already indulged such complaints. "I turned down invitations to speak in Istanbul, Moscow and even Paris in 2017, and instead visited Arizona, Alabama, Wisconsin, Indiana and small-town Pennsylvania," she wrote.

Peeved that this great sacrifice wasn't enough for the likes of Hastings—I already skipped a trip to Paris!—Sullivan finally took her reader up on his dare. She ended up choosing Angola, New York (chosen, I think, because it's a

---

1 Sullivan reported being threatened with a gun, being told by a reader that he would cut her breasts off with a knife, and being called the C-word.

DC reporter's perfect conception of an undesirable/nowhere-ish hole, a map dot between Erie and Buffalo) as a "heart of the country" locale.

There, she did just as Hastings suggested, hanging in "diners, flea markets, and pizza joints" for six whole weeks, in an effort to take the pulse of the commoner.

The awesome humor of a national news reporter needing to organize such an anthropological expedition to her own country to prove a connection to "real" people was clearly lost on Sullivan, but she at least tried. She came back with a number of conclusions.

She did concede the snarky, superior tone of reporters on social media probably grated. But the bulk of her conclusions pointed the finger back at her audience.

Here, she sketched out a particularly bad example of a man she met named Jason Carr, who sounded like a caricature from a Mike Judge movie:

> Much worse was my conversation with Jason Carr of Green Bay, Wis., a middle-aged member of the Oneida Nation who was visiting his girl-friend in western New York. Wearing a "Born to Chill" T-shirt and sitting behind the wheel of his Ford F-150 pickup truck in a KeyBank parking lot, Carr told me that media reports strike him as nothing but "a puppet show" that is "filtered and censored" by big business.
>
> He buys into the conspiracy theories that the United States govern-ment was responsible for the 9/11 attacks and that the 2012 massacre of Connecticut schoolchildren at Sandy Hook Elementary School was staged...
>
> I left the conversation shaking my head, knowing that, as is clear from the huge following of sites like the conspiracy-promoting Infowars, [Carr is] far from alone in his beliefs.

Sullivan tried to be generous in her assessment. Carr, she wrote, "was the excep-tion, not the rule." Moreover, she added, "His complaints didn't worry me as much as something else I encountered again and again: indifference..."

This led to her core conclusion:

> So many people were happy to complain vaguely about "the media," without really caring about the news, or following it with much interest. The concept of being a responsibly informed citizen? That was all too rare.

People just don't care, she concluded. Readers just won't do the work to be educated. They're too lazy to break out of the ignorance cycle: they're just irresponsible, bad citizens.

When I read that article, I don't exactly feel sympathy for Carr's political opinions, but I know what's going through his head. He meets Sullivan, who needs an invitation and a map to find an "ordinary" person, and though he can't articulate it, senses she's condescending to him. He throws his nutty belief system at her, she nods and takes it down in a notebook, then goes home and writes a piece about how people out there are too lazy to see the light.

In my experience conservatives hate reporters mainly because they see us as phonies. We reject the idea that we belong to a class, or that we have our own tribal beliefs. Sometimes the hypocrisy is something they've seen—upper-class liberals, railing about racism in the heartland from the comfort of an all-white suburban town, where they occasionally tip a Puerto Rican gardener or hire a Republican plumber. But a lot of it has to do with approach and tone, the way we openly write for and celebrate professional-sect audiences, unlike the columnists of the past, the Mike Roykos or Jack Newfields, who were unembarrassed to write in the language of the working person.

More than that, though: as a writer, it's always your fault when you fail to persuade someone, or you should always think it is. You may console yourself that some audiences are more difficult to reach than others, but if you're in the communication business, failing to communicate is a problem you should take personally.

People hate the media because they're too lazy to be informed is the reporting version of *They Hate Us for Our Freedom*. It's also standard within the industry, and really just an unfunny version of the classic Mel Brooks joke:

Your excellency, the peasants are revolting!

You said it, they stink on ice!

Trump's election unleashed a barrage of Sullivan-style investigations. One development was that a less overtly nasty version of The Peasants Are Revolting called "media illiteracy" began to be bandied about in academic and press-crit circles. Under this theory, hatred of the media arose out of the "confusion" of the digital age, in which people (read: dumb conservatives) had a hard time determining the validity of sources.

Part of the "media illiteracy" concept involves the idea that Fox is a giant evil misinformation platform designed to mislead uneducated people, which of course it is. But we run that story regularly, as though it's a surprise.

It's gotten to the point where the *Washington Post* even does stories about how Fox broadcasts the statements of the president of the United States without correcting him.

Why the fuck would they correct him? They're not in the news business. They're in the sell-ads-to-aging-anger-junkies-while-propagating-their-owner's-right-wing-ideas business. The only reason not to point this out is that it might make audiences wonder about the business model of other TV stations.

Still, the *Why Do They Hate Us?* question began to close once high-profile press critics like Jay Rosen of NYU started talking about a Trump-led "hate movement against journalists." The president's decision to escalate anti-press sentiment to the point of calling us "enemies of the people" has flipped the script.

Where Trump once rode to electoral victory by appealing to existing anti-press sentiment, and by mocking campaign coverage conventions that had been decades in the making, he is now described as the head of a top-down hate movement. He's becoming the source of the Nile. Now none of this is our fault!

Before 2016, journalists noticed the decline in trust in their profession, and sometimes wondered about it. Occasionally, we conceded that liberal political leanings of individual reporters were a factor.

There was also talk in the business that audiences were jealous of our cool jet-setting lifestyles. Factual fiascoes like the WMD mess, the aforementioned Rather's National Guard pieces, or my own employer *Rolling Stone*'s faceplant on the UVA rape case were sometimes mentioned as having contributed to loss-of-trust problems.

At very rare times, we considered that our insistence on covering events like Brett Favre's retirement decision or the Casey Anthony trial like Watergate or a moon landing might perhaps impact the public's ability to take us seriously. In my experience a reporter had to be in an advanced state of drunkenness before that one would come up.

Since the 2016 election, though, "Why do they hate us?" has become absolutely linked to Trump for most reporters. Audiences have similarly hardened. More than ever, we're stuck in a binary proposition.

Either the media is a liberal cult, as Goldberg insists, or audiences are as Sullivan describes them: hopeless ignoramuses who reject their duty to self-inform.

Neither take is accurate. The press is first and foremost a business, as commercial as selling cheeseburgers or underpants. We sell content, and what we don't sell is far more important than what we do.

If you want to scan the vast universe of things neither Fox nor CNN shows the public, just peruse "Project Censored" sometime. As in a sci-fi/dystopian movie, we only hear of certain crucial truths about our society when accidents happen— for instance, when a hurricane hits.

Katrina forced urban poverty into view for a time. Hurricane Florence caused the *New York Times* and others to finally notice the toxic manure lagoons created by corporate pig farms that have long been health hazards.

As in politics, there are huge areas of overlap in "left" and "right" media, between MSNBC and Fox. Both channels, despite seemingly opposite politics, need you to be identically receptive to advertising.

So neither channel will gross you out with stories about the *maquiladora* where Mexican workers are earning 70 pesos a day making your kids' toys. They won't scare you about the forests we're clearing around the globe to feed the cattle we turn into cheap hamburgers advertised in between segments.

And rarely will either bore you about bank bailouts in between Wells Fargo and Chase ads that are ubiquitously in your newscast, your Hulu feed, on the PGA tour, and plastered behind a serving Roger Federer at the U.S. Open.

There is a wide range of stories neither channel covers for other reasons, many of them involving the military or international financial institutions. But one story everyone can safely cover is how much we hate each other. There's no institutional or commercial taboo that story violates.

That's why 85 SENATORS, INCLUDING PROBABLY THE ONE YOU VOTED FOR, APPROVE OBSCENE $160 BILLION MILITARY INCREASE becomes "Trump snubs McCain during bill signing."

In the modern press, agreement routinely becomes discord by the time you see it. We addict people to conflict stories so that our advertisers can remind them to indulge other addictions, like McDonald's.

It's a perfect business model.

4. THE HIGH PRIESTS OF AVERAGENESS, ON THE CAMPAIGN TRAIL

I was saddened to read a story in the *Washington Post* this past summer about the shattered partnership of John Heilemann and Mark Halperin of MSNBC, Bloomberg, ABC, and *Game Change* fame.

Because of Halperin's sexual harassment scandal, Heilemann now refuses to work with his old comrade. This means the two will no longer be able to make assloads of money together being wrong about presidential politics.

Heilemann and Halperin were once an unfailing compass of American conventional wisdom. Whatever was true, they went the other way, and the national press usually followed. They perfected the art of commenting upon their own invented political narratives, a practice that brilliantly allows reporters to write about writing about what they write about.

What made these two pioneers in the hate-media business was the way they fused simple laziness with demeaning caricatures. They enshrined the practice of describing voters as dumb putty in the hands of DC political strategists, and perfected the art of turning one made-up hot take into eighteen months of articles, i.e. "Will Romney's Rush to the Center Succeed?" or "Can Candidate X Overcome [whatever]?"

Sure, if you're covering elections, you can investigate what politicians stand for. You can check who their financial backers are, and ask what that support might be buying, policy-wise. But that would be based on the assumption that audiences are best served knowing the real-life consequences of their votes.

The other route is to just make shit up. Set a rhetorical target, then spend years writing about who is and is not hitting it. You don't have to move an inch.

Remember the infamous "Which candidate would you rather have a beer with?" narrative? It basically got George W. Bush elected in 2000. Halperin and Heilemann didn't invent it, but they might as well have.

That cliché is probably dead now, since reporters feel guilty about declaring Trump the winner of the "beer test" last time ("Who wouldn't want to pull up a barstool to [sic] next to this guy?" asked *Slate* of Trump in February of 2016). But it spread havoc across five presidential races before hitting the Trump speed bump.

In polls at the start of the 2000 race, voters felt Al Gore would do a better job on virtually every issue, from the economy to protecting Social Security to education to naming Supreme Court judges to managing health care costs.

Bush was really struggling to find an issue to run on that year. Nobody remembers this, but Bush actually ran as a military pragmatist who would not use the army as global police!

Condoleezza Rice at his Republican Convention that year said America's armed services were "not the world's 911."

Back then, it was Al Gore who was saying new world realities would demand "we confront threats before they spiral out of control."

Whether he deserved to or not, there was every indication that Gore was going to win. Then, before the crucial third presidential debate, something happened.

A beer company, Sam Adams, commissioned a poll: Which candidate would you rather sit down and have a beer with, Bush or Gore?

By three points, 40–37 percent, Americans narrowly decided they'd rather have a beer with a recovering alcoholic than Al Gore.

That's right: this madness began as a publicity stunt by a beer company, looking to latch on to debate coverage as a way to score free PR.

Reporters loved the innovative poll. The "beer test" became shorthand for something they'd struggled over the years to articulate.

For decades, we'd run presidential candidates through humiliating marathons, making them divulge embarrassing family secrets on afternoon talk shows, trade scripted barbs with Lettermans and Lenos, and mock themselves on comedy shows like *Saturday Night Live*.

We wrote seriously about all sorts of things they did that had nothing to do with being president, but answered a lot of questions about their cravenness and their willingness to jump through media hoops.

We also systematically removed issue politics from races and gradually degraded the office, training voters to think of presidential candidates as boobs who would do whatever reporters asked of them.

They were like contestants on loony Japanese game shows of the *Takeshi's Castle* type, the ones that had morons gleefully diving face-first into rivers of mud while wearing Hamburger Helper costumes.

The big prize was the beer test. By 2004 the major news organizations were regularly commissioning this poll as a serious indicator. Bush walloped John Kerry that year in a Zogby re-hash of the Sam Adams quiz, winning with 57 percent of voters. A tradition was born.

Reporters love the beer test because it's a way of making elections about something other than politics. It's also a great way to make elections about us.

No crowd of millions ever banged down the door of *Time* magazine and demanded, "We want a president who's a good beer companion."

No, that idea came from a beer company, and reporters just happened to like it. It appealed to our caricatured idea of voters as brainless goons who can be trained to pick politicians using the same marketing techniques we use to sell soda or breakfast cereals. With tests like this, we never had to write about the policies.

Halperin and Heilemann could write thousands of words in a row about presidential races without so much as mentioning a policy position. They turned the Sam Adams ad into their idea of investigative reporting, devoting entire books to tales of political strategists conducting guerrilla wars behind the scenes in search of the perfectly average candidate.

In their two big campaign tomes, *Game Change* (about the 2008 race and McCain's failed "Hail Mary" choice of beer-test heroine Sarah Palin as running mate) and *Double Down/Game Change II* (which featured poker chips on the cover and was about Obama's quest to out-charm Mitt Romney), they unleashed blizzards of "likability" cliches. This is from *Double Down:*

The Obamans had been polling and focus-grouping on Romney for months. What they had discovered was that, while voters liked him

on paper—successful businessman, governor, family man, close to his
church—the more three-dimensional exposure they had to him, the
less favorable their impressions were... According to Joel Benenson's
research, 90 percent of voters had opinions about Mitt; his ratings on
the "cares about people like me" scale were abysmal...

"You live in Pittsburgh and you've got dirt under your fingernails,
who do you want to have a beer with?" a senior strategist for the reelect
observed to a reporter. "It ain't Mitt Romney. You're like, 'Shit, I'd rather
have with the black guy than him.'"

Halperin sold himself to other reporters as the oracle of the political elite. He
claimed to have his finger on the pulse of what he called the "Gang of 500," a group
of "campaign consultants, strategists, pollsters, pundits, and journalists who make
up the modern-day political establishment" and have the "inside dope" on where
the country is headed.

Another journalist might have just said "the people in my Rolodex," but
whatever. This "Gang of 500" was constantly telling Halperin the "inside dope,"
which often felt like pulled-from-his-ass storylines about candidates' strengths
and weaknesses. Nobody could get politicians to do the *Takeshi's Castle* obstacle
course better than Halperin. He and Heilemann are collectively the Skip Bayless
of political journalism, reducing politics to T-shirt-sized platitudes.

I saw this phenomenon up close in 2007–2008, when I had to cover the campaign of former *Law & Order* actor/Republican senator Fred Thompson.

Thompson introduced himself as a presidential candidate to the national
media via a bus tour in Iowa. Before he gave his first speech, however, there were
already multiple hot takes that reporters were playing around with on the bus. I
wrote down three I heard in the first hour:

1. Thompson is the only candidate who can beat Hillary Clinton;
2. Thompson is Reagan;
3. Thompson is too "low-energy" and "lazy" to be president.

There were real angles on Thompson, who had been a U.S. senator and, worse, a
longtime lobbyist who had represented everyone from nuclear power companies
to Haitian dictator Jean-Bertrand Aristide to the Tennessee Savings and Loan
Association. His wife worked for Burson-Marsteller, the PR/lobby firm that had

represented practically every corporate malefactor on earth, from Union Carbide to the makers of the Dalkon Shield.

But all I heard on the bus was a debate between reporters about whether or not Thompson was the next Reagan or a hapless lazybones, as if the two things were incompatible.

At the time, I had no idea that most of these takes had come from an early Halperin piece in *Time* called "A New Role for Fred Thompson."

Halperin noted, "Thompson is most often compared to Ronald Reagan, and the comparison is apt," but added, "critics question his endurance: he has a reputation for resisting a demanding schedule."

That summer was flooded with "lazy or not?" stories. "Lazy Fred," wrote *Slate* a week after Halperin, adding: "Is Fred Thompson too lazy to get nominated?" *Mother Jones* followed with, "Fred Thompson: Not Conservative Enough? Or Just Lazy?"

Carl Cameron of *Fox* blasted Thompson for using a golf cart in an August piece about "too late" Fred. The *New Republic* wondered if Thompson was enough of a "go-getter" and questioned his work ethic.

The press is selective in deciding when laziness is important and when you should give a politician credit for a "work smart, not hard" schedule. It is accepted wisdom, for instance, that Jimmy Carter worked too hard, but Reagan was a brilliant delegator.

The most honest take on this issue is that in the media, we mostly have no clue if a politician is working hard or not. It's easy to see stunts like the legendary "full Grassley"—the Iowa senator's pledge to visit all ninety-nine counties of his state—but we have no idea what's going on in between public appearances.

I've seen candidates with very light appearance schedules get passes from reporters on this question, with John McCain being a great example. McCain's idea of campaigning early in the 2008 race was a couple of midday stops to tell jokes at VFW halls. But unless someone like Halperin identified this as a problem, nobody would notice.

Fred Thompson, a political vet, understood that Halperin and the rest of the media had raised the "lazy" flag on him, and he wouldn't get out from under it until he saluted.

By the time he launched that first bus tour, he'd adjusted his public image accordingly.

He was like a pro athlete who blabbers agent-crafted remarks to counter sports-jock/Bayless-type criticisms. A parallel example would be newly traded New England Patriots receiver Josh Gordon talking about being ready to "work hard," after years of being criticized for his work ethic in Cleveland.

Thompson, too, told all of us he was "working hard" and ready to campaign all day long, if needed. "Saddle me up," he declared folksily. His aides, when they caught you in "private" chats (they made sure to do that with every reporter), pointed out their man was staying late to talk to voters, not ducking out after speeches as some writers had claimed.

A little later, in an Iowa debate, Republican candidates were asked to raise their hands if they believed climate change was real and caused by humans. Thompson snapped, "I'm not doin' hand shows." The other candidates cheered.

He was wrong and insane, but at least he was "standing out" and not being "passive" (these were other criticisms).

And just like that, no joke, the press started to warm to Fred Thompson. He went out on the trail with a "re-invigorated" (read: more aggressive) message. He railed against illegal immigration and said we needed to secure the border before we could have immigration reform. He said we should stay the course in Iraq because those *derned* terrorists were testing our resolve.

By the second time I followed Thompson, the shop talk on the bus was different. I heard things like, "He's not as dull as I thought" and "people fucking love *Law & Order*." His positions were actually a pale preview of Trump, but presentation-wise, everyone was impressed. He might actually be Reagan!

And it worked, sort of. Closer to the Iowa caucuses, Dana Bash at CNN did a bus-tour piece that asked, "Has [Thompson] found his mojo?" She wrote:

> To watch his campaign is to witness a candidate trying to shake the rap that he has no fire in his belly.
>
> His red meat speeches are redder. His arguments for why he should be President are sharper.

The love affair lasted a few weeks, until Thompson made the fatal mistake of reverting to form—in front of Halperin! In a little town called Waverly, Iowa,

Thompson skipped a walking tour and refused to put on a fire hat. "I've got a silly hat rule," he said.

He might have been influenced by the fact that there were only a few reporters there. But those two were Halperin and Roger Simon of CBS.

One "Fred Thompson's Lazy Day" headline later, and the candidate was toast. Michael Crowley of the *New Republic* wrote about the affair, pointing out that the entire Thompson campaign of late had been about "dispelling the laziness rap." Now, that mission officially failed.

"Memo to Fred," Crowley wrote. "It's a stupid and debasing process. But you can't fight it."

Exactly: you have to embrace it. This is how we got Donald Trump.

If Thompson had persisted that year as a more *energetic* science-denying, anti-abortion immigration hawk, he might have been the nominee. Instead he was pronounced "Lazy as Charged" and pummeled out of the race.

This is Punditry 101. You make up some meme like "lazy Fred" or "the Wimp Factor" (Bush I) or the "Bore Effect" (Gore), and insist the candidate needs to beat the rap to win. If the politician is obedient enough in trying to do so, you start talking about how he or she is "turning things around" or "reinvigorated," and the candidate will magically begin getting good press.

A classic example was 2012. Everyone in the press corps believed Obama was going to win that election against Mitt Romney. But to make things interesting, we started inventing storylines.

After the first Romney-Obama debate, for instance, it was said that Obama was "defensive" and "flat" and "wonky." My own local paper, the *Star-Ledger* in Jersey, said Obama lacked "punch," because he was "so intent on answering questions."

Obama after that debate told reporters they were right, that he was "too polite," and essentially vowed to be more of a puncher the next time out.

Heilemann/Halperin later described Obama's struggle in between debates to re-discover his own "likability." Clichés flew like sparks from an angle grinder. Could the President once again be the "I'd rather have the black guy" guy, with whom even a Pittsburgh steel worker with dirt under his fingernails would have a beer?

Obama's aides, the reporting duo told us, weren't sure. They recounted Obama's mock debates against John Kerry, who played the role of Romney in practices:

> Challenged by Kerry with multipronged attacks, the President rebutted them point by point, exhaustively and exhaustingly. Instead of driving a sharp message, he was explanatory and meandering. Instead of casting an eye to the future, he litigated the past. Instead of warmly establishing connections with the town hall questioners, he pontificated airily, as if he were conducting a particularly tedious press conference.
>
> While Kerry was answering a query about immigration, Obama retaliated for the earlier interruption by abruptly cutting him off.
>
> In the staff room, Axelrod and Plouffe were aghast. Sitting with them, Obama's lead pollster, Joel Benenson muttered, "This is unbelievable."

I do this for a living and I can't make sense of these takes. Obama was supposedly too passive in the first debate. Now he interrupts mock-Romney in a practice debate and his top aide David Axelrod is "aghast" because... why exactly?

Also, what's the line between being "explanatory" and having a "sharp message"? Was Obama supposed to *not* rebut attacks point by point?

Presidential debates are another pundit trick. They're significantly decided by the reaction of TV talking heads, who play the role of boxing judges. In some cases, a debate will reveal something important about a candidate, like the time Gerald Ford appeared not to know countries like Romania and Yugoslavia were Soviet client states.

In other cases, viewers will actually be more impressed by one candidate while watching the event. Then reporters run with an asinine post-game debriefing that changes the narrative. A classic example was 2000, when viewers thought Gore won until Republicans released a commercial with a loop of instances of Gore sighing while Bush spoke.

This was *off-camera* behavior. Before Gore knew it, he was being asked by Katie Couric if sighing was "presidential behavior." It became public legend that Gore lost the encounter (what does it mean to "lose" a debate, anyway? Isn't it just information you'll ponder in preparation for a larger choice you'll make later on?). Gore would later express astonishment that the news media could change his fortunes within eighteen hours.

We used to love stories like this because they highlight "the power of the medium," which is a less direct way of saying "the power of the press (to make bullshit a deciding factor)." What rational person cares if George H. W. Bush checks his watch during a debate? No one. But you might care if you're shown pictures of it five thousand times and told it matters.

In Obama–Romney, the big test was supposedly whether or not Obama could overcome his "polite" first contest. He probably would, wrote Heilemann/Halperin, because Obama's great strength as a politician was that in past crises, he always rose to the occasion. "In every instance, under ungodly pressure," they wrote, "Obama had set his feet, pulled up, and drained a three-pointer at the buzzer."

They were basically overlaying the plot of *Rocky III* on the 2012 race, except with basketball. Great champ has it too easy for too long, gets knocked off his perch, but looks phlegmatic in practice. Can he find the "Eye of the Tiger" in time for the big rematch?

Michael Bloomberg ended up paying a million bucks a year to these clowns for this kind of analysis.

Halperin/Heilemann wrote *Double Down* four years into Obama's reign. The politician who had run in 2008 on restoring habeas corpus, greenlighting drug re-importation, and bringing the troops home had delivered a very different presidency. He had given us a lot of information.

First-term Obama gave a massive blank check to corrupt Wall Street, expanded a revolting covert drone assassination program, and greatly widened the president's powers of secrecy and classification, while prosecuting leakers (and even journalists) in record numbers.

Halperin/Heilemann blew all of that off. In their prologue about the run-up to 2012, they barely mentioned Obama's record. The one descriptive line about policy was, "Change had come slowly when it came at all." Then they wrote a 386-page book about how Obama found his magic three-pointer just in time to get re-elected.

The larger press corps followed this pattern. When Obama showed up for the second debate and was more "oxygenated" and "lacerating" and threw "punch,

punch, another punch," headlines pronounced him "reinvigorated" and back on the road to victory.

The point of this kind of commentary is to lionize the politician who connects with voters on a level other than issues, and shows "aggression" and a "go-getter" spirit.

For decades, we told audiences that being "professorial" or "boring" or "answering questions" was a negative. We so predictably ripped politicians for these qualities that the smart ones like Obama learned to apologize for being "polite."

This is why it's such a joke that Heilemann—the only one of the two who still has a career—now professes to be shocked, shocked that the White House is manned by someone who grabs women by the crotch and verbally assaults everyone within earshot.

Trump embodies every quality these guys once celebrated: showmanship over substance, personal engagement over "explanation," extreme aggression, and an obsession with "winning."

Unsurprisingly, both Halperin and Heilemann planned to make a *Game Change III* about the Trump victory. They reportedly spent months in early 2017 getting gloating stories from the Trump White House about Trump's win. And they spent the early part of the campaign milking Trump for ratings to try to save their doomed Bloomberg show, *With All Due Respect.*

You can go back in time and see Heilemann and Halperin riding around the Wolfman ice rink in Manhattan on a big Zamboni emblazoned TRUMP with Trump himself. The two dorks in suits sheepishly asked him hard-hitting questions about whether or not he was nervous before an upcoming *Saturday Night Live* spot. "How are you feeling about it?" they asked, adding, "Do you skate?"

In the weeks before the election, after a year-plus of monstrous comments about everyone from Megan Kelly to fellow reporter Serge Kovaleski, Heilemann's big take on the Trump run was that it might have all been 4d business chess.

"Are the things he's doing now designed in a really, really cagey—and also kind of diabolical—way to build an anti-Clinton coalition he can monetize through another business venture after this is over?"

Then Halperin's career blew up in the wake of sexual harassment allegations, Penguin canceled their book deal, and Heilemann was forced to do a quick rebrand as the angriest anti-Trump antagonist on earth. When asked about Trump later by fellow NBC personality (and onetime fellow Trump supplicant) Joe Scarborough, these are the words that Heilemann used to describe Trump:

Utterly despicable, a classless man... Total scumbag... grotesque... repulsive... disgraceful, ridiculous, asinine...

But what would he be if you still had that book deal?

Assholes like Heilemann and Halperin are part of the reason voters picked Trump in the first place. People got so tired of watching politicians do stupid pet tricks for gatekeeping snobs that they voted in huge numbers for the first politician with the nerve to flip the script, which absolutely happened in this case. Trump had these idiots riding around on a Zamboni, for God's sake.

Now, of course, after years of casting Obama as *Rocky* and telling voters to pick the guy with whom you'd rather have a beer, the Heilemanns of the world are draping themselves in solemnity. They're denouncing voters for being dummies who refuse to take their civic duty seriously. And we wonder why people hate us?

5. MORE PRIESTS: THE POLLSTERS

Donald Trump was the least "electable" presidential candidate in modern history. He beat out even Lyndon LaRouche by a country mile.

Trump grievously offended nearly every voting demographic. He teed off on women, Latinos, Muslims, the disabled, "the blacks," veterans, and Asians ("We want deal!" he cracked, about the Chinese).

He retweeted, about Iowans, before the Iowa Caucus, the line, "Too much #Monsanto in the #corn creates issues in the brain?" This was after being confronted by a poll showing him trailing Ben Carson in upcoming caucuses.

Repeat: he ripped Iowa, Monsanto, and *corn* before the Iowa caucuses.

Additionally, Trump violated every idea we had about what a presidential candidate looked, acted, and sounded like. He threw water, bragged about his dong size, ranted about women's periods, and while doing so, didn't check countless other key "electability" boxes.

He had no "ground game," a characteristic normally cited as a crucial factor. He was also an adulterer and ignorant of the Bible, running in a primary whose constituents supposedly treasured religion.

By every conceivable standard of conventional wisdom, Trump had no shot. Even data journalists laughed at the notion that he could win.[1]

Nate Silver, the former baseball stats guru turned National Oracle™ (as *Gizmodo* called him), said Trump had a better shot of "cameoing in another *Home Alone* movie with Macaulay Culkin (or playing in the NBA Finals) than winning the Republican nomination."

---

1 I *publicly bet* on Trump to win the Republican nomination in August of 2015, but badly misfired in the general election.

But he won anyway. This should have proved "electability" was a crock, and killed it forever as a form of campaign analysis.

It did not. It lives on, as journalism's version of junk forensics. It's like the infamous "comparative bullet-lead analysis," a type of forensic science once used to link suspects to crime-scene bullets that turned out to be made up. Electability is the same kind of alchemy, about as scientific as chicken-bone divination, that nonetheless routinely impacts devastating real-world decisions.

"Electability" often amounts to pundits saying that because a thing just happened once, it will never stop happening.

Take a close race, like the 2000 presidential election. In it, independents broke late for George W. Bush, snapping a near-statistical tie.

A truly interesting statistical observation about that year would have been more in line with what Chomsky said about that race. His take was that in a sample size that enormous, a tie would only be expected in one situation: if people were voting for something random, like the presidency of Mars.

The amazing closeness of American elections has never made sense. In a country in which 10 percent of the population owns 90 percent of the wealth, you'd expect the very rich to be a permanent electoral minority. That it doesn't work out that way is odd. But this is not the kind of observation pundits tend to make. Instead, we peck around the surface.

The take from 2000 was about how independents behave when things get close. Pundits turned the observation about the late rush for Bush into a statistical law: *in tight races, undecideds tend to break for the challenger.*

This for a time was called the "incumbent rule."

Four years later, the "incumbent rule" was revisited to raise concern about George W. Bush's seemingly stagnant support levels heading into Election Day 2004, against challenger John Kerry.

When Bush won, suddenly everyone was wondering what happened to that incumbent rule.

Some cited a Democratic pollster, Mark Mellman, who wrote: "We simply do not defeat an incumbent President in wartime."

So that maxim was added to the other. Both became conventional wisdom: *Tight races tend to break away from the incumbent, unless it's in wartime, in which case they don't.*

Reporters built up a stack of these "laws of campaigning." We became alchemists in big conical hats, sorting through giant tomes at the start of each race, to see if paths to victory for each candidate could be found in our mazes of rules.

The trick was using polls to convince voters to interpret political news through someone else's eyes, instead of their own brains. You may like the policies of candidate X better, but "polls say" (this use of the passive voice is key) you should vote candidate Y, if you want to win the election.

But "Polls say" is often just "we say," in disguise—in the same way a man-on-the-street quote is often just the first person found who agreed with a point the reporter wanted to make.

In elections past, "Polls said" an "electable" candidate was someone capable of "crossing the aisle," a "fiscal conservative" (whatever that meant), not "soft on defense" and possessing of certain personal characteristics: married, with kids, heterosexual, tall, presentable, religious, and preferably with military experience.

Both parties and their main donors consistently threw, and throw, their money behind candidates who check all of these boxes. This person becomes the presumptive frontrunner. Campaign reporters would then trail along—I've watched this many times—and prod would-be voters at events to comment on the candidate's superior "electability."

This was particularly an issue with John Kerry. If you were a reporter following Kerry, you felt like you'd died and woken up in a vat of boiling grease. The man was pure distilled boredom. He had no clue why he was running for president.

The only thing Kerry seemed to enjoy on the campaign was "orange baseball," a game in which he'd roll an orange from the front section of his campaign plane down the aisle into the press section.

The vets on the plane explained this was an old tradition (apparently Nancy Reagan was really into it as well). But Kerry bowled more oranges than any candidate they had ever seen.

If we were taking off, Kerry would lean his huge head into the aisle, flash a dazed smile, and drop an orange on the carpet. As the plane accelerated upward, the fruit would fly down the aisle, gaining speed throughout, and smack the piles of camera equipment at the back of the plane, if it didn't first bounce into the face of a sleeping reporter or bash an unsuspecting stewardess in the kitchen. Kerry would smile equally at each of these outcomes.

The "fun" soon became weird. The female reporters in particular found the whole thing obnoxious. Up front, you could plainly see that Kerry's team was trying to talk to him about stuff, but he was focused on that orange. On one flight we had two going at once.

What was up with this dude? All we knew about Kerry was that he was supposedly more "electable" than Edwards (who was "too angry" on class issues) and Dean (who was "too liberal"). And this was, after all, the "electability" election. In 2004 the buzz was that nothing was more important than electability.

How did we know that? Because everyone on the plane said so. There were literally thousands of articles about Kerry and "electability" that year.

Matt Bai of the *New York Times* later summed up 2004 as follows: "In this year's campaign, electability became the issue itself."

After playing the orange game on Kerry's flights, reporters would jump out in search of fodder for "electability" stories. At events, which after all were filled with Kerry supporters, they'd ask questions like, "Do you think Kerry can beat Bush?"

"Uh, yes," the person would say. "I think he can beat Bush."

Next morning, you'd see the story:

John Q. Dinglehat of Hologram, New Hampshire wants to see a Democrat in the White House—and thinks John Kerry is just the man to make it happen. "I think he can beat Bush," Dinglehat says.

Pollsters and pundits alike framed Kerry as the "beat Bush" candidate. "Seen as the Best Candidate to Beat Bush, Kerry primed for a N.H. Victory," the Gallup service wrote, just before the primary.

At that and other primaries that year, the National Election Pool exit poll questionnaire asked voters if they cared more about having a nominee with whom they agreed on policy, or one who "can beat George Bush."

And just like that, electability really did become the driving issue of the race, when it never had been before.

In 2000, New Hampshire voters answering exit surveys had listed "best chance to win in November" as their primary reason for choosing a candidate just 7 percent of the time.

By 2004 they were listing it as the primary reason between three and five times as often. In Iowa, an amazing 50 percent of voters listed it as their chief concern. We were asking the fuck out of that question.

Soon enough, as Kerry racked up primary wins, our own language started to bounce back to us. This is from the *Washington Post*:

> Patricia Coan of Fairfax, a retired medical practice manager, said: "I voted for Kerry for the same reason most Democrats are voting for him—he can beat George Bush."

The phenomenon worked in reverse with other candidates. Reporters would pester people: "Will you vote for Edwards even if someone else has a better chance to win?"

Or: "Does it bother you that Kucinich has no chance to win the election?" I'd hear reporters laying this on people in August and September of 2003, months before the New Hampshire primary.

Dean actually got the following question in an online Q&A in November of 2003: "How do you address the common criticism: 'I like Dean's policies, but I don't think he can beat Bush?'"

The whole "electability" question usually implies a) there's a candidate in this field who's most likely to win, and b) there's a candidate who appeals to you on a policy level, and c) those candidates are not the same person.

To this day people believe this is the case. Generations of voters have been trained to consider the politician who represents their views as unlikely to be "electable."

Most people are terrified of throwing their vote away, so they'll steer clear of any candidate the press tells them has no chance. Particularly when the incumbent is odious, voters won't vote their own interests and conscience. They actually think it's their civic duty not to.

The trick works best with political minority groups, who've been trained to vote according to how they're told a larger plurality thinks. Until pretty recently, if you were nonwhite, female, single, childless, or gay, you were typically told you had to choose between a slew of straight white candidates who "polls said" had an actual chance.

That dynamic is still true if you belong to any non-traditional political persuasion. If you're an anarchist, a socialist, a "populist" (this term can mean almost anything), a nationalist, a Green, even a libertarian (the Ron Paul kind, not the Peter Thiel/Koch Brothers kind), you'll hear that "polls say" people are not ready to elect your type of person.

This effect is so powerful that it caused Barack Obama to underperform with black voters early in the 2008 race. Obama did not get the early backing of a lot of black churches, and leading African American Democrats like John Lewis initially steered clear.

This was not because Obama was a poor candidate, but precisely because he was a "plausible" one. African American voters, the buzz went, were genuinely afraid he would win the nomination, then lose to a Republican.

"They didn't know him, a), and, b), they thought it was a long shot," said Jesse Jackson. "Black voters are comparatively conservative and practical."

When Obama made enough gains that year for black voters to start moving in his direction, suddenly there was a new party line: Latino voters were the new "firewall" protecting Hillary Clinton.

It goes without saying that language about "firewalls" is crazy and insulting. It implies the nomination is the property of the presumptive frontrunner, and challengers are destructive forces. In this case it was openly argued before the primary in California (where fires are sort of an issue) that Clinton's best hope was the historical Latino distrust of black candidates.

"The Hispanic voter—and I want to say this very carefully—has not shown a lot of willingness to support black candidates," a Clinton pollster named Sergio Bendixen told the *New Yorker*. Robert Novak later summed up: "Clinton Gambles With Latino Firewall."

The "polls say" trick also works, sadly, with labor. Every year, even in the primaries, unions endorse candidates with poor records on labor, because they buy the "electability" pitch.

Sometimes small locals will back the obvious pro-union candidate, while national leadership will give the big endorsement to the more ambiguous frontrunner. This was the case with Clinton over Sanders in 2015–2016.

But big labor voting against big labor is a regular theme. I watched this at an AFL-CIO conference in Whitfield, New Hampshire in 2003.

At the event, each Democratic candidate made a plea for the labor vote. Two were longtime union favorites: Richard Gephardt of Missouri and Ohio's Dennis

Kucinich. These politicians fulfilled every single organized labor wish list. Gephardt had a 100 percent rating with the national AFL-CIO, as did Kucinich, who among other things called for a repeal of NAFTA and the WTO.

But the group in the end decided to back Kerry, who had voted for Most Favored Nation status with China, was a staunch NAFTA defender, and strongly believed in global trade policies, all policies traditionally opposed by labor.

"We need a seat at the table," is what one of the union men told me, implying that it was better to back a weak-on-labor Democrat with a shot than a good one with none.

If labor wouldn't back a lifetime labor advocate like Dick Gephardt, would college kids vote for Kucinich?

After all, Kucinich was the only candidate who treated college students like grownups and embraced idealistic policies like a Department of Peace. While other campaigns tried to win over "youth" by passing out T-shirts with cutesy names ("Deanie Babies" and "Liebermaniacs") or giving away free hot dogs, Kucinich went the other way.

At the University of New Hampshire in Durham, he refused to dumb down his speech and quoted the likes of Jung, Barbara Marx Hubbard, Thomas Berry, and the humanist sociologist Morris Berman.

In a preview of issues that would become extremely popular among Democrats years later, he said his campaign was about changing the priorities of the country away from military spending and foreign intervention, and toward greater investment in education and health care. He sat down and opened up the floor to discussion, and the "stump speech" became a sit-in, where people talked about all sorts of things, including their personal lives, depression, drugs, etc.

Kucinich ultimately got a standing ovation (as both he and Gephardt had at the AFL-CIO conference). Afterward, though, few students said they would even consider voting for him.

"[Kucinich is] everything that I personally would want in a President," a grad student named David Wilmes told me. "But... it's going to have to be someone like Kerry or Edwards."

Why?

"Well," he said. "It's probably going to have to be someone who's tall."

I told Kucinich about this exchange. He sighed and said that until people learned to vote according to their own beliefs and preferences, politics would be a "mirrored echo chamber, where there's no coherence."

This term, "no coherence," defined modern American politics for a generation, when almost nobody voted for the candidate they personally liked the most.

Middle- and lower-middle-class Republican voters still endorse tax breaks for billionaires. Labor votes against labor. Inner-city minority voters endorse candidates who pledge to lengthen prison sentences and put more cops on the streets. Right-wing voters driving around on Medicaid-funded scooters applaud candidates who rail against the consumers of "free stuff."

Very few campaign journalists ever raised an eyebrow about this, though, until polls stopped being able to predict it. This is a kinder way of saying that in 2016, voters started to blow off polls, which threw the whole business into disarray.

I hate ripping on Nate Silver. For one thing, I was a big fan of *Baseball Prospectus*. For another, his essays on polling are always interesting and fun to read. To me he's been a victim in a larger con.

"Electability" was essentially conventional wisdom in search of scientific recognition. When fivethirtyeight.com appeared on the scene, campaign reporters—I heard this—felt their made-up takes were finally being sanctified by data. I remember, in particular, a debate about Sarah Palin in the later stages of the 2008 race.

Reporters were torn. Palin seemed to be the candidate you'd rather have a beer with, but she was also clearly, you know, unfit for office, which bothered a lot of people covering her. How to square the contradiction? They'd normally be celebrating the "beer" candidate, but what to do now?

Silver at that time wrote an article explaining that a vice president is by definition assuming office during a crisis. After all, the president has just died. Therefore, experience counts more than "vision." In sports terms, you'd rather have the major-league ready player than the upside prospect.

"I think Americans can feel sympathy for Sarah Palin, can believe she's the sort of person they'd want to have a beer with," he wrote, "and still find her a detriment to McCain's case for the White House."

Reporters breathed a sigh of relief. The "beer test" was still a thing, just not in this particular situation! Nobody had to come out and say, "All that stuff we've been saying about beer was irrelevant and irresponsible."

After two election cycles of near-perfect prognostication—he got 99 out of 100 states right in the 2008 and 2012 races—Silver was elevated to God status by campaign reporters. There were stories like "Triumph of the Nerds" that described him as a "big winner" after elections.

The problem was that Silver's predictions were based on a generation of voter behavior skewed by mountains of our goofball campaign reporting and idiotic conventional wisdom. Should voters ever tune us out, all that data would become meaningless overnight.

This happened in 2016, when Silver outlined a Unified Field Theory of presidential campaign narratives. There were six stages of campaigning, he said, and each portended doom for Donald Trump.

The stages were: Free For All, Heightened Scrutiny, Iowa and New Hampshire, Winnowing, Delegate Accumulation, and Endgame.

Heading into the 2016 election, there were clues that the power of conventional wisdom was waning. A 2015 Pew survey, for instance, showed declining interest in "electability." I personally was getting that sense less from polls, and more from the increasing frequency of being told to fuck off at campaign events, particularly Republican ones, i.e. the press was now being tuned out before we even asked questions, let alone before we told you who was and was not "electable."

The thing was, nobody in the press had any clue what would happen if people stopped listening to our "electability" horseshit. There was no data on this. We were about to find out.

Trump demolished Silver's "six stages." He lost Iowa, and even underperforming media expectations there didn't dent him. He accelerated during the "Winnowing" period. As Silver predicted, the Republican Party did indeed do everything it could to stop him in the "Endgame," but that may have helped Trump win the nomination, because Republican voters by then hated the Republican establishment and used Trump as a vehicle to express this.

Official endorsements turned into a negative, not a positive, so having less than 5 percent of them didn't hurt Trump. As such, the so-called "establishment primary" was not a factor.

Silver, to his great credit, ultimately realized that "conventional wisdom" had infected polling. He warned about going too far in the other direction, but his basic take was that "polls may be catering to the conventional wisdom, and becoming worse as a result." This was in 2017.

He'd already had a dramatic change of view during the 2016 race. By the time the election rolled around, he was giving Trump a 29 percent chance of winning, which was higher than just about everyone else.

There was a big lesson in this for everyone, or there should have been. Politics, despite the fact that it talks about itself as baseball all the time ("inside baseball" is the favored term of people who think they're playing it), is not baseball. In baseball, batters don't intentionally strike out because they're told the pitcher has high strikeout rates.

Data journalism works a check on conventional wisdom. When they combine is when you get problems. The two genres can be as hard to separate as humping dogs. Even after the Trump fiasco, the product of such unholy unions—"electability"—is still running loose.

A summer 2018 piece in the *New York Times* about the likely Democratic field echoed ancient articles about the likes of Mitt Romney and John Kerry. We were told to be wary of extremists like Elizabeth Warren and Bernie Sanders, and go with something tamer and nearer to the "center":

> For all the evident support for Mr. Sanders's policy ideas, many in the party are skeptical that a fiery activist in his eighth decade would have broad enough appeal to oust Mr. Trump...
>
> Mr. Sanders's generational peer, Mr. Biden, 75, is preparing to test a contrasting message this fall... Mr. Biden has struck a gentler chord than Mr. Sanders and Ms. Warren, delivering paeans to bipartisanship and beckoning Democrats to rise above Mr. Trump's demagogic taunts.

Michael Shearer of the *Post* argued something similar:

> Like several other Senate candidates eyeing 2020, Warren has endorsed a suite of expensive policy proposals that have made some in the party nervous...
>
> For this reason, some Republicans have signaled that they would welcome a Warren run in 2020. Stephen K. Bannon, a former aide to

Trump, dismisses Warren as "the weakest candidate the Democrats could put up."

The easiest way to predict what kinds of "electability" stories you'll see in an election season is to look at the field of candidates and see which ones have a lot of lobbying and ad money behind them.

Those candidates will be described as electable. Everyone else will get the "polls say" treatment. Be wary of our version of junk science.

6. THE INVISIBLE PRIMARY: OR, HOW WE DECIDE ELECTIONS BEFORE YOU DECIDE THEM

C all it the Original Lie of campaign journalism, the serpent-and-the-apple story of manipulative political reporting.

It stares you in the face at the outset of each campaign season. You'll typically see it in a graphic.

On Fox, it's YOU DECIDE. ABC has been going with YOUR VOICE, YOUR VOTE. CNN prefers AMERICA'S CHOICE.

As much as possible, the press underscores the *you*-ness of elections. It's all about you! *You* get to choose! We're just tabulating the results!

Except the networks do not actually believe this. Most of the top campaign analysts in the biggest print outlets don't believe it, either.

It doesn't take much digging to find different analyses of what elections actually are, or what they're supposed to be, in the eyes of the pundit-o-sphere. The real slogan should be:

YOU SORT OF DECIDE!

Or:

2020: YOU DECIDE. AFTER WE DECIDE.

Here's what Nate Cohn wrote in the *New York Times* in early 2015, as part of an argument for why Donald Trump could never win the nomination. Check out the odd language:

Grass-roots conservatives and liberals may resent it, but many analysts—including me—argue that the outcome of presidential nominations is shaped or even decided by party elites.

Why would *only* "grass-roots conservatives and liberals" resent the idea that elections are decided by party elites? Shouldn't everyone think that's nuts?

Sadly, they don't. Most campaign analysts see the campaign season as a referendum on their ability to steer electorates. When we talk about "party elites" deciding elections, what we really mean is that institutions like the press, the two political parties, and corporate donors can throw up insuperable obstacles to anyone they please.

Cohn phrases it as follows:

> Party opposition is even worse. It ensures a chorus of influential critics in the media and a well-funded opponent with endless resources for advertisements to echo the attacks. Grass-roots support and super PACs can help compensate for a lack of broad support, but they probably can't overcome broad opposition. The voice of the elites is too strong and influential.

Here's how the process usually works, bearing in mind that Donald Trump is and was an all-time outlier.

At the end of each election cycle, key donors, along with corporate consultants and leaders of party organs (like the Republican National Committee, for instance), will informally talk about what went wrong and how to fix it. These ideas may then be batted around in a formal proceeding like the drafting of an electoral "autopsy" or "postelection report."

After 2012, for instance, Republicans were convinced they needed to soften on immigration to close the gap with Democrats. The RNC report on the loss of Mitt Romney laid out a whole series of reforms they thought would be necessary, including, "We must embrace and champion comprehensive immigration reform."

Then the few hundred people who actually matter in Washington will get their heads together and quietly decide which candidate is going to get the money for the next run. That candidate ends up with a few hundred million bucks and a head start with the press. This is how the *Times* described it in a different piece:

> The endorsements and donations garner mainly positive media attention for a candidate, and the candidate's poll numbers then typically increase.

These increases generate more positive media coverage, which in turn generates more endorsements and donations, and rivals are winnowed out of the competition.

This is the so-called "invisible primary." The term comes from a 2009 book written by a group of academics and published by the University of Chicago Press, called *The Party Decides*.

The book's four authors took on the proposition that parties had become increasingly irrelevant in modern politics, as decision-making left the smoke-filled room.

The history here is important. In March of 1968, incumbent president Lyndon Johnson, probably stunned among other things by his poor performance in the New Hampshire primary against antiwar challenger Eugene McCarthy, abruptly decided not to run for re-election. Vice President Hubert Humphrey decided to run in his place as the choice of the party establishment. But it was too late in the game for him to formally participate in primaries.

So the race ended up being between two candidates who were actually on the ballot—Eugene McCarthy and Bobby Kennedy—and one who was not, Humphrey. Kennedy would be assassinated before the convention.

In the convention in Chicago that summer, Democratic party bosses nominated Humphrey on the first ballot despite the fact that the other two candidates had won the votes. At the time, bosses could still control delegates without having votes behind them.

In an effort to quell the fury of Democratic voters (particularly young antiwar voters) Humphrey, in characteristic fashion, made a Mephistophelian bargain.

He accepted the nomination for that year, but agreed to create a commission that would reform future elections. The subsequent McGovern-Fraser commission created the system of "pledged delegates" we have today that puts more power in the hands of actual voters, by more formally tying delegates to the decisions voters make at the ballot.

The authors of *The Party Decides* let us in on a secret: the McGovern-Fraser commission didn't actually disenfranchise party bosses and donors! Actually they still control things a lot!

The "invisible primary," they argued, was and is a pre-primary period in which party bosses "scrutinize and winnow the field before voters get involved, attempt to build coalitions behind a single preferred candidate, and sway voters to ratify their choice."

The authors went on to list countless examples of pre-primary money and endorsements as having been deciding factors. In 2000 Bill Bradley and Al Gore were equally sucky campaigners, but Gore had 82 percent of the party endorsements, and more money, so—win, Gore. George W. Bush in the same campaign was another pre-anointed nominee. Mondale in '84, same thing. Bob Dole in '96. And so on.

The Party Decides is packed full of (I think unintentionally) unpleasant metaphors about our democracy. In one particularly hard-to-follow section, the authors describe something they call the "restaurant game":

> Here, then, is a coordination game that better captures what may happen in the invisible primary. We call it the restaurant game...
>
> Imagine that a large number of people are trying to coordinate on a place to eat and that, if a majority manage to go to the same restaurant, they will get some benefit, such as a price discount. At the same time, all want a restaurant that matches their culinary preferences, which differ. Some diners, whom we may call purists, are more finicky than others.

Note: if you're discussing campaign dynamics in America, you can't avoid terms like "purist" or "purity." These are descriptors invented for people who insist on voting for the candidate of their choice, like for instance an antiwar voter who won't vote for a pro-war candidate. Snobs! In the politics-as-eating metaphor, a purist is just an annoying customer who won't just eat what's served. They go on later, venturing into a long, odd discussion about voter-customers ending up in a "fish-house" instead of Denny's:

> If, as diners continue making choices, the fish house continues to draw a large and diverse crowd, even some diners with intense preferences for food other than fish might conclude that they can get a decent meal at the fish place—and earn the group discount as well. This restaurant game would play out differently in different conditions. If the diners are very hungry, they might converge more quickly than if they had just feasted. It would also matter if the town has only one good restaurant, many good restaurants, or none...

I'm not sure what the fish house is supposed to represent, but basically the authors seem to be suggesting that under certain conditions, a lot of people who would rather eat something other than fish, will eat fish:

YOU DECIDE (TO EAT FISH. WHEN YOU
DON'T NECESSARILY WANT FISH). 2020!

Here's another analogy *The Party Decides* folks came up with: running for the nomination is like figure skating:

Skaters do not determine the number and kinds of jumps and spins they must perform. Nor do they determine the standards of performance. Nor, above all, do they choose the judges, who are selected by the larger figuring skating community to implement the community's rules of competition and its standards of judgment. Skaters win not by pleasing themselves or their coaches or even the crowd in the arena, but by pleasing the judges and the insider community they represent...

In sum, skating is not about *pleasing yourself.* It is about fulfilling the orders and desires of the insider skating community. Class dismissed. The cafeteria is now serving fish.

When this odd book came out, it had a big impact on many reporters. Campaign writers quickly learned to love talking about the "invisible primary" in humblebragging fashion: *Let us tell you what goes on behind the ropeline!*

The creepy subtext of these stories—that someone else decides your vote, before you decide your vote—was rarely commented upon.

In 2016, Jeb Bush won the Republican "invisible primary." This was all but officially announced before the race began. Romney's 2012 finance chair, Spencer Zwick, said in February of 2015 that anyone who "wants to be taken seriously running for president" (read: seeks assloads of money from my donor list) needed "to be in a similar place" to Jeb Bush policywise.

A little over five months later, Bush reported having $114 million in PAC money. Pretty much the same process unfolded for Hillary Clinton on the other side, as Clinton was declared the runaway winner of the "invisible primary" in the spring of 2015.

Reporters tend to describe the winner of the "invisible primary" as more electable and the wiser choice. In some places you will see voters who reject the party-approved candidate described as "off the reservation" or "stubborn."

Here's David Frum—once a neoconservative Bush speechwriter, today a darling of the Democratic intelligentsia—talking about what happened in the 2008 and 2012 races, when Republican voters kept resisting the candidates ordained for them by donors:

> Big-dollar Republican favorites have run into trouble before, of course. Rudy Giuliani imploded in 2007–08; Mitt Romney's 2012 nomination was knocked off course as Republicans worked their way through a series of alternative front-runners: Rick Perry, Herman Cain, Newt Gingrich, and finally Rick Santorum.
>
> But Giuliani lost ground to two rivals equally acceptable to the donor elite, or nearly so: Mitt Romney and John McCain. In 2011–12, the longest any of the "not Romneys" remained in first place was six weeks. In both cycles, resistance to the party favorite was concentrated among social and religious conservatives.
>
> The mutiny of the 2016 cycle was different...

Ironically, about two years out from the election—November–December 2018 this time around—is when reporters are most open about these processes. Around this time you can find any number of stories out about the "invisible primary" and who's winning it. (Incidentally, why is it called by such a catchy name? Why not the "establishment primary"? The donor primary? The back-room primary?)

"The invisible primary comes into view," NBC announced, in a piece about 2020 Democratic hopefuls. The article is full of enough loathsomeness and nonsense to fill a few notebooks, but here's a sample, from the always-lovable ex-Republican (and now Democratic) hitman David Brock:

> "For all these other candidates, the first question is: Where are you going to get the money?" said David Brock, a prodigious fundraiser who speaks with donors often and runs a constellation of Democratic groups and super PACs. "If you can't answer the question of where you're going to get the money, you're not going to go anywhere."

This is coming from a man whose candidate in the last race, Hillary Clinton, lost despite nearly doubling Trump's fundraising.

The "invisible primary" was core belief for campaign reporters through 2016, when the Trump campaign exploded the thesis. It wasn't just that Trump won the nomination in defiance of party chiefs, it was that the party-approved candidate, Bush, was not remotely competitive.

This (along with the surprisingly vibrant challenge of Bernie Sanders on the other side) spoke to a massive collapse in the influence of political elites with voters. But that issue has not been addressed head-on by the press.

The standard take instead is to treat the Trump episode as an aberration, a bad weather event, as Jonathan Bernstein of *Bloomberg* did in his "invisible primary" piece:

> This is the time that party actors—politicians, campaign professionals, activists, donors and so on—can really make a difference. They may or may not be able to control nominations (I think they generally can, Trump notwithstanding). But they certainly can influence them...

The point of all of this is that most experienced campaign reporters understand that money and the preferences of donors and the party chiefs play a crucial—and typically deciding—role in picking a party's nominee.

But it ruins the narrative to keep bringing up the smoke-filled room once the campaign gets going. So the "invisible primary" stories tend to recede pretty early.

That's when you'll start getting the hot takes about how this or that bloc of voters will really decide things this year. Forget the donors! This is the year of: Soccer Moms! Evangelicals! Gun Owners! NASCAR Dads! Millennials! Millennial Women! Office Park Dads *(*seriously)!

These stories are designed to shift attention away from the "invisible" actors and bring you back to that place where YOU DECIDE—not nineteen billionaires with their checkbooks out at a lunch table at the Monocle in DC, two years before Election Day.

The second part of this is that the back-room nature of the nominating contests is camouflaged as the season wears on, by selling up the intense divisions of the general election.

The more we turn up the heat on the red-versus-blue hatred down the stretch, the less voters think about chummy early processes like the "invisible primary." And boy, do we have a lot of ways to make things heated.

7. HOW THE NEWS MEDIA STOLE FROM PRO WRESTLING

In Virginia in early 2015, a thirty-five-year-old pro wrestler by the name of Daniel Richards followed Donald Trump in amazement. In a creepy way, he understood he was watching a kindred spirit.

"He was doing what I do," he said.

Richards would later capture fame with a hilariously campy wrestling persona called "The Progressive Liberal." He enters small arenas, largely across Appalachia, wearing a shirt emblazoned with Hillary-Clinton-faces, screaming things to fans like, "You vote against your economic interests!"

The hardcore country crowds go nuts. Richards was and is a heel act. Pro wrestling depends on the core format of a villain versus a hero, in industry terms a heel versus a "babyface," or "face."

Out of this format springs an infinite number of storylines—partner betrays partner, hero "turns" heel, adversaries unite to fight for the flag or a woman. But it all starts with a bad guy, entering the ring with a swagger, shouting vile stuff at the crowd to get things nice and warm in the arena.

"A heel's job is to bring heat," says Richards.

When Richards saw Trump on TV, he recognized right away what he was watching.

"He was a vintage WWE entertainer," he said.

One thing was different, though. "A pure heel wants to be booed by everybody," says Richards. "Trump is unique in that he said things that would trigger the left, but there are people on the right who will love him for what he says."

He pauses. "So he's a heel, but he gets the babyface pop from his base."

A heel's taunts are designed to inspire a prudish reaction. The babyface sometimes responds to provocations with naïve dignity, not expecting the surprise kick to the face the whole audience knows is coming.

Trump, always the instigator, taunted Jeb Bush and his Mexico-born spouse, Columba, early in the race. He suggested the Florida governor "likes Mexican illegals because of his wife."

Jeb refused to engage directly. He said only that he was "proud of his wife" and Trump was "totally inappropriate and not reflective of the Republican Party views."

Politico compared Jeb's tepid response to Trump to Mike Dukakis's infamous failure to lash out at CNN's Bernard Shaw for a 1988 debate question that began, "If Kitty Dukakis were raped and murdered..."

Comparisons to Dukakis are deadly enough in American politics. But it got worse. Around that time Jeb appeared on a show with his mother, Barbara Bush. Trump, playing textbook heel, ripped Jeb for needing his "mommy."

Bush again reacted like an aggrieved aristocrat. "I won the lottery when I was born 63 years ago and looked up and I saw my mom," he said, in a debate. "My mom is the strongest woman I know."

"She should be running," Trump quipped.

This was crude, but from a pure wrestling standpoint, Richards recognized the move. "I totally dislike Trump," he says, "but you had to laugh at that. [Bush] was not equipped to deal with that situation."

There's a convention in wrestling where the heel breaks the rules, but the crowd expects the face to fight back. For ages, hitting with a closed fist was "illegal" in WWE, but heels were always punching people.

"The babyface will never throw a punch until the heel does it," Richards says. "But when a babyface doesn't fight back, no one is going to get behind him."

This happened to Jeb, and Trump danced on his grave by going on *Morning Joe* and declaring, "I thought he was going to push me harder to apologize." Translation: What a wuss!

There's real drama in wrestling, but it's theatrical drama, not the sporting kind. It's never clear how audiences will respond to any script. The roles of good guy/bad guy may be predetermined, but audiences may respond more to one performer or the other, based upon who acts his or her role better.

As such there's a gray area with heels and faces. "Sometimes boos are cheers," Richards explains.

Richards cites Steve "Stone Cold" Austin, a classic heel. In 1996, Stone Cold defeated Jake "The Snake" Roberts, a Bible-thumping face. After Austin whipped him, he gave a speech as Roberts was being carried out of the ring. "You sit there and you thump your Bible," he said. "Talk about your psalms, talk about John 3:16—Well, *Austin 3:16* says I just whooped your ass."

"'Austin 3:16' became the biggest-selling T-shirt in wrestling," Richards says. "Austin got so popular, he had to turn face."

Audiences love a good heel. They go wild when king-douchebag types like Randy Orton stand flexing their pecs and preening in the middle of the ring, another Trump specialty (the preening, not the pecs). Trump's incessant bragging about his money is the political equivalent of doing a "crotch chop" (look it up) in the ring.

Richards saw the parallels right away. But almost no one in blue America spotted this, least of all the press corps. This was malpractice on one level—to be that out of touch with so popular a phenomenon was inexcusable—but it proved dangerous also, as reporters didn't recognize that they were sliding into a known business model.

As far back as 1987, *Wrestlemania* attracted 93,173 customers to one Silverdome show in Detroit. The genre has been massively popular for decades. But few political reporters have ever watched wrestling. They didn't get Trump in the same way they don't get WWE.

In the late fall of 2015, when Trump started to rise again in the polls, I started to see reporters on the trail carrying around *Mein Kampf* or *The Paranoid Style in American Politics*. They were looking for political parallels in the past.

The book they should have been reading was *Controversy Creates Cash*, by former wrestler/wrestling producer Eric Bischoff, of now-defunct World Championship Wrestling (which was put out of business by Vince McMahon's WWE). Bischoff was himself a famed heel act. His book is a field guide to how wrestling uses provocation and fake narratives to drum up fan interest and make money.

He wrote:

> When you watch wrestling, what you see looks fairly simple. It looks like a staged, choreographed fight between two people who supposedly have an issue, something that they're fighting over... What you really don't see is the skill and the art that's required to engage the third person in that ring. The third person in the ring is the audience.

Without crowd engagement, you've got a bunch of goons in underpants flipping each other, a meaningless story. The presence of a big howling crowd confers legitimacy and power to the event. Everything therefore becomes about building crowd energy. Without that, there are neither villains nor heroes.

There's a fine art to deciding when to have a champ lose, or be humiliated, or turn heel, or whatever. Managing that dynamic is a privilege of the promoters, a carefully guarded trade secret called *kayfabe*.[1] It's considered a major sin in wrestling to "break kayfabe," i.e. slip out of character, admit to the fakery.

The problem, as Bischoff explains, is that the business always wants for real heels. You can't have crowds without heroes, and you can't have heroes without great bad guys. But nobody wants to be the villain forever:

> Sometimes I see it in guys who are really experienced—they don't want to be the bad guy. They don't want to get booed. But for a story to be successful, there has to be a villain. You have to have, or at least perform, the characteristics that people truly hate. You have to be a liar, a cheat, a sneak, a coward—and the fans need to believe it.

Trump is a born heel. These exact words are now used in headlines to describe him: liar, cheat, coward and, most recently, traitor.

When Trump performed *Wrestlemania* in 2007, in an event tabbed "The battle of the billionaires," he played the face, in a "bout" against WWE founder Vince McMahon (they both had partner fighters for the match).

In the match, you could see the heel urge coming through. Trump got tired of McMahon's rap and sucker-tackled him, "winning" the fight with shots to the back of the head and face. (For those unfamiliar with this event, Trump and McMahon

---

1 The term "kayfabe" is thought to have originated as carny slang for "protecting the secrets of the business." The term "kayfabe" itself may ultimately originate from the Pig Latin form of "fake" ("ake-fay") or the phrase "be fake."

were actually "fighting"). He was perfect in the role and *Wrestlemania* fans—who are a pretty decent sample of what America is like "out there"—loved him.

Throw an attention magnet like Trump into a political journalism business that feeds financially off conflict, and what you get is the ultimate WWE event. It's a cross of *Ali G* and *Wrestlemania,* a heel act using real credulous reporters as props. The drama was fake—sort of—but the profits and the political consequences were real.

***

In late December of 2015, Trump seized control of the race thanks to a hurricane of invented drama. In a speech in Grand Rapids, Michigan, Trump teed off during the bathroom break Hillary Clinton had taken while in a debate with Bernie Sanders.

He said of Clinton's debate disappearance: "I know where she went. It's disgusting, I don't want to talk about it. Too disgusting, don't say it, it's disgusting."

He then went off on a tangent, saying Hillary got "schlonged" in her 2008 run against Barack Obama.

Schlonged! Did he say that?

The whole press corps scrambled to red alert.

Both the *Washington Post* and the *New York Times* had stories about "schlonged" up before midnight. The *Times,* ever proper, would say only "Trump Goes Vulgar In Swipe At Clinton." The *Post* went the route a lot of papers would travel, using Trump's utterance as an excuse to say "penis" or "large penis" as many times as possible:

"'She was favored to win, and she got schlonged,' Trump said, turning a vulgar noun for a large penis into a verb."

By morning, many of the other campaigns issued official comments. The Clinton campaign predictably denounced "the humiliation this degrading language causes all women."

A few hours later, Trump tweeted this flame of news into a full-on wildfire.

"Once again, #MSM is dishonest," he wrote. "'Schlonged' is not vulgar. When I said Hillary got 'schlonged,' that meant beaten badly."

This was the Mike Myers "A sphincter says what?" routine from *Wayne's World.* Trump's tweet was plainly designed to get straight reporters to repeat his bad words for him, even escalate them on his behalf.

Within hours, the *Daily Caller* was taking Trump's side in the controversy, using a perhaps-unintentional triple entendre: "Trump Doubles Down on 'Schlong,' Veteran Journalists Back Him Up."

Meanwhile, the *Washington Post* by that first night was running chin-scratching analyses like, "Donald Trump's 'Schlonged': A linguistic investigation." With its unique brand of unimaginative pretentiousness, the paper somehow managed to cite quotes from both Ben Franklin and Harvard University professor Steven Pinker. The Pinker quote read:

"Headline writers often ransack the language for onomatopoeic synonyms for 'defeat' such as *drub, whomp, thump, wallop, whack, trounce, clobber, smash, trample,* and Obama's own favorite, *shellac* (which in fact sounds a bit like *schlong*)."

All of this column space devoted to "schlong" was not going to other subjects.

Just prior to Trump's "schlong" comments, Barack Obama had signed the Cybersecurity Information Sharing Act, a landmark law giving the government access to more of your private data. The Fukushima disaster was still causing hundreds of tons of radioactive water to spill into the ocean. A new study had even been released suggesting search engines had poorly-understood abilities to influence elections—these same papers would care a lot about this later, but not now.

Everybody was having too much fun with "schlong." To make sure things stayed that way, Trump tweeted again late that second night, at 10:47 p.m.:

"When I said Hillary Clinton got schlonged by Obama, it meant get beaten badly. The media knows this. Often used word in politics!"

Now he was transparent. Trump went from "she got schlonged" to "Hillary got schlonged" to, after thinking about it a few more hours, "Hillary Clinton got schlonged *by Obama*."

That last iteration had such obvious and horrific metaphorical connotations that they scarcely needed to be said out loud. Yet Trump's opponents and would-be foils in the media did so anyway, repeatedly.

By the next morning, on December 23 Hillary ally and chief media attack dog David Brock was barking Trump's own words back into the ether. Brock said "Hillary schlonged by Obama" was "racist" and made Obama out to be a "black rapist."

CNN tracked down still-viable Republican candidate Chris Christie for comment. Christie, in absolute seriousness, said he had "plenty of thoughts" about "schlonged," but "didn't want to talk about it."

In a *Forbes* article, "Donald Trump and 'Schlonged': The Long and the Short of it," author Susan Adams interviewed Rabbi Benjamin Blech, author of *The Idiot's Guide to Learning Yiddish*. He said, "Please don't use that word in my company."

Adams asked the question anyway.

The rabbi went along, saying *schlong* not only meant a penis, but was "especially used to describe a large member, as in, 'I was in the locker room, and boy, I saw his schlong.'"

This was a Gilbert Gottfried set by now. Trump got David Brock to call Barack Obama a "black rapist" and had a female reporter from *Forbes* magazine interviewing a rabbi about admiring schlongs in locker rooms. All that was missing was a traveling salesman and a barn.

Trump created a giant free promotion machine in the news media, which seemed never to grasp what he was doing. Either that, or it did, and didn't care.

"They were suckers for it," noted Richards. "They're giving him the oxygen he needs. It feeds right into what he's doing."

What was he doing? Trump's run seemed to begin as a publicity stunt. The press was free to ignore the candidate during this stage of the race. At the very least, it didn't have to build giant skyscrapers of nonsense around everything that slipped out of his mouth.

But there was synergy between a game show host building up his Q rating and a commercial news media whose business model thrives on conflict and was often starved for the real thing. Reporters who'd spent years concocting dubious features about the "Gore Bore" problem or the "Wimp Factor" now had a real presidential front runner talking about "schlonging" a female rival. *Ka-ching!*

By the day after Christmas—just five days after all this insanity started—NPR was entering "schlonged" in the list of possible "words of the year." Trump meanwhile was managing to turn all of this into a referendum on Bill Clinton, who made the mistake of jumping in and describing "schlonged" as part of Trump's "penchant for sexism." Trump turned around and blasted Clinton's own history with women, and got even "enemy" publications to bite. A huge triumph was the

December 28, 2015 piece in the *Washington Post*: "Trump is Right: Bill Clinton's Sordid Sexual History is Fair Game."

There was unabashed glee in the coverage. CNN's features were produced to the hilt, with old-country *Fiddler on the Roof*-style music cued up when they interviewed Yiddish experts. Atrocious puns flew in every article.

Pundits raided Nexis in search of prior uses of "schlonged" for the sheer pleasure of repeating them in print, as the *Daily Beast* did in recounting a 2007 Jimmy Kimmel sketch about "donkey-schlonged counterparts."

Trump turned the *Washington Post* and the *New York Times* into what the wrestling world calls "dirt sheets."

Once, these were paper pamphlets circulated to help fans keep up with taunts and smears and other wrestling gossip. Sometimes they contained whispers about the personal lives of performers. Editorially, their standards were all over the place: wrestlers often complained they got things wrong. Either way, they were effective as hype mechanisms. With Trump, we transplanted that dubious format onto the country's top campaign coverage outlets.

Trump's whole platform was a heel routine, down to his foreign policy. "We don't have victories anymore," he'd say. "We used to have victories, but we don't have them now."

He didn't just rip America, he taunted it, unspooling long homilies to our weakness and decline that were designed to whip crowds into an impotent furor.

This is exactly like bad-guy foreign wrestler Cesaro telling Ric Flair: "America, no matter how great you once were, you have *nothing* left—except maybe a bar tab you can't pay!" Trump's diatribes against the "elites" in DC, meanwhile, aped the screeds against the wrestling "corporation" that elevated hero-of-the-common-man wrestlers like the Rock and Steve Austin. This was where Trump stole his "populist" act (if he got anything from *Mein Kampf*, it's less obvious).

Coverage of this crossover insanity drove spectacular growth across the cable, TV, and digital news sectors in 2015–2016. Just on CNN, MSNBC, and Fox alone, Trump led a boom that saw a 167.4 percent rise in ad sales in 2016 compared to 2012.

The campaign press played the shocked commentator in perfect deadpan, in part because they were genuinely clueless about what they were doing. They never understood that the proper way to "cover" pro wrestling, if you're being serious, is to not cover it. It is, after all, bullshit.

"With anyone else," says Richards, "this might have been a week's worth of news stories."

***

The longer Trump hung around in the race, the more the *Wrestlemania* audience began to take his side. They could see through the fake outrage in papers like the *Post.*

After all, if you think the guy shouldn't be making America think about Hillary Clinton getting "schlonged" by Barack Obama, don't repeat it fifty thousand times. Would you put it in a headline if it were about your daughter? No, but you would if you wanted to sell newspapers or, in the case of David Brock, score political points on Trump's negatives (we later found out the Clinton campaign was praying for Trump as an opponent for this reason).

Bischoff in his book noted that heels after a while start to demand hero's welcomes—a mistake, he says. "You have to want people to hate you," he wrote. "They should be throwing shit at you."

But Trump started to demand cheers along with the boos. He was shooting for big doses of both. His entrance at the Republican National Convention—sauntering through a white-lit corridor into the Q arena in Cleveland—reminded me of the "Scott Hall walkout," a famed moment in heel-preening.

His over-the-top arrival by taxiing jet at an Albuquerque rally later that year recalled about a dozen WWE events, like Lex Luger arriving by helicopter to bodyslam Samoan giant Yokozuna.

Then he won the election, which felt like a production error. Trump was supposed to lose. It even seemed he wanted to lose. That's how the script should have gone. He was such a lurid villain that under normal circumstances, crowds probably would have rallied any dope in a white cape sent to fight him to a 20-point win.

Unfortunately, Trump ran into the one candidate capable of pinning herself. It was a rare WWE act where a real match broke out.

***

Pro wrestling is more sophisticated than it looks. A lot of care is put into tending subtle questions of character and narrative arc. Take out the steroids and it's an inspired art form, a sports-entertainment hybrid that echoes troubadours and traveling morality plays. And the moves are kind of awesome, once you get into it.

But as a model for either national politics or journalism, God help us.

It turns out to be a business formula that works all too well. While Trump subsequently started trying to squeeze out of his heel role by inventing a new foil called "Fake News" ("He's trying to turn face using the media," quips Richards), the media doubled down on white hat/black hat politics.

Trump has a tendency to WWE-ize everyone in his orbit. On the campaign trail, this worked for him. People like Jeb Bush and Marco Rubio and Hillary Clinton proved inept whenever they tried to fight using those tactics.

The press, though, profits from sheer noise, drama, and divisive "heat" the same way Trump once did. When reporters after 2016 began bowing to reader pressure to "call Trump out," they gladly entered the ring with him.

Top reporters now regularly do the outraged-hero, finger-pointing routine whenever they're within a mile of Trump. Jim Acosta's confrontations with the president, for instance, seem culled straight from WWE outtakes.

Trump's early presidency turned into a heel/hero promotion, with Bob Mueller in the face role. It was an important story, but the probe also sold papers in ways unrelated to its actual political or legal meaning. Mueller was cast as a hero conquering evil, a symbol of hope—Mueller on votive candles, Mueller as the subject of "All I Want for Christmas is You" sets on *Saturday Night Live,* etc. Obviously, we never saw anything like this with Lawrence Walsh.

Political coverage in the Trump era has become increasingly focused on questions of character and storyline. A cynic would say this is how Trump himself wants it. He gets the press focused on "Da Nang Dick" tweets about Senator Richard Blumenthal instead of diving into the impact of things like his tax cuts or deregulatory schemes.

I don't think it's that simple. The Trump era has moved the whole political media into the WWE space, where most stories are just entries in our ongoing love/hate relationship with Trump. We ignore *everything* else, not just Trump's subtler evils.

The problem with any coverage strategy based on a villains-versus-heroes storyline—and this has become a feature of both right-wing and "liberal" media—is that it boxes in editors. What if a character your paper has built up as a villain says something true, or does something righteous? What if one of your good guys turns heel? How do you admit the truth of that without puncturing audience expectations?

In a controlled entertainment like the WWE, where heels and heroes never deviate from script, this is no issue. But reality breaks kayfabe all the time.

***

In October of 2017, the Pew Research Center did a study on news stories involving Trump. They discovered a few interesting things.

The percentage of stories including a Trump tweet was higher among "liberal" and "mixed" outlets (CNN, ABC, CBS, and NBC counted as "mixed") than the percentage in right-leaning outlets. You are more likely to read a Trump tweet in *Politico*, *Vox*, *Slate*, or on CNN than you are in *Breitbart* or the *Daily Caller*.

The folks at fivethirtyeight.com suggested reasons for this. Their Claire Malone wrote:

> Is this where we tell our readers about journalism business models and how it's more expensive to do reporting that involves investigation? Because honestly, I think that has to be taken into account.

It's true. There is a financial pull toward research-free stories. Writing 1,200 words of jokes about a Trump tweet costs less than sending a reporter undercover into a Mexican *maquiladora*. But that's not why we do the one and not the other.

We do it because quick-and-dumb would still provide better bottom-line investigations, even if you could take cost out of the equation. Real evil typically appears as institutional greed and inattention, and is depressing. People should never enjoy reading about the truly awful, and they don't—which is why we spend less time on the water in Flint than body-language analyses of Ivanka Trump. You can't "love to hate" the Flint water crisis. But you can love a good heel act.

Character sells. Reality, not so much.

Get used to a world of heels and heroes, with not a whole lot in between.

8. HOW READING THE NEWS IS LIKE SMOKING

The news is an addictive product.

Like cigarettes, this product can have a profound negative impact on your health. Almost without exception it will make you lonelier, more anxious, more distrustful of others, and more depressed.

We do this on purpose. Even at the reporter level, some of us know what we're doing.

When you order a Double Whopper and fries, nobody at the BK counter tells you to stop jogging and lay off salads and apples. But the cashier can probably guess that'll be a consequence.

It's the same with us. We know we're in the emotional manipulation business. We know we're training you to unmoor yourself from reality and adopt self-destructive habits.

After a lifetime of following the news, most customers will lose—usually forever—the ability to understand what they're getting into. There are no warning labels on the news. If there were, here is what they might say:

THE NEWS IS A CONSUMER PRODUCT

If you take away nothing else from this book, please try to remember this.

Years ago I trained myself in a trick. Before clicking on any article, I imagine the title of the news outlet emblazoned on a cigarette box or candy wrapper (as in, "I'm going to run outside for an MSNBC").

This news-as-smoking similarity begins with the ritual of consumption.

Especially in the cell phone era, consuming both products is idiosyncratic, private, and designed to be pleasurable.

You get the same rush from pulling the dense metal phone out of your jeans that a smoker gets withdrawing a softened cardboard Marlboro box.

My phone cover has a waffle-patterned back to it. If I close my eyes, I know exactly how it feels. Close your eyes and try it. You can probably do the same thing.

Before they target your lungs, cigarettes win you over with smell and touch and sound: that coffee-like aroma, the brittle feel of the rolling paper, the whooshing noise of a spark becoming a flame.

When you read news, it's the same. The feel of the depressed circle of a phone control button is a pleasing sensation. Scrolling is a similar tactile trigger to grinding a lighter with a thumb.

The bright color of your favorite news outlet's logo is designed to be as soothing as the familiar mint green of Kools, or the red circle of Lucky Strikes.

The magic begins after you click.

In 2017, Facebook's former VP for growth Chamath Palihapitiya said he was guilt-ridden over helping push a socially destructive product that fed off "short-term, dopamine-driven feedback loops."

Napster founder and fellow onetime Facebook executive Sean Parker said something similar, talking about the "little dopamine hit" that you get from likes and other rewards. It was, he said, an experience designed to exploit human "vulnerability."

Most educated people understand addiction is a danger of Internet use generally. The hunched-over, phone-obsessed individual has become a meme in modern art and commentary.

But few have tied it to the news.

Internet-fueled addiction is frankly just a new quirk to the crass consumer experience that is (and has been for some time) the news.

The notion that you are reading the truth, and not consuming a product, is the first deception of commercial media.

It's the same with conservative or liberal brands. In both cases, the product is an attention-grabber, a mental stimulant.

The core commercial activity involves an ad stuck in front of an eyeball, though you may also pay a subscription, or less commonly, a newsstand charge. The involuntary surrender of your personal data may also be part of the consumer price.

In all cases, however, you're paying something in exchange for the experience of reading an article or watching a report.

All the commercial actors make more money the more you read or watch. The business, therefore, is geared toward keeping you glued to the screen.

This leads to the second deception of the news business:

YOU DON'T NEED TO WATCH THAT MUCH NEWS

You will never have the political power to do something about all the terrifying problems we wave at you.

The human brain just isn't designed to take in a whole world's worth of disturbing news. Most of us have enough trouble with the more mundane problems of finding inner peace and securing happiness for our loved ones.

We know this, but keep winding you up anyway.

In fact, the tension between the sheer quantity of horrifying news and your real-world impotence to do much about it is part of our consumer strategy.

We create the illusion that being informed is a kind of action in itself. So to wash that guilt out—to eliminate the shame and discomfort you feel over doing nothing as the world goes mad—you'll keep tuning in.

The "You don't actually need to be watching this all day" rule would be true even if news stories were sorted logically and according to social importance.

They aren't:

WE ARE NOT INFORMING YOU. WE CAN'T, ACTUALLY

Irony alert: the most important news story in the world is the inability of the ordinary news consumer to understand the news.

This is no dig against readers. The world has just grown so complex that the majority of serious issues are beyond the understanding of non-specialists.

Take "the economy." The average citizen has basic ideas about money. We shouldn't spend more than we have. People should pay their debts. And so on.

But how many people know what a derivative is? An interest rate swap? An auction rate security?

Just the process for issuing the public bond used to pay for the skating rink where your kids play is a morass so complex it took federal prosecutors nearly a decade to train themselves in the language of it, when they tried (and failed) to bust bankers who rigged that game to steal money.

I covered the Dodd-Frank financial reform act in 2010–2011. The Senate and the House were working to come up with new guidelines for the clearing of derivatives. In the least impenetrable terms I can think of, they were trying to establish a mechanism for settling swap transactions in the way exchanges settle stock trades.

But not a single elected member knew anything about clearing derivatives. Only one or two had staff members who were in any way acquainted with the issue. Except for one or two academics who volunteered time between classes, the only people who could understand the bill were paid lobbyists. This issue had profound importance because the opacity of the swap market was a major factor in the 2008 crash.

So, talk about horrors: not only is the structure of the modern economy inaccessible to ordinary consumers, it can be inaccessible to the people setting public policy. Often, it's beyond the CEOs in relevant industries (AIG sank in part because executives did not understand its own financial products).

There are similar complexity issues in almost every field, from energy to medicine to pollution science to nuclear weapons maintenance.

If we in the press were being honest with audiences, we would tell them: the world is so complex, you cannot ever hope to be truly informed. We can tell you a few broad strokes, but that's it.

Or, if we were truly acting out of concern, we would make educating audiences about the basics of complex fields urgent priorities.

But we could never make that stuff sell. So we find other material.

Most journalists are failed humanities majors. Literature degrees are common among our kind (I have one). If we have expertise in anything, it's telling stories.

That's mostly what we do. Rather than try to get you up to speed about complex problems, we build up characters and storylines, using soap-opera techniques.

About those stories:

WE SELL IDENTITY

In *Bias,* that Bible for people who loathe and fear the "liberal media," Bernard Goldberg looked at a curious episode in the late eighties and early nineties, when the press randomly decided to care about homelessness.

Goldberg cited a study examining 103 network TV stories on homelessness, along with twenty-six news articles. He quoted analyst Robert Lichter:

> "Only one source in twenty-five," Lichter concluded, "blamed home-lessness on the personal problems of the homeless themselves, such as mental illness, drug or alcohol abuse, or lack of skills or motivation. The other 96 percent blamed social or political conditions for their plight..."

In sum, Goldberg's gripe was that reporters didn't interview enough people who thought homelessness was a personal failing.

He's right. I would argue he's also an asshole. But, technically, not incorrect.

Homelessness, generally speaking, has always been a serious problem. Current levels are about three times what they were when Ronald Reagan became president. Goldberg was in the ballpark of the right question: why were the networks freaking out about it back then, and not before or after?

Among other reasons, reporting on homelessness in the Reagan years was a popular means of decrying the "Greed is good" era. Talking about the issue became a way of showing you cared.

This was satirized by Bret Easton Ellis in *American Psycho*. His deranged killer Patrick Bateman, while dining at an upscale restaurant called "espace," interrupts everyone's overpriced dinner to give a speech about all of the things the news tells him to care about.

Bateman's fellow moussed-banker pal Timothy Bryce challenges the table guests, saying, "What about the massacres in Sri Lanka...? I mean, do you know anything about Sri Lanka, about how, like, the Sikhs are killing tons of Israelis over there...?"

This is basically everyone who reads the news. Most people don't know anything about it, of course.

Anyway, Bateman corrects him ("Come on, Bryce, there are a lot more important problems than Sri Lanka") and gives a list of things "we" must do to fix the world.

"We have to provide food, and shelter, for the homeless," he deadpans.

Like Bateman's Oliver Peoples glasses and herb mint facial mask, concern for the homeless was just another fashionable thing to wear.

The Bateman character later kills a homeless person and his dog for fun, which I doubt many news consumers have done. But most audiences did forget about homelessness pretty much instantly once we in the media stopped babbling about it.

By an amazing coincidence, the drop in coverage came exactly as officials in cities like New York began forcing the homeless out of "civilized" areas by mass-arresting them for things like obstructing pedestrian traffic. Out of sight, out of mind.

American Psycho was a book about how the American idea of personality is constructed around things we buy. We may be insane monsters inside, but we work hard to have good consumer taste on the surface. Ellis understood that most of us, when we read the news, are really just telling ourselves a story about who we like to think we are, when we look in the mirror.

The main difference between Fox and MSNBC is their audiences are choosing different personal mythologies. Again: this is a consumer choice. It's not the truth, but a truth *product*.

People who watch Fox tend to be older, white, and scared. They're tuning in to be told they're the last holdouts in a disintegrating empire, Romans besieged by Vandals.

Fox runs the stories that pop out of Nexis, featuring a standard list of cultural villains, usually liberals, feminists, atheists, immigrants, terrorists, or any of a number of handout-seeking political constituencies.

When a liberal celebrity says something stupid—which happens about once every two seconds—it goes straight on the air (they have a whole archive of Lena Dunham bits).

Fox is basically a neverending slasher flick for the Greatest Generation. The only thing that varies is what Marx-fluent monster leaps out of Camp Crystal Lake. Antifa is a good recent foil. The network was trying to squeeze content out of the New Black Panthers for a while.

People who watch MSNBC, meanwhile, are tuning in to receive mega-doses of the world's thinnest compliment, i.e. that they're morally superior to Donald Trump. The network lately has become a one-note morality play with endless segments about Michael Flynn, Michael Cohen, and Paul Manafort. This isn't the first time they've used this model.

The coverage formula on both channels is to scare the crap out of audiences, then offer them micro-doses of safety and solidarity, which come when they see people onscreen sharing their fears. There is a promise of reassurance that comes with both coverage formulas.

This is critical, that you're encouraged to have consumer expectations, even though news should be unpredictable. Even sports fans expect disappointment about half the time. Not news audiences today:

WE'RE SELLING SAFE SPACES

The worst sin in the tobacco business is to upset customer expectations. Every cigarette must be the same. If even once you light up a Camel and taste strawberries or pelican guano, your brain will never forgive the brand.

The news business now works the same way, even though it shouldn't.

Reporters are supposed to challenge their audiences. Did you buy one of the 110 billion non-biodegradable plastic bottles sold by Coca-Cola last year, and if so, would you like to see a picture of where it might have gone?

Did the politician you voted for go back on his or her promises? Did your tax dollars pay for the bombing of women and children in foreign countries? Do you even know where we're at war?

There's a widespread belief now that "bravery"[1] in a reporter is someone like Jim Acosta asking tough questions of someone like Donald Trump. But Acosta's viewers hate Donald Trump. Wake me up when he takes on his own Twitter followers, or gets in his boss Jeff Zucker's face about the massive profits they've all been making off Trumpmania.

We don't challenge audiences. I know one TV reporter who did a story about a murder in a poor region of the South. After the piece was cut, the news director ordered that interviews of chief characters be re-shot as standups by the reporter, a typically good-looking, well-dressed, educated northeasterner.

The reason? Images of poor, inarticulate people are disturbing to audiences, especially upscale ones (read: people with disposable incomes who can respond

---

1 This kind of behavior is braver in places where journalists get killed, like reporters I knew who investigated Vladimir Putin, including Anna Politkovskaya and Yuri Scheckochikhin.

to advertising). That's why we don't show poverty on TV unless we're laughing at it (*Honey Boo Boo*) or chasing it in squad cars (*Cops*).

In the same way, if we've spent time building your identity as a person who despises and fears Donald Trump, and has ardent hopes he might soon be removed from office, we can't upset that.

Which brings us back to MSNBC. The network's recent all-Russiagate format is indistinguishable from the pioneering way the Clinton-Lewinsky scandal was monetized in the late nineties by MSNBC.

People forget that MSNBC, before it found its current niche as an anti-Trump network, was just a conventionally crappy news organization.

Launched in July of 1996, it had just a few hundred thousand households tuning in as 1998 approached. Then they made a decision to become, as former NPR ombudsman Alicia Shepard put it, the "first all-Monica, all the time network."

Keith Olbermann, then host of "The Big Show," began running a nightly segment, "The White House in Crisis," which spun Lewinsky stories virtually every night.

Another MSNBC show, *Hardball* with Chris Matthews, extended its breathless format and began rebroadcasting at 11:00 p.m. during the Lewinsky period. All its top-rated shows were about the Clinton scandal.

Olbermann's audience grew 148 percent in 1998. *Hardball* went from 252,000 households in 1997 to 559,000. Most conventional media did the same. The AP ran a whopping 4,109 stories on Monicagate in its first year of coverage, and had twenty-five reporters on the story full-time.

The top three networks devoted 1,931 minutes to the subject in 1998, more than the next seven subjects combined (and much more than a 1998 story that would have major implications for a later economic collapse, the repeal of the Glass-Steagall Act that had kept the investment banking, depository banking, and insurance businesses separate).

As they are now, talk shows were full of speculation that the president would imminently leave office. "I think [Clinton's] Presidency is numbered in days," said Sam Donaldson on ABC in the fateful last week of January 1998.

This was pure manipulation: creating expectations in emotionally vulnerable audiences, holding out the possibility of huge imminent news, which guaranteed people would keep checking not just daily, but by the hour, the minute.

Fox did all of this and then went a step further. It milked the Lewinsky story through unapologetic cheerleading for the demise of Clinton.

Unlike other outlets, which merely sought to cash in on sensation, Fox openly villainized Bill and trashed all the characters in the story. They even ran a poll asking if Monica Lewinsky was just an "average girl" or a "young tramp looking for thrills."

Openly taking sides gave Fox a consumer advantage. For certain viewers, it was more like a pep rally than journalism. No matter what happened, Fox was always going to have a predictable take, one it was unembarrassed by.

Meanwhile, Keith Olbermann was leaving MSNBC and moving back to sports, later claiming his "White House in Crisis" work gave him moral "dry heaves".

The new model was what author Deborah Tannen called "two side fighting." In the Lewinsky affair, outlets began either being for or against the Clintons, and you knew what you were getting before you tuned in.[2]

Not long after Monicagate, Fox assumed the top spot and stayed there for fifteen years, making $2.3 billion in profits in 2016 alone.

I've run into trouble with friends for suggesting Fox is *not* a pack of lies. Sure, the network has an iffy relationship with the truth, but much of its content is factually correct. It's just highly, highly selective—and predictable with respect to which facts it chooses to present.

The worst of Fox's excesses are editorial comments, like Sean Hannity saying Halloween teaches kids to beg for handouts, or Brian Kilmeade saying Americans "keep marrying other species and other ethnics" and "Swedes have pure genes," or Glenn Beck saying of Obama, "this president has exposed himself as a guy over and over and over again who has a deep-seated hatred for white people." It obviously denies scientific consensus on issues like climate change and has introduced some horrific deceptions into America's belief systems, the birther controversy being the most notable.

2 Because of this, the real scandal of the Lewinsky affair—what we later came to understand as a #MeToo question—was largely uncovered. The conservative Fox, run by serial harasser Ailes, was obviously never interested in that angle. The increasingly pro-Clinton non-Fox media, however, wouldn't cover it either, focusing instead on the legitimacy of the special prosecution investigation and subsequent impeachment. The popular take on the case was epitomized by Chris Rock's "He got impeached for *what*?" take.

But the network's bread-and-butter coverage doesn't require crossing such lines. It mainly picks real things that happen to coincide with their brand and their propagandistic objectives, and runs those stories over and over. A staple of its coverage is the American tourist butchered, maimed, or abducted in a third-world country, or any murder in which the suspect is an immigrant, etc.

For instance, the same Fox that spent years going ape over would-be perjury, obstruction of justice, and extramarital sex in the Starr investigation is suddenly dead silent about a somewhat similar narrative involving Donald Trump paying off porn stars. People don't tune in to *Fox* to hear bad news about their team.

The network is now a lot sloppier, factually, than it once was, having learned over time that its audiences don't notice or mind screw-ups. The lesson of *Fox* in this sense should scare anyone who works anywhere in the business, because a lot of the *Fox* business model—if not its political content—is standard practice.

By the summer of 2016, I predicted the press would soon be divided in a way that left media audiences permanently sheltered from any narratives their "side" might find troublesome.

If you're a consumer of one media brand, the polls will tell you Trump is trending up: he's five points ahead at the beginning of 2018. Pick another brand and you'll learn only 38 percent of Americans plan to vote for him, and he's in dire trouble. You can tell yourself any story you want about the future.

During the heat of the Russiagate Panic, if you chose one brand, you'd read often about the "beginning of the end" of the Trump presidency. Pick another and you'd read there are basically no legal avenues for removing Trump prematurely that don't involve a Republican Senate's unexpected cooperation.

I work in this business and don't know who to trust. The situation recalls the landscape of third-world counties, where the truth has to be pieced together from disparate bits reported by news outlets loyal to different oligarchical factions.

Companies are nurturing emotional dependencies for cash. The key is to always report negatively about the other audience, but never about your own. They're bad equals you're good, and endlessly spinning in that cycle creates hardened, loyal, dependent followers.

A 2016 Pew survey found remarkably similar numbers of Democrats and Republicans—58 percent of the former, 57 percent of the latter—said members of the opposing party made them "frustrated."

The survey showed 52 percent of Republicans believed Democrats were "closed-minded," while 70 percent of Democrats felt that way about Republicans.

We're not encouraging people to break these patterns. If anything, we're addicting people to conflict, vitriol, and feelings of superiority. It works. Companies know: fear and mistrust are even harder habits to break than smoking.

9. SCARE TACTICS: ALL THE FOLK DEVILS ARE HERE

In the mid-sixties, a South African sociologist named Stanley Cohen focused on a seemingly parochial topic.

He was interested in news headlines about gangs of "Mods" and "Rockers" clashing at seaside holiday resorts around Great Britain. The narrative had taken the nation, and the world, by storm.

In 1964, the Mods and Rockers were not yet fully distinguished and had little concrete group identity. Rockers roughly speaking had wavy hair and fashioned themselves after American groups like the Hell's Angels (though they listened to different music). Mods had cropped or shaved heads, listened to soul, ska, and R&B, and favored tailored clothes. I'm reliably informed by one former Mod that the costume was "parkas, Ben Sherman shirts, Wrangler jeans and jackets, and Doc Martens... we also rode scooters, in contrast to the Rockers' minibikes." According to media narratives in sixties Britain, these dueling young deviants, minds addled by new forms of music, were desecrating British holiday resorts. The victims were middle-to-upper-class Britons enjoying traditional seaside holidays.

Cohen went back, sussing out the first "Mod-Rocker" clashes, to see how closely the real tales matched tabloid descriptions. One of the first occurred at the small town of Clacton, on the east coast of England. During Easter, 1964, the small town was sopping wet and suffering its coldest temperatures in eighty years. The shopkeepers were testy about losing tourism money, and young people in the area (the town was a hangout for kids from the East End of London) were grumbling over rumors that some restaurant doors would be closed to them. On that Easter weekend in 1964, a few members of the groups threw rocks at each other on the streets. A couple of beach huts were destroyed. One youth fired a starting pistol in the air. A few were arrested.

Not much of a story.

The press thought otherwise. The Monday after these happenings, every paper in London with the exception of the *Times* carried the Clacton events on the front page. They included the following headlines:

DAY OF TERROR BY SCOOTER GROUPS
YOUNGSTERS BEAT UP TOWN—97 LEATHER JACKET ARRESTS
WILD ONES INVADE SEASIDE—97 ARRESTS

Cohen began to look at other clashes and noticed a pattern. As he wrote:

> The next lot of incidents received similar coverage on the Tuesday and editorials began to appear, together with reports that the Home Secretary was 'being urged' (it was not usually specified exactly by whom) to hold an inquiry or to take firm action...

Straight reporting gave way to theories especially about motivation: the mob was described as "exhilarated," "drunk with notoriety," "hell-bent for destruction," etc.

Reports of the incidents themselves were followed by accounts of police and court activity, as well as local reaction. The press coverage of each series of incidents showed a similar sequence.

Before long, the stories went international. There were articles in America, Canada, Australia, South Africa, and other nations. In Belgium, a photo of the disturbances came over the caption, "West Side Story on English Coast."

A keen observer of language, Cohen smelled fabrication in some of the stories, if only because they were "too stereotypical to be true." But he couldn't prove that the many "interviews" tabloid journalists supposedly scored with would-be Mods and Rockers had been invented.

When Cohen looked more closely, he found much that was incorrect in the national reports. Local newspapers were better.

"Not only are the reports more detailed and specific," he wrote of the locals, "but they avoid statements like, 'all the dance halls near the seafront were smashed' when every local resident knows there is only one dance hall near the front."

Cohen found other problems. The "Mods" and the "Rockers" were uniformly described as "affluent young people," who came to resort towns in a kind of zombie haze.

The fable of "affluent" gangs was elevated in part because of a story—true, as Cohen found—that one of the youths arrested in one of the clashes offered to pay his £75 fine by check. That the cheeky kid didn't have a checking account and was just pressing the buttons of the locals was not reported.

The Mod-Rocker clashes peaked with infamous episodes at the beachside towns of Margate and Brighton. As Cohen discovered, nothing earthshaking happened in any of the cases. Locals actually spoke warmly of the clashes as having increased tourist traffic.

Moreover, regional coverage put the cost of the damage at Margate—made famous by the sensational *Daily Mirror* headline, WILD ONES 'BEAT UP' MARGATE—at a whopping... £400.

The papers worked overtime to keep the narrative of out-of-control youth alive in the homes of prim and proper Englanders. Any story they could possibly tie to the Mod-Rocker clashes hit the papers, even if the link was tenuous.

On May 18, 1964, for instance, The *Dublin Evening Press* published:

TERROR COMES TO ENGLISH RESORTS. MUTILATED MOD FOUND IN PARK.

This turned out to be a story about a man in his early twenties found stabbed in a Birmingham park a day before a reported "clash" at a nearby resort. The only thing "mod" about him was that he was found in a "mod jacket."

A national furor set in. Lawmakers everywhere rushed to get "Malicious Damage Bills" into law, and campaigns against youth music and movies abounded.

There was not a single editorial in any major newspaper that dared play down the threat. Editorials frequently came in tandem with calls for action of an increasingly intense variety.

After an incident at Whitsun, the *Evening Argus* printed twenty-three letters; seven proposed corporal punishment! There were calls for "using fire hoses on the crowds, tear gas, hard labour schemes, flogging, long prison sentences," and "banning the offenders from the town."

Perhaps most important, the tabloids—staffed as they were with people who had few skills, moral or otherwise, beyond being occasionally clever writers—began to master the art of creating dehumanizing symbolic language for both groups.

The favored epithet was "wild ones," but that was soon accompanied by other descriptors: "vermin," "ratpack," "ill conditioned odious louts" (*Daily Express*), "retarded vain young hot-blooded paycocks" (*Daily Sketch*), "grubby hordes of louts and sluts" (*Daily Telegraph*), "their bovine stupidity... their ape-like reactions to the world" (*Evening Standard*).

Cohen found the most omnipresent descriptors were *boredom* and *affluence*. These descriptions played into belief systems of target audiences who were desperate to believe young people were simply lazy, drug-addled, spoiled monsters. In fact, the Mods and Rockers both were mostly undereducated and working class.

In 1972, Cohen would publish a book, *Folk Devils and Moral Panics*, that described all of this. *Moral panic* has as a result become a permanent part of our lexicon. "Folk devils" were what Cohen called the targets of these instant manias.

Not a reporter, Cohen nailed many of the techniques that make journalism work.

Thanks to Christopher Nolan, pop audiences now know magicians rely upon a basic premise of a pledge, turn, and prestige, i.e. a promise to change something ordinary into the extraordinary. Show the audience a common top hat, pull a rabbit out of it.

In examining the mod-rocker mania, Cohen noticed tabloid reporting worked on a similar premise.

Reporters depicted ordinary life, then showed it disrupted and distorted by contagion. The scare coverage implied future problems and put audiences in a siege-like mentality. They'd been trained to wait for delivery: more violence, more social disruption, more headlines.

This set of circumstances led to something that another sociologist, Leslie Wilkins, deemed the "Deviancy Amplification Spiral."

This was an academic term for "using invented problems to drive people actually crazy." It went something like this:

1. LESS TOLERANCE *leads to*
2. MORE ACTS BEING DEFINED AS CRIMES
leads to
3. MORE ACTIONS AGAINST CRIMINALS
leads to
4. MORE ALIENATION OF DEVIANTS
leads to
5. LESS TOLERANCE OF DEVIANTS BY CONFORMING GROUPS *leads back to* #2, etc.

With this circular method, you could take small incidents and blow them into national terrors in a snap, and God only knew when any of it would stop.

***

All this research was groundbreaking and impacted the thinking of sociologists and academics around the world from the early seventies on.

It did not, however, much penetrate the consciousness of editors and news directors, who continued to profit off moral panics whenever possible. They ran audiences through the same Satanic spin cycle for decades.

American news consumers will remember many of the worst examples.

During the sleepy years of the later Cold War, shlock magazines like *Time* and *Newsweek* constantly tried to sell us on the next "folk devil" invasion.

Editors knew: the target middle-aged magazine reader plopping down in the chair of a doctor's waiting room is desperate to find company sympathetic to the confusing changes in their once-lovable children.

Why is little Johnny suddenly so taciturn? Could it be the drugs? The glue? The music? The alarming new sexual mores? Pick up *Newsweek* and find out!

Weeklies for decades cycled through TEENS: HORNY AND OUT OF CONTROL covers. If you look back you'll notice, humorously, there's usually a well-placed female teen derriere on the front of such efforts.

Teen pregnancy has been another favored topic. To scare the pants off parents, mags will make sure the third-trimester horror on the cover looks no older than eight.

The mystery of your suddenly aloof child's brain, your child as tyrant who needs a hell of a spanking (think of the "corporal punishment" letters in Cohen's study), and, of course, your child as potential rifle-toting mass murderer are other popular themes.

Moral panics were once very likely to involve a "something is corrupting your otherwise angelic youth" theme.

The "Dungeons and Dragons" terror of the early eighties was an example. Some of us are old enough to remember the absurd scare flick *Mazes and Monsters,* starring an early version of America's most dependable moral-panic frontman, Tom Hanks.

Often the panic came hand in hand with a ready legal solution. Tipper Gore's "Parents Music Resource Center" freakout over heavy metal lyrics was an eighties re-hash of Mod-Rocker fear. The solution, thankfully, was tame: warning labels. The same craze today would likely result in a Heritage Foundation council working with iTunes to secretly remove morally threatening music.

Reporters were always allowed tons of leeway when investigating moral panics. The thinnest statistical reeds would do.

Time ran an infamous "CYBERPORN" cover in 1995 showing a shocked kiddie looking aghast into the evil glow of a computer screen. The reader is left to imagine the awful image the boy must be seeing.

The piece was based on a bogus *undergraduate* research report about rising cyber-threats by a mysterious figure called Marty Rimm, who disappeared shortly thereafter.

Time writer Philip Elmer-Dewitt later wrote eloquently about being too young to realize he'd been duped. In retrospect, he wrote, the piece was the worst combination, i.e. good writing, bad facts:

"One *Time* researcher assigned to my story remembers the study as 'one of the more shameful, fear-mongering and unscientific efforts that we ever gave attention to.'"

Nonetheless, the *Time* cover caused political figures like Ralph Reed and Chuck Grassley to spring into action demanding censorship of the Interwebs.

Another early *Time* cover telling parents to worry about the impact of video games may not have predicted mass social contagion, but did hint at a future football star ("GRONK! FLASH! ZAP!").

There were constant variations on "techno-panic" themes, suggesting new technologies would addict children to profanity, violence, peeping, sexual deviancy, and other terrors.

Moral panics tended to have the most profound consequences for "folk devils" who were politically underrepresented. The War on Drugs has arguably been the most devastating ongoing panic of all, dating back to the unintentionally comic *Reefer Madness*.

It would be impossible to calculate how many unnecessary years in jail have been handed out to dealers and users thanks to blunt moral-panic stunts like George H. W. Bush holding up a bag of crack supposedly bought outside the White House (the offender had actually been lured from across town).

We've had terrors over Y2K, SARS, Bioterror/Anthrax, day care molesters, and countless other devils.

There was even a hoax scare over teens using a Zambian hallucinogen called *jenkem*—brewed from fermented human waste—that turned out not to have any confirmed American cases. But it made for good copy. "Jenkem: Stay Alert or Call it a Hoax?" wondered ABC in 2007.

***

A few sociologists over the years have noted that moral panics benefit the interested players in a particular way. There is symbiosis between big commercial news outlets and state authorities.

Scare the crap out of people, and media companies get richer, while state agencies get more and more license for authoritarian crackdowns on the "folk devil" of the moment. A perfect partnership.

The crack story exemplified this.

TV stations glamorized the "wars" on the streets, got great ratings, yet rarely got to the heart of what the crack epidemic was: a way for cocaine cartels to expand the consumer base beyond the saturated market of upper-class buyers of powder coke. Crack was just the cartel version of a corporate marketing ploy to rope in poorer consumers.

Poor crackheads scared the public so much, authorities wishing to fight them got almost anything they asked for. The most infamous reform was the so-called

"100-1 sentencing laws," which gave crack offenders sentences one hundred times longer than powder offenders.

This is the hallmark of the moral panic scenario. It's a real story, but it's exaggerated, often wildly, and comes wrapped in proposals for authoritarian solutions.

***

The only thing preventing moral panic from becoming the dominant model of commercial press in the past was that we in the media had other ways of making money.

As Jim Moroney of the *Dallas Morning News* explained to me, newspapers in the pre-Internet days were cash machines. They had their own networks of trucks and distribution points, and if you wanted to find a worker for hire or sell a car, the local paper was the only game in town.

"These were scarcity businesses," is how he put it.

It was the same with local radio and TV stations, limited in number because each needed FCC licenses. There were only so many 30-second spots on the air.

If you had a radio show or a daily newspaper, you didn't have to wind up the local Junior Anti-Sex League to torch-bearing action every week to sell copies. You made enough on classified and local ads that you could safely not indulge in fear-mongering, if you so chose.

Smart people, however, understood that the instant this cash cow disappeared, the media business would change forever. No less an authority than Marshall McLuhan, in his famed book *Understanding Media,* wrote way back in 1964:

> The classified ads (and stock-market quotations) are the bedrock of the press. Should an alternative source of easy access to such diverse daily information be found, the press will fold...

In the Internet age, the news media has lost classified ads, and the instant relay of stock market quotes, which made empires out of services like *Reuters* and *Bloomberg,* no longer much impresses business consumers.

We're left to hunt other game.

Accelerated by social media, moral panic has become the last dependably profitable format of modern news reporting.

Until recently, crime has been the great example. Despite what the public believes, crime has been declining in America for nearly three decades.

Because so much news programming depends upon beliefs to the contrary—to say nothing of politicians who depend upon scare tactics and "tough on crime" platforms to get into office—we rarely hear about this, thanks to a number of scams the press employs.

One is cherry-picking sources for crime stats. Every crime reporter will tell you there are two major outlets for national crime statistics, particularly violent crime: the annual reports by the FBI, and the Bureau of Justice Statistics.

Both are outputs of the Department of Justice, but the BJS uses the same methodology every year (it's based upon broad surveys of households, asking people if they were victims of crimes) and tends to report less alarming statistics.

Newspapers inevitably use FBI stats, which use varying methodologies and somehow always come out a little scarier.

Going by the FBI, violent crime fell 49 percent between 1993 and 2017. By the BJS, violent crime fell 74 percent during the same period.

But the public doesn't believe it.

There have been twenty-two Gallup surveys asking about violent crime since 1993. In eighteen of them, Americans believed crime was rising. Significantly, the numbers change if you ask people about crime in their neighborhoods, where most people see flat or declining dangers. Thus the typical belief system of an American media consumer is: crime may be down in my area, but it's surely way up somewhere else.

It's easy to play with numbers. NUMBER OF KILLINGS SOARS IN BIG CITIES ACROSS U.S., wrote the *New York Times* on July 18, 1990.

Read carefully:

Murder rates have increased steadily over the past several years. After reaching a peak of 10.2 killings per 100,000 population in 1980, the rate fell to 7.9 per 100,000 in 1984 and 1985, a decline that officials attribute to the drop in numbers of people in their teens and 20's. The rate has since rebounded, reaching 8.4 in 1988, the last year for which the F.B.I. has figures broken down in that way.

In other words, the *Times* in 1990 could have written the murder rate was down compared to 1980. But they chose to use the more recent swing upward as a hook. In the long run, of course, violent crime declined after 1990, and has overall since 1980. 1988 proved a high-water mark.

The only brake on this kind of behavior in the past was the potential that another news outlet might call BS. This rarely happened, since even rival news agencies tended to collectively benefit from any scare. But the possibility at least existed.

Today, in a politically cleaved media landscape, reporters know there is less danger than ever that their target audiences will be exposed to dispositive information. Rival publications do not reach rival audiences. MSNBC viewers do not read the *Daily Caller* and vice versa.

Moral panics therefore rage on, essentially unchallenged, in every corner of the political universe.

The 2018 "caravan" of Central American immigrants was a classic moral panic. Immigrant stories frequently are. The caravan had all the hallmarks, with simplistic symbolic language describing the "invaders" ("criminals," "gang members," etc), along with the classic over-prescribed authoritarian solution—troops were literally told by the president they could consider a rock in the hands of an immigrant to be a firearm, i.e. shoot them if so engaged.

President Trump later walked back the idea, but this was all a typical panic tale.

Not having interviewed the people arriving, I couldn't tell you which group of reporters is correct on one of the other central questions. Were the migrants attempting simple immigration, i.e. were they just looking for better living conditions, in which case their journey was technically illegal? Or were they seeking asylum from violence or political oppression, which is legal under international law and requires the host country to grant hearings?

Who knows? It was probably a mix of both. One thing, however, seems certain. Seven thousand migrants was not an "invasion."

This would have been a minor, if depressing, story, were it not in the eye of a furious maelstrom surrounding the politics of Donald Trump. It might not have been reported at all in the Bush or Obama years.

Similar to the crime story, the immigration furor has mostly rested upon the pumping up of anecdotal information about border crossings. Placed in proper context, we're talking about a problem (if it's even that) that's declined significantly since 9/11. It's the Mods and the Rockers clashing at the border, only on a much bigger scale, with much more prominent political players mixed up in the cultural argument.

The same kinds of reporting techniques increasingly dominate anti-Trump media, however.

The constant drumbeat of "It's the beginning of the end" stories about "bombshells" causing the "walls" to "close in" on Trump—so comic that a mash-up of such comments dating to Trump's first week in office has gone viral—is a case of straight-up emotional grifting.

Editors know Democratic audiences are devastated by the fact of the Trump presidency, so they constantly hint at any hope that he'll be dragged away in handcuffs at any moment. This is despite the fact that reporters know the legal avenues for removal are extraordinarily unlikely.

Such puffing of false hopes is the most emotionally predatory behavior that exists in journalism.

If you do a TRUMP'S FINAL DAYS story in *Politico* in September 2018, there's no penalty when he's still in office weeks later. These stories get a lot of hits.

Meanwhile, the rare articles in the liberal press warning audiences not to expect a Nixon-like exit tomorrow—like the *Guardian* piece from July 2018, WHAT LIBERALS (STILL) GET WRONG ABOUT TRUMP'S SUPPORT—tend to disappear quickly.

Even worse has been Russiagate, which became a serious problem throughout the business for a variety of reasons, among them the fact that it delayed the necessary journalistic process of examining what really happened in 2016. On top of that it's also been a clear case of moral-panic journalism.

The press, for instance, has stopped making distinctions between individual Russians and "Russia," assuming somehow one Russian must be in communication with the other 150 million.

When special prosecutor Robert Mueller submitted in a filing that an Olympic weightlifter promised "political synergy" to Trump lawyer Michael Cohen (an overture Cohen "did not follow up on," according to Mueller himself), the press jumped. Here is Franklin Foer of *Slate,* who wrote some of the first Russiagate pieces:

> Cohen was talking "political synergy" with the Russians in November, 2015. November, 2015! That's further back than most timelines of collusion usually begin.

So "a weightlifter" becomes "the Russians" instantaneously, and the minor fact of the communication never going anywhere is left out. Imagine if a "Putin lawyer" contacted Hulk Hogan and the Russian press reported "CONTACT WITH AMERICA!!!"

We would think this was crazy. We would also think it was crazy if a Russian weekly magazine tried to scare readers by showing the Mormon Tabernacle Choir invading the Kremlin. But this happened with *Time* magazine, one of many to confuse St. Basil's basilica with the Kremlin on a cover showing the beautiful onion-domed church taking over the White House.

But this kind of nuttery is typical of what happens in these tales.

The reporting surrounding the infamous "Internet Research Agency" ads was also a virtual copy of Cohen's findings about how statistics can be bent to fit narratives.

In the fall of 2017, the *New York Times* worked hand in hand with a collection of unnamed sources, congressional authorities, and self-interested think-tankers (who've been gobbling up grant money to study the new red threat) to create a devastating portrait of Russian subversion via Facebook ads.

This is from a monster ten thousand-word piece by Scott Shane and Mark Mazetti called THE PLOT TO SUBVERT AN ELECTION. The money quote:

> Even by the vertiginous standards of social media, the reach of their effort was impressive: 2,700 fake Facebook accounts, 80,000 posts, many of them elaborate images with catchy slogans, and an eventual

audience of 126 million Americans on Facebook alone. That was not far short of the 137 million people who would vote in the 2016 presidential election.

The "126 million" stat has been quoted and re-quoted over and over, despite it actually representing a remote hypothetical. In Senate testimony, Facebook executives said the statistic represented the number of people who "may have been served" by one of the 80,000 posts over the course of a *194-week* period—over three full years—between 2015 and 2017.

Facebook executive Colin Stretch testified before the Senate that during the same period, "Americans using Facebook were exposed to, or 'served,' a total of over 33 trillion stories in their News Feeds."

This means the IRA content represented a whopping .0000000024 of all impressions seen during this time. The BBC, conspicuously not an American outlet, was one of the few agencies to put the IRA numbers in context, calling the ads a "drop in the bucket."

Does that mean the IRA ads are a non-story? No. They are certainly concerning and worth investigating. But this is one of many instances of the scale of an issue clearly being exaggerated.

Moreover, it's been hard not to notice the usual moral-panic symbiosis in full effect. The prolonged scare has translated into heightened profits for media companies, and aggressive calls for increased powers of censorship and enforcement for government, ironically to control the spread of "fake news."

What Stanley Cohen described over fifty years ago was a pale preview of what was to come. Cohen saw a primitive effort by cash-hungry tabloids to slap simplistic, symbolic labels on "deviant" groups.

The tabloids were highly effective in creating an "ick" factor around their Mod and Rocker villains, even stripping them of sympathetic characteristics they had in real life, like working-class backgrounds. Without public defenders, media audiences were free to despise them without restraint, and embellish their anti-portraits in their heads.

In America in the eighties and nineties there were usually people to counter such public panics. For every Tipper Gore, there was a Frank Zappa or Dee Snider appearing for the defense.

In our new cleaved and atomized landscape, those brakes are gone. Every demographic has its own folk devils, who go undefended.

Conservative media long ago fixated on libs, commies, terrorists, Islamicists, tax-and-spenders, feminazis, and countless others. No one on Fox pleads for context.

#Resistance media now has devils of its own: deplorables, white supremacists, Trumpites, Bernie Bros, neo-Naderites, false equivalencers, dirtbag-lefters, and countless others (a new craze is labeling socialists like Corbyn and Sanders anti-Semites).

Without any way to put an end to such passions, the new normal will be coexisting, dueling panics: the caravan versus Russiagate, "the beginning of the end" versus "How the Left lost its mind," *Breitbart* versus *The Palmer Report.*

Few audiences of any of these outlets will realize they're engaged in similar behaviors to those of hated antagonists.

The only constant will be more and more authoritarian solutions. In the social media age, we can scare you as never before. Which means politicians will have an easier time obtaining permission for censorship, surveillance, immigration bans, and other expanded powers.

This is the major departure from the *Manufacturing Consent* age. In 1985, the popular demons were objects of universal terror, usually an external threat— Soviets, Sandinistas, the AIDS virus.

Today pockets of media consumers demonize one another, calling for dueling crackdowns. We have become our own worst enemies, and the longer the cycles play out, the more authoritarian our future will look.

10. THE MEDIA'S GREAT FACTUAL LOOPHOLE

On Friday, January 18, 2019, Special Counsel Robert Mueller took the unusual step of releasing a statement essentially shooting down the latest "bombshell" in the Russiagate story, which had been released by BuzzFeed earlier that day. The BuzzFeed story said Donald Trump directed his personal lawyer, Michael Cohen, to lie to congress, which would potentially have been a felony.

After the BuzzFeed piece broke, Democrats not only wasted no time calling for impeachment, but within hours began fundraising in response to the story. This is from a mass mailing issued that same day by DNC chief Tom Perez:

"Huge news just broke that indicates Trump's former attorney Michael Cohen lied to congress under the specific direction of Donald Trump himself... If you're committed to holding Trump accountable... today is an important day to show it. Donate $3 right now to help Democrats..."

Mueller's statement said, "BuzzFeed's description of specific statements to the special counsel's office, and characterization of documents and testimony obtained by this office... are not accurate." It was an extraordinary step, one an official in that position rarely takes unless it's necessary.

It wasn't the first time it happened. Testifying before the Senate Intelligence Committee in June 2017, former FBI director James Comey shot down a *New York Times* story from February 14 of that year suggesting Trump campaign officials had had repeated contacts with "senior Russian intelligence officials."

Asked by Idaho senator James Risch about that story, Comey said, "in the main, it was not true."

The *Times* story had been sourced to multiple "current and former American officials." How could it have been wrong? Or was Comey wrong?

Both stories belong to an ancient tradition of reports, predating Russiagate, that live in a precarious loophole in the American system of media.

The public largely misunderstands the "fake news" issue. Newspapers rarely fib outright. Most "lies" are errors of omission or emphasis. There are no Fox stories saying blue states have lower divorce rates, nor are there MSNBC stories exploring the fact that many pro-choice Democrats, particularly religious ones, struggle with a schism between their moral and political beliefs on abortion.

Most of what's "fake" is in the caricature: of our own audiences, and especially of despised groups. As even Noam Chomsky said, newspapers are "full of facts."

With one exception.

There is a loophole that involves a procedural flaw in Western journalism's fact-checking tradition. It's gotten worse with time. The offending story type nearly always has the same elements:

It involves national security or law enforcement;

It's sourced to unnamed officials;

The basic gist of the scoop is classified or otherwise unconfirmable.

On August 25, 1986, the *Wall Street Journal,* citing multiple unnamed sources, stated without qualification, "The U.S. and Libya are on a collision course."

The article said the American intelligence community had new information that Muammar Qaddafi was planning terrorist acts and we therefore intended to bomb the crap out of him. Oh, and he was possibly facing an internal coup, too.

"There are increasing signs that [Qaddafi has] resumed planning and preparations for terrorist acts," the *Journal* wrote.

Other outlets, including the *New York Times* and the *Washington Post,* later picked up the story. International tensions heightened.

Big story! But the whole thing was a crock. It was an American-generated "deception plan" designed to make Qaddafi nervous. We found out only because another unnamed person leaked the memo explaining as much (the memo had been written by Reagan national security adviser John Poindexter) to Bob Woodward.

I call these stories "four-sourced clovers," because the number of unnamed sources claiming to bolster such questionable scoops has, humorously, grown over time.

The "senior Russian intelligence officials" story James Comey was forced to shoot down in 2017 had four unnamed sources. So did one suggesting Trump was about to fire the Fed chair. Luke Harding had two for his recent *Guardian* bombshell about Paul Manafort supposedly having met with Julian Assange (that story is still unconfirmed).

Some of these stories begin with a single high-ranking intelligence official speaking to a reporter (or team of reporters) at an esteemed paper like the *Times* or the *Washington Post*. The reporters might ask for additional confirmation. The official may give them some names. The reporter(s) call the names.

The names might belong to agency subordinates, or to retired officials now working at think tanks or private "research" agencies. Those sources confirm the initial story in its particulars.

So you get four sources, or maybe six, but depending on the story type, it may really just be one story that's been cycled through four friendly heads. It's a game of telephone, with the reporter at the end.

Incidentally: it's a red flag if the call is coming from the official, as opposed to the reporter calling the officials. The average intelligence official wouldn't stop to tell you if your child was on fire. When they start cold-calling agencies, and/ or rotating scoops by doling them out to different outlets and papers each week, that's a huge red flag.

When you see one of these stories, check to see if that reporter has a history of national security pieces. If he or she does not, if this transmission of classified scoops is taking place in the context of a new relationship, be extra wary.

Why? Because relationships matter in journalism. Reporters theoretically must be willing to go to jail to protect their sources. Similarly, no good source will want to burn a reporter with whom he or she has a long-standing relationship.

It's not easy for any security official to find a journalist with the intelligence, integrity, and wherewithal to successfully protect their identities. When an official finds a reporter who's proved he or she will not burn them by running off-the-record disclosures, the official will tend to want to protect that relationship. The official therefore will not knowingly dump a big steaming pile on that reporter's lap.

So for instance, there was a pretty good chance the particulars of the story were correct when David Ignatius of the *Washington Post* printed the first "bombshell" about Michael Flynn having had phone calls with Russian ambassador Sergei Kislyak. It's an open secret in the business that Ignatius is a favored reporter of the CIA.

God only knows who his source was on the Flynn story, but it sure was interesting that he ran a slobbering two-thousand-plus-word profile of departing CIA director John Brennan shortly afterward, somehow managing not to mention Brennan's infamous episode of lying to congress about hacking the computers of Senate staffers.

We know the CIA folks aren't going to toss Ignatius in the Judith Miller memorial shame-dungeon. There were some other things in that Flynn piece that raised eyebrows, but the gist of it was almost certainly dead-on.

In so many other cases, you just can't be sure. Remember these stories?

ISRAEL RAMPS UP CAMPAIGN AGAINST GAZA AID FLOTILLA, 2011

When Israel effected a naval blockade of the Gaza strip, pro-Palestinian activists (including the likes of Alice Walker) organized to try to break through with boats to deliver humanitarian aid. In advance of the arrival of those flotilla-challenging civilians, Israeli authorities told every reporter with a pulse they had firm intel violence was planned.

This is from the above *Washington Post* article about the story:

> On Tuesday, Israeli newspapers were filled with reports from unnamed military officials, charging that sacks of chemicals, including sulfur, had been loaded onto flotilla vessels with the aim of using the materials against Israeli soldiers. The reports, citing military intelligence sources, said that some activists had spoken in preparatory meetings of their desire to "shed the blood" of soldiers and had threatened to kill those who might board their ships.
>
> "Coming to kill," said a headline in the Maariv newspaper over a photo of one vessel.

About a month later most of the activists, stuck in Greece, gave up and went home. Five months later a few boats tried to break through, and "activists from nine nations surrendered peacefully."

It's possible Israeli officials really did have intel about planned violence. Whether they did or not, telling the whole world about it in advance pre-justified almost anything that might later have taken place on the seas.

This is one of the most common varieties of these tales, intel agencies salting audiences with scary warnings, so later action looks more proportionate.

There were examples of this in the months prior to the Gulf of Tonkin incident as well, before the Kosovo campaign, really before any military action it's standard. This doesn't mean it's wrong, but it sure is tough for a civilian reporter to check.

US OFFICIALS INCREASINGLY CONCERNED IRAN COULD ATTACK ISRAEL, MAY 18, 2018

In the summer of 2018 CNN helpfully relayed concerns of "several" unnamed officials who warned Iran might be on the "cusp" of an attack against Israel. It might have been true. Who knows? The language of the piece seemed pulled from *Team America World Police*: "Iran is about to attack Israel—isn't that right, Intelligence?"

> Intelligence is not clear on when an attack could come and what form it would take, they said, with one official noting that "if there is an attack, it might not be immediately clear it's Iran."

So there may or may not be an attack, and if there is one, it might not look at first like Iran is behind it, although you might want to assume they are, if it happens, and we're not saying it will.

How do you confirm that?

These stories aren't always about national security. Take, for instance, this piece:

EVIDENCE SUPPORTS OFFICER'S ACCOUNT OF SHOOTING IN FERGUSON, OCTOBER 23, 2014

Having written a book about the controversy surrounding the grand jury investigation of a police killing, I know this is very dicey territory for reporters. The central conundrum with grand jury investigations is that sources will often reveal bits of testimony, but almost never put their names behind their information for the very good reason that they're typically prohibited from doing so by law.

I say almost never, because some grand jury witnesses feel strongly enough about what they're doing to take the risk. I had three grand jury witnesses in the Eric Garner case come forward by name. The *New York Times* got a key witness to put her name to the information that she'd been instructed by prosecutors not to use the word "chokehold."

In the above *Washington Post* account of the inquiry into the shooting of Michael Brown by officer Darren Wilson in Ferguson, the sourcing appeared to be a weird game of racial telephone:

> *More than a half-dozen unnamed black witnesses have provided testimony to a St. Louis County grand jury that largely supports Wilson's account of events of Aug. 9, according to several people familiar with the investigation who spoke with* The Washington Post.

So: unnamed black grand jury witnesses told other unnamed "people familiar with the investigation" who in turn told the *Washington Post* that testimony largely supported Wilson's account of a righteous shoot.

Not to delve too deeply into this case about which many people have very strong opinions, but the actual legal issues in the Wilson-Brown case were subtle. There were multiple sticking points. One was the whole issue of why Brown was stopped in the first place.

Most of the American public saw the gnarly footage of Brown stealing cigars from a convenience store. But Brown was actually stopped for the legally meaningless offense of "blocking traffic." Wilson also allegedly saw cigars in Brown's hands, conveniently providing the probable cause for arrest, at which point Brown supposedly tried to reach into a squad car and take Wilson's gun.

The sequence of events from there supposedly involved Wilson firing twice from the car, hitting Brown once on the thumb and missing with the other shot. Brown then fled and was 160 feet away when he turned around, at which point Wilson fired ten more times, in self-defense (I'm being generous not putting that in quotes).

That the grand jury ultimately decided to accept this account could already have been inferred from the fact that they returned no bill in St. Louis County prosecutor Bob McCullough's effort to indict Wilson. McCullough, who ostensibly was the one seeking that indictment, sounded more like a defense counsel after the grand jury's decision. He described eyewitness accounts that Brown had attempted to surrender as having been "completely refuted by the evidence."

Okay, then. We get it, the grand jury decided to believe Wilson's story. So what is the point of the *Washington Post* piece? The major piece of information in it is that six *black* witnesses provided accounts that "largely" supported Wilson's version of the shooting.

These black witnesses did not speak to reporters directly, as witnesses had in the Garner case, to me and to *Times* reporters Al Baker, David Goodman, and Benjamin Mueller. Instead, their accounts were relayed to the *Post* reporters via the telephone game, through "people familiar with the story," whose races were of course not mentioned.

It should be noted that prosecutors are barred from providing information to the public about what's discussed in a grand jury proceeding. If they want to do it, they normally have to ask a judge, as prosecutor Dan Donovan did in the Garner case. Donovan got permission from Judge Stephen Rooney to tell the public he'd called fifty witnesses and shown them sixty exhibits over nine weeks.

When various groups asked the same judge to break the grand jury seal for other information, they were denied.

The same thing happened in Ferguson. Although we got to hear through the *Washington Post* that someone characterized the testimony of six black witnesses as supporting Wilson's account, at least one actual grand juror in the case was mad enough to sue to ask permission to tell his side of the story.

The unnamed juror (who couldn't offer a name) sued because he or she felt the public's impression of the grand jury's work was "not entirely accurate." The plaintiff said the case had a "stronger focus on the victim" than other cases the grand jury heard, i.e. the juror felt prosecutors were trying to put Michael Brown on trial more than Wilson.

The judge struck down the suit.

This is a perfect example of the "four-source clover" effect. You've got multiple unnamed sources telling reporters something they really can't check in any conventional way. They could have used their names if they had so chosen, but did not.[1]

---

1 Regarding the unnamed Ferguson sources: perhaps they'd have risked a penalty to offer their names. But others had taken that same risk in other cases—like the Garner case—because they felt strongly enough about what they felt was the truth that they were willing to incur consequences to tell their stories. The same is very rarely true for unnamed sources. In some cases, as in the Chelsea Manning case, an anonymous source is taking a big risk. But most of the anonymous sources in the above examples were probably bosses, not underlings. Why would the head of the CIA need to be nameless? A general? A chief of police or D.A.? Always take that into consideration. What is the purpose of the anonymity? Is it to protect someone's job or freedom? Or to insulate the person against political consequence if the story goes sideways?

Meanwhile another person literally goes to court to ask permission to give the world his or her name and tell his or her story, and is denied.

One of the most infamous varieties of this story involves drone strikes, as in:

U.S. DRONES AND YEMENI FORCES KILL
QAEDA-LINKED FIGHTERS, OFFICIALS SAY

It used to be a big deal for America to be at war. When eight thousand American troops spent three days shooting Cubans hiding behind palm trees on the island of Grenada, apparently to rescue six hundred medical school students, the country was transfixed. War! Shooting! Helicopters! *Awesome!*

The press swarmed over the island and Tom Brokaw got to do a special report complete with rat-a-tatting "Breaking News!" typewriter sounds that included a graphic with two hastily composed computer warships (they looked like trace jobs from *Battleship* pieces) sitting outside the harbor at St. George.

Today we bomb people basically nonstop and it never makes the news. The average American had no idea we were at war in seven countries last year, and that was just the official disclosure.

In addition to actions in Syria, Afghanistan, Iraq, Somalia, Libya, and Niger, we'd been aiding the Saudi bombing of Yemen for nearly 1,100 consecutive days on December 11, 2017, when the Pentagon submitted its latest "where the hell we're currently at war" summary—also known as a section 1264 report, which has to be delivered to Congress every six months under the National Defense Authorization Act.

That's about as much as the military is required to tell us these days about what it's doing. We were already occupying a third of Syria before the military really bothered to tell anyone. The *Washington Post* informed us somewhat after the fact that we intended to stay in country on an "indefinite" basis. Congress neither debated nor authorized this action.

So in a world where not just wars but occupations can safely be left out of the news, imagine how the reporting works on individual bombings.

The government as recently as last spring asserted in an American courtroom that it had the right to authorize "lethal action" against even an American citizen without indictment, probable cause, even notice, due to a series of legal loopholes so preposterous they would impress Kafka.

So our drones are in the air constantly, searching out the enemies of democracy. How does someone get on the Kill List? Ususally through a combination of human intelligence and algorithmic analysis. In the Obama years there were meetings cheerfully known as "Terror Tuesdays," in which lists of soon-to-be-dead were approved.

You can get on the list by being a "military-aged male" in one of our "small war" zones, by carrying a weapon, by calling the wrong cell phone number, and for dozens of other reasons. So we have a list (known as the "Disposition Matrix") and our flying robots zoom around the globe, crossing borders without permission, dropping payloads whenever we think we've spotted one of our targets.

We hit with surgical precision. In fact, we're so good, we've killed the same terrorist twice on dozens of occasions.

This is how totally without ethics our intelligence sources are, and how lazy newspapers are—we don't even notice when we report the same terrorist killed by drone on different dates in different countries!

Here we are, in the *Guardian,* killing *Cole* bomber Fahd al-Quso in Yemen in May 2012:

Fahd al-Quso was hit by a missile on Sunday as he stepped out of his vehicle... The drone strike that killed Quso was carried out by the CIA after an extended joint surveillance operation with the US military, two American officials said, speaking on condition of anonymity because they were not authorized to speak to the media.

And here we are, in the *Telegraph,* killing him in Pakistan, two years before:

One of the FBI's most wanted terrorists was killed alongside a Briton by a drone attack in Pakistan last month targeting al-Qaeda operatives planning a Mumbai-style attack in Europe, according to reports...

In all, there were four different publicly reported bombings in which al-Quso was supposedly the target. We killed him those two times in Yemen and Pakistan, but we also tried to kill him on at least one other occasion in Yemen.

The *New York Times* cited non-government sources in saying we hit al-Quso's car on July 14, 2011 (he's called al-Qusaa in their piece). One estimate places the total number of people killed in efforts to kill al-Quso at forty-eight.

A non-profit in England took over a year to count just the publicly double-killed terrorists. The London-based Reprieve organization found that 1,147 people were killed by drones in efforts to kill just forty-one men.

Twenty-four men were reported killed or targeted multiple times in Pakistan. Those attacks resulted in 874 people dead, including 142 children. Just in pursuit of Ayman al Zawahiri, we killed seventy-six children (he's still alive).

Jennifer Gibson, the lawyer who did this research for Reprieve, was amazed that all of this was out in the open.

"It's not like this happened once," she says. "It happened over and over and over."

There are several issues here. If we're reporting someone killed more than once, someone who is not Fahd al-Quso or Baitullah Maisud or Qari Hussain is actually dying in each case. Yet read the accounts of all of these bombings and see if you notice a pattern, as in the case of the *Times* report referred to above about how drones killed "Qaeda-linked fighters":

WASHINGTON — American drones and Yemeni counterterrorism forces killed more than three dozen militants linked to Al Qaeda's affiliate in Yemen over the weekend in one of the largest such attacks there in months, officials from both countries said Monday.

At least three airstrikes were carried out against Qaeda fighters in a convoy and in remote training camps in southern Yemen. They were militants who were planning to attack civilian and military facilities, government officials said in a statement.

Unnamed "officials" tell us the "militants" killed were planning to "attack civilian and military facilities."

True? Possibly. How would a reporter really know? One thing we do know, however, is we kill a significant number of civilians, and children, and these people never appear in the information handed to reporters.

Pick out any one of these stories at random. Suspected IS spokesman Aziz Azam was supposedly killed in an "IS hideout" in Afghanistan in late December of 2018.

Was he the only one killed? Who else died? Nobody is ever mentioned.

Remember that MOAB bomb we dropped on ISIS caves in Afghanistan early in the Trump presidency that sent an entire couch full of Fox analysts into painful tumescence? Remember them gushing about how that's "what freedom looks like"? Remember Geraldo Rivera saying "one of his favorite things to watch" is "dropping bombs on bad guys"?

In that orgiastic case we dropped a twenty-one thousand-pound bomb, which initial reports said killed thirty-six "militants," and "no civilians were affected by the explosion."

By the next day, April 15, 2017, the death toll was "at least 90 militants," and none of them were civilians!

How about that for precision! *America, fuck yeah!*

When I studied in the Soviet Union, a Russian friend told me a joke about what a typical *Pravda* headline looked like:

АВИАКАТАСТРОФА - ЖЕРТВ НЕТ!
(AIR CATASTROPHE - NO VICTIMS!)

Most Russians at least had the decency to not believe this stuff in private. But Americans swallow similar absurdities on a regular basis.

We know our open-ended bombing campaign kills children, in quite large numbers. So how can anyone with even half a brain think that we can drop the largest non-nuclear bomb on earth, have it hit a group of people, and seriously believe no innocent people were killed?

In a lot of these "four-source clover" stories, reporters technically don't do anything wrong, at least according to the tenets of the profession. We're taught: it's okay to run stories, so long as multiple reputable sources are saying the same thing.

In rare cases it's even considered acceptable to try to push a story forward with one unnamed source. Some of the most famous stories in history were broken this way. Watergate was a great example.

The issue is with the assessment of "reputability." To me, reporters have been burned so often by government officials from nearly every national security agency that there should be a big disclaimer on any article sourced entirely to these no-named:

Four current and former officials from an agency with a record of lying to the media that dates back to the U.S.S. Maine said today...

There are lots of good journalists who would disagree about this. There are gut calls we make in this job. A rule I go by: when the info your unnamed source puts out is actually derogatory to the government, you might be more inclined to act on a hunch.

But so many things are beyond confirmation, and we run them anyway. The errors are piling up fast enough that we might want to reconsider the practice.

***

Most officials have no mandate to protect a news outlet's reputation. They'll happily burn anyone and not lose a wink of sleep. They've been doing so for decades. TV channels and newspapers to them exist to be used politically.

In some cases an official will develop a working relationship with a reporter who perhaps semi-knowingly transmits dicey, "trust us"–style information (this is similar to the way short-sellers have working relationships with financial reporters). But just as often, the news outlet is in the dark. They're assuming a person with a government title won't screw them, despite extensive evidence to the contrary. They always think: "This is different from My Lai, the missile gap, the Pentagon Papers, the 'Soviets planned the papal assassination' story, WMDs, the seventy-plus American backed foreign coups, and countless other incidents. In this era, my era, officials don't lie."

Wrong. They lie constantly and always have, yet for some reason, we allow them to keep doing it.

***

One last note. One of the reasons this trend is worsening has to do with class changes in this business.

The old days were obviously no panacea. Reporters until recently almost uniformly were white men, and this had an obvious deleterious effect on journalism.

However, back in the day, reporters often came from a different class than the people they reported on in government. A newspaperman in the forties or fifties socially was somewhere between a plumber and the administrator of a typing school. Often he was not college-educated.

Celebrated radio man Walter Winchell worked for a newspaper called the *Graphic* early in his career. Legend has it he was asked in those days if he worked at a newspaper.

He supposedly joked in reply: "Yeah, but don't tell my mother. She still thinks I'm a piano player in a whorehouse."

That might be an apocryphal story. In fact, it's almost certainly bullshit. But it rings true enough, and gives a clue about where the newspaperman thought he was class-wise back then.

Meanwhile the worthies who established the OSS and later the CIA were almost exclusively products of the Ivy League. The clichés about the Bushes bringing their goofball Skull and Bones sensibility to secret service governance were true. The secret agent was a silver spoon creature.

There was therefore a natural antipathy—at least a little—between some reporters and the self-appointed philosopher-kings who worked in secret agencies and spent their days deciding what the world map would look like.

That antipathy is gone today. Reporters, especially national ones, often come from the same schools as FBI and spy chiefs, and they worship the big brains at Langley. There's an obsession with credentials and resumes that would make reporters of the Sy Hersh school puke.

When unnamed "officials" with secret clearances call reporters today, reporters wet themselves. They'll print anything they're told, and they don't even need to be bribed or intimidated into doing it. This is a major reason these unconfirmable stories are so easy to place now.

The press used to be at least a bit of a tough crowd. Now, it's a laugh track, and the joke is on us.

11. THE CLASS TABOO

"Journalism has evolved into a career with significant entry barriers, one of which is the unpaid internship. This makes the profession whiter, wealthier... and less concerned with public policy issues that affect the poor and even the middle class."

—Dana Goldstein, *The American Prospect*

In the late 2000s, the British Cabinet Office issued a report called "Unleashing Aspirations." It found journalism to be one of the most socially exclusive professions in the country, noting:

- 98 percent of journalists born since 1970 were college-educated
- Less than 10 percent came from working-class backgrounds
- A journalist on average grew up in a family in the upper 25th percentile by wealth

In America the change came in stages. When journalism became cool after *All The President's Men,* upper-class kids suddenly wanted in. Previously a rich American kid wouldn't have wiped his *tuchus* with a reporter.

Ironically, *All the President's Men,* which made reporting glamorous, was about adversarial journalism. But the next generation of national political reporters viewed people in power as cultural soulmates because, at least socially, they were.

While sportswriters for a while remained hardscrabble, cigar-chewing types who hammered team owners and managers for every tiny mistake, political reporters became professional apologists, constantly telling us how hard it is for politicians to win elections and run things.

By the 1990s and 2000s, the new model for political reporting was found in books like *Primary Colors* or *Game Change,* which celebrated politicians and their aides, and looked at things from their point of view. Leadership was hard!

If a candidate had to fib or back off a campaign promise, the new generation of scribes explained a politician's job was to accept the "burden of morally ambiguous compromise."

Reporters were forever trying to re-create the American Camelot. In each presidential race, any halfway decent-looking young Democrat was described as "Kennedyesque." In 2004, *both* Democratic candidates, John Kerry and running mate John Edwards, won the moniker (the newspapers' current Kennedy-to-be is Beto O'Rourke).

In the next Camelot, reporters this time around wanted to be counted with the Best and the Brightest. They wanted, literally, to be courtiers.

By the time Barack Obama ran for president, the transformation was complete. Obama, most everyone in the national press corps agreed, was our generation's long-awaited Kennedy (German reporter Christoph von Marschall even wrote a book called *Der schwarze Kennedy* about Obama). Those who followed his campaign wanted to be passengers on his ride, "part of history."

I remember stepping on Obama's campaign plane for the first time and seeing the press section plastered in photos. It looked like a high school yearbook office at the end of a semester. Apparently, there was a tradition of reporters taking pictures of themselves covering Obama. They often posed with the candidate, and pasted the pics on the plane walls.

I liked Obama well enough at the time, but thought: "Man, this is not a good look." A reporter who allows himself or herself to be photographed arm in arm with a politician is asking for trouble. If I did it, I knew, police would find a hundred bodies buried under the candidate's lawn the next day.

There was something to the whole courtier thing, however. By that time in history, to even get on the plane as a reporter, you had to jump over a slew of cultural and financial obstacles.

The aforementioned unpaid internship was just one. Another was travel cost: the price tag for a news organization to send a reporter on the campaign trail was thousands of dollars a day, which limited traveling press to the richest corporate outlets. There are no alt-weeklies on the trail.

The Internet accelerated the class divide. Big regional newspapers increasingly became national or even global in mind-set. In the digital age it made more sense to design coverage for a sliver of upper-class readers across the country (who could afford subscriptions and responded to ads) than the whole bulk of readers in in a geographic area around Boston, New York, Washington, or L.A.

Because news organizations were targeting those audiences, it made sense to pick reporters who came from those ranks as well. By the mid-2000s, journalists at the top national papers almost all belonged to the same general cultural profile: liberal arts grads from top schools who lived in a few big cities on the east and west coasts. This was less true of reporters at more regional newspapers, who very often were more adversarial and took on local industries and politicians with more gusto than their national counterparts.

The only variable was their approach to the job. But that was about to become uniform, too.

***

I first met Thomas Frank in the third week of August, in Denver, Colorado, at the 2008 Democratic National Convention. I was covering the campaign for *Rolling Stone* and was thrilled to meet the author of *What's the Matter With Kansas?*, a bestseller I'd admired for its originality and quick-witted prose.

I was in my mid-thirties and Frank, a bit older, was holding forth at a lunch table full of writers and Democratic aides.

The backdrop was the coming coronation of Obama, a politician who for many at the table (at the time, anyway) represented something optimistic and new. Frank, the bestselling writer, was ripping off one one-liner after another, holding everyone's attention.

I don't remember the conversation, but I do remember Frank giving me his business card. He had a smile that stretched from ear to ear as he put it in my palm and pointed: "It's in the shape of Kansas!"

I looked down, felt the irregular edges of the card, and burst out laughing. Frank had another quality national political writers increasingly lacked: he was funny.

What's the Matter With Kansas? was an engaging book with a serious premise. It was designed to be the answer to a question that a lot of self-described liberals were asking at the time: why had working-class Americans abandoned the party of Roosevelt to vote Republican in such huge numbers?

Frank answered the question through the perspective of his home state, attempting to describe the complicated and often anguished thinking of work-ing-class Kansans. In his eyes, the conquest of such voters by the Reagan Revolution had been a historic switcheroo:

> The great dream of conservatives ever since the thirties has been a work-ing-class movement that for once takes their side of the issues... In the starkly divided red/blue map of 2000 they thought they saw it being realized: the old Democratic regions of the South and the Great Plains were on their team now, solid masses of uninterrupted red, while the Democrats were restricted to the old-line, blueblood states of the Northeast, along with the hedonist left coast.

Neither caricatured nor lecturing, *What's the Matter With Kansas?* explained countless resentments built up among working-class voters over religion, edu-cation, economic inequities, and other issues. Many of these resentments were understandable, even if they'd also been carefully cultivated by GOP strategists.

In the eighties, these groups had wasted no time stepping in when Democrats, in a moment of insanity that has now stretched across decades, decided to punt away their working-class base:

> The Republicans... were industriously fabricating their own class-based language of the right, and while they made their populist appeal to blue-collar voters, Democrats were giving those same voters... the big brush-off, ousting their representatives from positions within the party and consigning their issues, with a laugh and a sneer, to the dustbin of history.

What's the Matter With Kansas? was a prescient portrait of a Democratic Party that was transforming into what Frank would later term a "party of the professional class"—urban, obsessed with its own smartness, worshipful of meritocracy and credentialing, and exquisitely vulnerable to accusations of elitism.

The book was no cookie-cutter analysis. It wasn't typical Republicans Suck/Democrats Suck marketing (drearily, there was one shelf for each in most bookstores back then). Frank came to painful conclusions, including many about his own party, and was unafraid to communicate them to readers.

This to me was what journalism was supposed to be about, asking why things happen and being willing to be surprised or even upset by the answers. If Democrats could hear hard truths like the ones in *What's the Matter With Kansas?* they were in good intellectual health.

Years later, it looks like some of that was a mirage. Frank today suspects the more difficult parts of *What's the Matter With Kansas?* were just overlooked.

"Everyone remembers the first few pages," he says, which were about the failures of the Reagan revolution. The thornier sections about the strategic and moral errors of the Democratic Party were closer to the end.

"Nobody read it all the way through," he says now, laughing.

***

It's the third week of August, 2016, almost eight years to the day from the 2008 Democratic convention. I'm in Des Moines, Iowa, listening to Donald Trump speak on the dirt floor of the State Fairgrounds. It smells of pigs and horseshit in the building. Trump is preaching to a crowd that seems half biker, half farmer.

It's not Kansas, but I'm reminded of Thomas Frank.

Trump's speech is almost word for word a recitation of the talking points Frank had warned in *What's the Matter With Kansas?* were in danger of being lost forever to the Democratic Party. The New York billionaire is, of all things, appropriating the language of the original Populist movement.

"The White House will soon become the People's House," he said. "This campaign... it's going to help everyone. These are people who work hard and don't have a voice. Their voice has been taken away."

Populism has become a hot topic in recent years, with countless furious articles devoted to the subject. Big northeast dailies like the *Times* and the *Post* have devoted innumerable critiques of both current brands, the right-wing version pimped by Trump and the more traditional version, recently revived by the likes of Bernie Sanders.

The original Populists of the 1890s were a left-based movement of farmers and the working poor. They had fiery rhetoric but fairly modest goals. They sought a graduated income tax and public railroads, and railed against the "money power" of the Northeast.

Then as now, their movement was reviled as crude and uninformed by the upper-crust voices of papers like the *New York Times*. The really devastating criticism came from celebrated writer William Allen White, who penned an essay about the state most associated with the movement, called... "What's the Matter With Kansas?"

The essay, which Frank ironically referenced in his book, denounced with thick sarcasm the efforts of the less equal animals in the American barn to try to govern themselves. White's position was that fist-shaking Midwestern ignorants needed grownups with degrees to run things for them. White particularly thought Populists should keep their calloused hands off the economy, writing:

> What we need is not more money, but less capital, fewer white shirts and brains, fewer men with business judgment, and more of those fellows who boast that they are 'just ordinary clodhoppers...'

White's essay might as well have been written today, perhaps by a writer like Max Boot of the *Washington Post*, who in winter of 2018–2019 tweeted:

> What's wrong with elitism? Shouldn't we want the best qualified people to run government just as we want the best qualified to fly airplanes, perform surgery, design buildings, etc?

Trump politically was and is a million miles from the ideals of the original Populists. However, in 2016, he constantly invited ridicule from smarty-pants national media figures of the Boot type, knowing it could only burnish his "populist" credentials.

That August, with Steve Bannon as his campaign manager, Trump added a twist, selling himself to audiences as a savior of African Americans.

"I thought about Abraham Lincoln, Abraham Lincoln is a pretty good Republican," Trump cracked that day in Iowa. "It brings me to a subject that is important and personal for me. Nothing means more to me than making our party the home of the African-American vote..."

Snickers shot through the press section. As that summer wore on, I noticed the traveling press seemed only able to deal with Trump on two levels, disgust and ridicule. Which made sense, maybe, if you were only focusing on Trump the TV personality.

But presidential campaigns are not all about candidates. They're more about the people who vote for candidates. Movements often precede their eventual leaders.

The challenge in covering Trump ought to have been to ask: What predisposed people to this person's appeals? What created an opening for Trump?

For nearly a year on the trail I'd been astonished that the answers to this question seemed so elusive to colleagues. The racial/nativist element was heavily covered, from the "they're bringing rapists" episode on day one of Trump's campaign to his confrontation with Univision anchor Jorge Ramos.

But there were many other things going on, and they weren't exactly hidden. It took about two minutes of surveying any Trump audience to hear comments like, "Fuck it, why not?" and "I'll vote for anyone who isn't a politician," or, "We have to try something."

This spoke to a profound pessimism and disillusionment that preceded Trump, whose appeals were clearly designed to hoover up long-simmering frustrations.

Contrary to what was reported, Trump speeches tended to be policy-based and often as much about class as race or nationality. He talked about exported jobs, soaring drug costs, and the conspiracy of bought-off pols in both parties who made these problems possible.

Whether he was a realistic solution to these or any problems was a completely different question. But his pitch was working. Why?

In the summer of 2016, hundreds of reporters descended into the hollowed out ex-industrial towns where Trump was finding success, ostensibly to answer that question. These places were often in a state of near-devastation, overrun with unemployment, debt, an opiate crisis, and, unique in industrialized countries, declining rates of life expectancy. People in these places were pissed, and had been for a while.

But newspapers rarely commented on this. By the summer of 2016, Trumpism became very nearly synonymous with terrorism, i.e. something whose origins you didn't need to ask about if you were a good citizen. Terrorists hated us for our freedom, Donald Trump won votes because he was racist, and that was all we needed to know.

Articles began to appear attempting to prove no other rational explanations existed for the Trump phenomenon. People who had real economic issues—or who had other legitimate gripes, like war vets returned from the Middle East—preferred Democrats, we were told.

Again, the term "economic insecurity" began to be laughed at that summer, and before long its very use was denounced as, itself, a coded form of racism. "White working class" would join its ranks later.

Meanwhile, Hillary Clinton was struggling. Only once during the general election did she attract a crowd bigger than ten thousand people (in Arizona, where her campaign was delusionally devoting resources, instead of focusing on places like Pennsylvania and Wisconsin).

Absurdly, instead of asking the people in these Trump crowds why they were there, reporters more often dialed long distance to ask other big-city pundits and academics to explain what was going on.

The explanations that came back were bizarre. "Trump [is] regularly... going to places where he is most beloved, not where the ground game is most competitive," GWU professor Lara Brown said.

The Clinton campaign claimed the small crowds were intentional. Reporters actually bought this.

"We've gone into the less populous areas for a reason," said Clinton communications director Jennifer Palmieri, insisting they were targeting key voters who just happened to live in sparsely populated regions.

In the rare cases when mainstream American news outlets even mentioned the seeming lack of enthusiasm for the Democratic campaign, they dismissed it with bizarre tautologies.

"Trump is trying to get massive crowds," explained Chris Cillizza of the *Washington Post*. "So no one should be surprised when he gets them."

Apparently Hillary Clinton wasn't trying. So, no big deal. That Trump would later be ridiculed for his delusions about crowd size was beyond ironic, considering how much time those same press critics spent explaining away the enthusiasm gap in 2015–2016.

There was another explanation out there for the enthusiasm problem, but no one wanted to hear it.

***

Thomas Frank published *Listen, Liberal* in March 2016, just as Trump was wrapping up the Republican nomination. It was written at a time when Clinton was expected to be the next president.

The book warned, however, that even with victory probably ahead, the Democratic Party had serious unresolved problems. These began with the fact that there was a major disconnect between perception and reality among the national press about the financial situation "out there":

> According to official measurements, the last few years have been a time of brisk prosperity, with unemployment down and the stock market up. Productivity advances all the time. For those who work for a living, however, nothing seems to improve. Wages do not grow. Median income is still well below where it was in 2007...

Every page of *Listen, Liberal* contained similar warnings that voters were not doing as well as newspapers insisted, and this discontent would eventually express itself.

When Trump defied expectations and won, Frank composed an afterword to *Listen, Liberal*. It pointed to the curious press myopia about the election:

> [Reporters] persistently overlooked what was driving his uprising. Stories marveling at the stupidity of Trump voters were published nearly every day during the campaign. Articles accusing Trump's followers of being bigots appeared by the hundreds, if not the thousands...

Frank wasn't saying bigotry didn't exist, just that it was only part of the story. "Trump was a bigot, yes, and this was inexcusable, but he also talked about trade," he wrote.

Frank noted the hypocrisy of Trump, whose own brand of shirts and ties were made overseas. But he was "giving voice to people's economic frustration."

The reaction to *Listen, Liberal* was different from the reaction to *What's the Matter With Kansas?* Even though the new book sold well, and foreign news outlets were as interested in his work as ever, American media colleagues reacted with curious diffidence.

The book was reviewed a bit less, discussed on public radio a bit less. Cable news more or less stopped calling Frank to be a guest. He wasn't bitter about it, just puzzled.

"I'm not complaining. I'm happy with how the book was received," he says. "But compared to the interest they used to have in my writing, and compared to the interest from foreign media, it's a noticeable drop-off. That is a fact. I felt like I was saying something they didn't want to hear."

Frank's 2016 experience was a part of that big cultural change in the business. However, it was more like the last chapter in a story than the first.

"There's been a huge die-off of journalists of a certain type," explains Frank. "Remember Mike Royko, the columnist from Chicago? He wrote from a blue-collar perspective, in a blue-collar voice." He pauses. "There are no more Roykos. That's gone. It's a dead genre."

The tough-talking, bard-of-the-streets, people's columnist of the Royko or Jimmy Breslin school once held exalted positions in most big cities. These larger-than-life figures had begun to vanish from American newspapers in the eighties and nineties.

They were replaced, en masse, by representatives of what Frank calls "Ivy League monoculture," pundits like Boot and David Brooks and E. J. Dionne and Ross Douthat, whose ideas about politics were tied up more with modernity than class. These were voices for the yuppie set, urban, educated, white collar, in perpetual awe of productivity and corporate innovation.

Frank didn't really belong to the Royko tradition. He grew up in Mission Hills, Kansas, which he described in *What's the Matter With Kansas?* as "the wealthiest town in the state." He had a doctorate in history from the University of Chicago.

He was, in other words, exactly the kind of smart-setter chosen to replace the provincial Roykos, Breslins, Terkels, and Herb Caens when a new wave of editorialists began appearing in the nineties and early 2000s. (As a private school kid from Massachusetts, I was part of the same phenomenon.)

The Royko era had its own problems. Though journalism over the years has found a few homes for women like Nellie Bly or African Americans like Les Payne, the lead columnist job in the hometown paper was almost always a white guy, and it was a great thing when the business at least began to diversify.

But in fixing one problem, another was created. The blue-collar voices lost were not replaced.

Frank represented a link to that vanishing tradition because he at least tried to search out the perspective of working-class voters. He was celebrated for this in the Bush years, when his work could be offered by upscale Democrats as evidence regular people were being conned by Reaganites into "voting against their interests."

However, the moment his writing became too much of an indictment of the failures of the professional political class in general (read: Democrats as well as Republicans) he joined an increasingly long list of people whose point of view was no longer much in demand, on TV or anywhere else.

A University of California professor named Joan Williams went through something similar. She came from a family with working-class origins and felt she had some insight into Trump's base, in particular via memories of her father-in-law who hated professionals but admired entrepreneurs.

After Trump was elected, Williams wrote a piece for the *Harvard Business Review* called "What Many People Don't Get About the U.S. Working Class" that among other things took Democrats and their proxies in media to task for being clueless when it came to addressing the legitimate concerns of a sector of society that was losing job security and the dignity that came with it. She wrote:

> For many blue-collar men, all they're asking for is basic human dignity (male varietal). Trump promises to deliver it.
>
> The Democrats' solution? Last week the *New York Times* published an article advising men with high-school educations to take pink-collar jobs. Talk about insensitivity.

Her article was full of nuanced, uncomfortable observations about why working-class people voted for Trump. It clearly struck a chord, becoming the most-read online piece in the history of the publication, with over 3.7 million readers. She wrote a follow-up book immediately. But it hasn't exactly won her a lot of friends.

"It's been hard," she says. "I've written a lot of things that weren't published."

She says the "intelligentsia of the professional managerial elite" seems remarkably blind to the fact that working-class Americans are paying attention to how our political and financial pie is being divvied up. They know, she says, that "opportunity has been incredibly more concentrated in a small dense metropolitan area," and they're angry about it.

Williams has spent her whole life writing about difficult topics like racism and sexism, but nothing has approached this for the discomfort level. "It's been the toughest subject I've ever had to take on," she says.

Academics like Williams have fewer places to get the word out, among other things because there's no longer much space for alternative viewpoints of any kind. The 2016 race coincided with another mass die-off, the Ice Age of newspapers in general.

"By now, there are only two newspapers left, the *New York Times* and the *Washington Post*," Frank says. "And they're identical. They say the same things. It's an incredibly limited ecosystem."

A whole genre of journalism, what you might call the empathetic analysis, was disappearing. This approach was already mostly gone from conservative media by the early 2000s (none of those Ann Coulter–style books about treason featured much empathy for "liberals"), but post-Trump it began disappearing from blue-state media as well.

As a result of all these factors, the modern press spends a lot of time doing what papers did in the age of the original Populists, rolling eyes at "clodhoppers" in flyover country. The worship of urban experts is so out of control that asking rich city folk what's good for the not-rich is normal practice. The following headline, for instance, is not from *The Onion*:

OCASIO-CORTEZ, WARREN TAX PLANS ANNIHILATE MIDDLE CLASS:
FMR. BAIN CAPITAL MANAGING DIRECTOR

The sheer number of articles wondering if Trump's win suggests there's "too much democracy" these days conveys more about who is doing the analysis than it does about the political situation.

Politicians and journalists alike have absolved themselves of any responsibility for what's gone wrong, settling instead for endless finger-pointing at people who are irredeemably stupid and racist—who just "have bad souls," as Frank puts it. This convenient catchall explanation makes the op-ed page the place where upscale readers go to be reassured they never have to change or examine past policy mistakes, even if it means continuing to lose elections.

In his latest book, *Rendezvous With Oblivion*, Frank calls this a "Utopia of Scolding":

> Who needs to win elections when you can personally reestablish the rightful social order every day on Twitter and Facebook? When you can scold, and scold, and scold, and scold. That's their future, and it's a satisfying one: a finger wagging in some vulgar proletarian's face, forever.

The irony of 2016 is that it was the ultimate example of what happens when political leaders stop listening to voters. They'd been tuning them out for a generation, sticking them with the costs of pointless wars and dramatic economic changes like the vast wealth transfers caused by a succession of exploding financial bubbles. Ordinary people were told, not asked, how to deal with things like the NAFTA-sped export of the manufacturing economy. Finally, voters hit back with a monster surprise.

The media was supposed to help society self-correct by shining a light on the myopia that led to all of this. But reporters had spent so long trying to buddy up to politicians that by 2016, they were all in the tent together, equally blind. Which is why it won't be a shock if they repeat the error. You can't fix what you can't see.

12. HOW WE TURNED THE NEWS INTO SPORTS

The biggest taboo in American media has nothing to do with race, gender, or class. It involves the news itself.

Ever notice no one ever says, "Hell if I know" on a cable news show? Despite the fact that most media figures have huge knowledge gaps about the news (which, after all, is *the set of all things on Earth*), we're trained to offer opinions even when we have no clue.

Part of this has to do with the internal logic of news media, at its core an entertainment product. It triggers suspension of disbelief if someone on air admits to not knowing the history of Kurd-Turk relations, or the hierarchy of Venezuelan socialism, or the rules of a government shutdown.

We're also training audiences to fear being caught not knowing, and to believe it's shameful to be ignorant of news. You think Wolf Blitzer doesn't know what's going on in the Sri Lankan civil war? Who's the reigning party in Japan's House of Councilors? Who's currently occupying Idlib?

(Wolf Blitzer doesn't retain much, apparently. He finished with –$4,600 on *Jeopardy*. Asked for a five-letter word describing an "economic crash" he replied, "What is a crash?" In another category he was told in advance that the answer would contain three letter "E"s. His guess was "Annotated." Wolf Blitzer reads a teleprompter. Don't ever feel inferior to Wolf Blitzer.)

News companies don't just want you feeling ashamed of not knowing the news. That's desperate marketing, ring-around-the-collar tactics. They want you so emotionally invested that your psyche falls apart if the wrong story appears on screen. We want you awake at night, teeth chattering, panicking about things over which you have no control.

When networks went in the direction of building this kind of audience for news, they knew exactly how to do it, because they had an existing, successful business model. They knew what the perfect news consumer looked like because he was already reading the sports page.

News purveyors knew: if they could find a way to cover politics like sports, and get news consumers behaving like the emotional captives we call sports fans, cash would flow like a river.

How to pull that off? The main thing is, don't break the spell.

A professional sportscaster in America may do just about anything in public, even things that from the outside appear to stretch the absolute limits of human idiocy.

He or she may howl like a child over a missed free throw, treat Jeff Fisher like Stephen Hawking, report the seventh round of the NFL draft like the Nuremburg trial, ask an athlete to measure his bicep mid-interview, or even fart on the air.

The one thing Mr. Sportscaster can't ever do is remind audiences it's just a game. He or she can't ever tell them it's okay not to care.

In fact, the two most taboo lines in all media in America are *I don't know* and *I don't care*. The dynamic is more grotesque and ridiculous in sports, as one radio man found out in early 2019.

***

In mid-January, as the New England Patriots were getting ready to play the Kansas City Chiefs in the AFC title game, a Boston-based sports radio host named Fred Toettcher was invited by a Chicago radio station called *670 The Score* to talk football.

"I'm not even sure who invited me," Toettcher said later. "I got a text from a producer."

The Chicago show was called *McNeil and Parkins.* Hosts Dan McNeil and Danny Parkins pilot AM 670's afternoon slot using a typical modern sports-talk format, i.e. a room full of homerific meatheads who cheer their teams at all costs and egg their fan bases on to do the same.

The city of Chicago had no skin in the Chiefs-Pats game. But neutral cities will often invite one radio personality from each market to come on and hype a big event.

What you're looking for if you're a producer of one of these segments is a caricature of each city, so hosts can poke fun. From Kansas City you want a slow-talking cowpoke who literally eats barbecue during the interview. From Boston, you want a thin-skinned racist with a Dorchester accent who wears Patriots underpants—basically, an extra from *The Departed*.

Toettcher was invited on so a couple of guffawing jocks could make Boston jokes.

If you didn't have Google, having Toettcher play the "Boston" role in this segment made at least some sense. He does co-host the top-rated sports program in Boston. Along with Rich Shertenlieb, their *Toucher and Rich* show on Boston's 98.5 FM just pulled a 10.8 share in the coveted morning slot in 2018's Fall Nielsen ratings.

A ten share is hot stuff in sports radio. If a sports program is pulling those numbers, you can assume it's a fan favorite.

Boston's *Sports Hub* and *670 The Score* were once broadcast partners under the national CBS umbrella. However, in late 2017, there was a merger of two major national sports radio networks, CBS and Entercom. This temporarily put Boston's two bitter sports-talk rivals—CBS's *"Sports Hub"* and Entercom's WEEI—in the same corporate tent.

For reasons too boring to explain here, *Sports Hub* was eventually forced out of the CBS/Entercom family to eliminate a potential antitrust problem. This landed *Toucher and Rich* and the rest of the *Sports Hub* programs with new ownership, under a consortium called The Beasley Group.

I bring this up only to point out that had this Chicago-Boston interview taken place a few years earlier, it not only wouldn't have been hostile, it couldn't have been hostile, because that would have been CBS-on-CBS crime.

In fact, Toettcher had been a guest on *The Score* countless times back in the days when 670 was a sister station, and had never gotten any grief.

"I'd been on there like, twenty times," Toettcher recalls.

Now, however, Toettcher wasn't a fellow CBS personality. He was just a jock from an unaffiliated Boston station, fair game. *The Score* even plugged his upcoming segment by misidentifying his station:

"Coming up next, Fred Toettcher, from the *Toucher and Rich* show, WEEI Boston..."

As Toettcher later explained on the air, "I think they assumed we were part of Entercom because of the sale."

In any case, Toettcher got on air with McNeil and Parkins and was asked if he was excited about the game. Verbally, he shrugged.

He explained he'd been doing Boston sports for years and in a yawning voice said, "[the Patriots] always just win." If they did happen to get to the Super Bowl, he joked, "I'd have to go to Atlanta where there's three hours of TSA to get back here, and I'm not looking forward to that."

The Chicago guys jumped all over this.

"It sounds like you don't want them to win," said Parkins, the younger, skinnier half of the Chicago duo.

Toettcher sighed. "I don't care," he said. "I just want it to be interesting."

Toettcher really didn't care. He's from Atlanta.

"I'm not a fan of the Patriots," he says now. "My audience *knows* I'm not a fan of the Patriots."

Everyone who listens to sports radio in Boston knows this about *Toucher and Rich*. Their schtick is two out-of-town, laid-back rock deejays who don't hide the fact that they don't really care about the Patriots, Celtics, Red Sox, or Bruins. Part of the charm of the show is the hosts' total indifference to the results of games in a sports-crazy town.

The Chicago hosts didn't know this, but one senses that even if they had, they wouldn't have believed it. They listened in stunned silence as Toettcher went on to explain what the one nice thing about the Patriots winning in Kansas City would be, from his point of view.

"I spent eight years in Atlanta, so I'd like to see friends there," he said. "But I don't care who wins this game."

The Chicago guys started to explode with laughter. Toettcher cut them off.

"Wait, you guys always care?" he asked. "If there's a Chicago team in a championship, you always have a rooting interest?"

"Yeah!" said Parkins.

"Yeah, we're Bears fans," said McNeil.

"Boston's seen too many titles if you don't care who wins the championship game," said Parkins.

Toettcher explained again. "I'm not from here. My allegiances lie elsewhere. But listen, it helps the bottom line when they win, so..."

The Chicago hosts were determined to have Toettcher get into character. They wanted him to pump up the Patriots. They even opened their interview of the Atlanta native to the tune of "Shipping Up to Boston" by the Dropkick Murphys, famous for being on the soundtrack to *The Departed*. Then they tried to bait him by playing a mumbly quote from Bill Belichick.

"Something tells me, Fred, that no one in Boston cares that [Belichick's] not the greatest quote, right?" asked Parkins.

Probably they were guessing Toettcher would defend Boston's legendary curmudgeon. But Toettcher, who is not a sports guy but a comic and a rock deejay, brightened at the chance to have fun with the Belichick theme.

"Actually, there are two things that get [Belichick] going," he quipped. "One is talking about punters. The second is a little music by *Bo-n-n-n* Jovi."

Dead silence.

"He, uh, immediately lights up," continued Toettcher, who'd expected a laugh. "That is... a way to the man's heart."

More silence. Toettcher realized he was in for a difficult interview.

"Alright," Parkins finally said. Then, addressing his co-host, he added with sarcasm, "If we ever get [Belichick], Mac, Bon Jovi's the way we'll start him off."

The agonizing interview went on like this. At one point the duo pressed Toettcher on the Patriots using the "nobody believed in us" card.

They seemed to want him to defend this. Toettcher not only called it "crap," but pointed out that Patriots receiver Julian Edelman was charging $30 for BET AGAINST US T-shirts, and "if you buy one of those, you're a dope."

More silence. The hosts clearly wanted a Boston homer, and what they got was a rock radio personality from Atlanta making fun of the Patriots and their fans. It went on a bit longer, the *Score* hosts thanked Toettcher, and he hung up.

Some time later, Toettcher had a bad feeling about the interview. He cued up the podcast version of it online.

Listening, he found out that ten seconds after he'd gone off air, the Chicago crew started busting on him.

"Let's hope," they said, "our next guest has more enthusiasm for the topic."

McNeil went on a rant about what a terrible guest Toettcher had been. "Fred went down on three pitches," he said. "I don't think we need to call him again."

The Chicago crew pored over his "I don't care who wins" comment like it was an anomalous blood test result.

"I bet he doesn't act like that on the air in Boston. I don't think that would go over real well with Patriots fans," McNeil concluded.

"Yeah, it's a Jets fan doing sports in Boston pulling a ten share," quipped Parkins.

"Oh, *really, really,*" groaned McNeil.

The Chicago hosts were wrong. *Toucher and Rich* strikes exactly that indifferent tone. The show is a genuinely interesting experiment in media.

The two were holdovers from the rock station WBCN. When CBS launched the new all-sports format at the *Sports Hub* in 2009, it decided to keep the pair on in the coveted morning drive slot.

"I think the idea was to see if we could get a younger audience," Toettcher explains.

Toucher and Rich runs counter to conventional assumptions about how sports media (and, increasingly, the news media as a whole) works in this country. Despite being the top sports show in maybe the most virulently sports-mad city in America, the hosts go completely off-script.

They don't troll other cities, don't feed hometown paranoia about referees or national media, and don't fellate the local sports heroes. They do nothing to make audiences feel like Boston or Boston teams are inherently better than other cities.

Instead, they make fun of how absurd pro sports is in general and do a lighthearted, informative morning show that reminds fans not to take themselves or anything else too seriously. They have regular interviews with local sports figures like Celtics president Danny Ainge, but you don't turn off the program ready to dive off a building if the Celtics lose a game.

The sports format *Toucher and Rich* parodies is standard almost everywhere in the country.

Sports journalism—especially local sports journalism—is usually pure manipulation. (The stations are also often owned or sponsored by local teams, so there's a mandatory rah-rah factor as well.) Sports media strategy is based on the idea that the core audience has a powerful dependence on the local team, and will tune in to anything that reaffirms its slavish rooting interests.

The flip side of cheering is hating, so part of that formula is hating everything about rival teams and fan bases.

Most sports media trains audiences to see the world as a weird dualistic theology. The home city is a safe space where the righteous team is cheered and irrational worship is encouraged. Everywhere else is darkness.

Opposing fans are deluded haters. Increasingly most local fan bases are encouraged to see the national sports media as arrayed against them, too.

Long before Donald Trump trained followers to see CNN as fake news, countless local fan bases learned to despise ESPN as a corporate villain out to undermine their team.

The local sports personalities inevitably encourage this, too, feeding conspiracy theories about everyone from Chris Mortensen to Curt Schilling. "Why does ESPN hate us?" is a message-board topic for virtually every fan base in every major sport.

The paranoia about both national media and the opposing fans is now such a central part of the fan experience that for some modern fans, the dread of an opposing city reveling in their city's loss outweighs the potential satisfaction of winning.

There are Red Sox fans who'd prefer to not make the playoffs at all than lose to the Yankees there, and vice versa.

Because of all of these factors, the local on-air sports personality is now almost always a feverish rooter with a conspicuous regional accent who puffs up every local player and feeds the paranoia/inferiority complexes of callers.

Toettcher over the years has been amazed at how far counterparts in other cities will go to play up the "other cities suck" act.

He tells a story about 2016, when the Atlanta Hawks beat the Celtics in the playoffs. A local Atlanta sports station, *92.9 The Game*, hosted by Rick Kamla (who is from Minnesota, not Atlanta) cooked up a "Boston sucks" song and performed it at a local bar.

The song was called "Shipping Them Back to Boston" and was, you guessed it, a parody of that same "Shipping Up to Boston song." The opening lines:

What's up, Boston? Whatcha got now? You drowning in chowder?

"The chowder thing drives me crazy," says Toettcher. "Why do you hate *soup?* What's wrong with you?"

Kamla sang the next portion of the song:

Atlanta rocks and Boston sucks and I'm only telling the truth
　　Way to go on that brilliant idea to trade away Babe Ruth
　　It was wicked awesome beating you, and now you're home just like
the Knicks
　　You may have more championships, but we have more champion
chicks!

"Champion chicks?" Toettcher says. "Seriously?"

When *Toucher and Rich* first got hold of the recording years ago, they had some fun on the air with Kamla and his song. This is a persistent parody theme in their show, the notion that a person who isn't from City X will get a broadcast job there and suddenly transform into the world's biggest Texans or Yankees or, in Kamla's case, Falcons fan.

A sportscaster who gets into that mode will inevitably start to pander to the audience, willing to say anything for ratings. As Toettcher put it on air, they become like a man who's so desperate to get a woman in bed, he tells her on the third date he's interested in having children.

What follows is a symbiotic stupidity cycle. Fans become conditioned to having their dumbest ideas ratified, and sportscasters every day have to go deeper and deeper into the jungle of homerism to keep callers happy.

"Basically they'll say anything to make fans emotionally dependent on the team," Toettcher says. "They'll say, 'I'll be the pied piper. I'll hold up the banner. And you'll love me and love me and love me.'"

Toettcher explains he and Shertenlieb don't use the same formula because it's annoying.

"You've got someone who's just telling you what you want to hear over and over," he says. "That would be the most annoying person to hang out with."

Also, he says, it's not natural.

"If you're a Patriots fan and you're at a dinner, and some guy there says he's a Kansas City sports fan, what are you going to do, get up and leave? No. You'd be polite. That's how people behave, in real life."

I asked Toettcher if he'd noticed at all that this same on-air strategy had spread to political media.

"Definitely," he says. "Since Trump's been President... It's just like sports. You pick a side and that's your identity. There's a lack of nuance. A lack of gray area."

The phoniness, the constant hyping of conflict, the endless stroking of audience prejudices and expectations, these all started as staples of sports media. But now that same commercial formula has moved down the dial.

"It's exactly like the political discourse on TV," Toettcher says.

***

News stations are a lot more careful to prevent such outbreaks of disbelief-suspending honesty. They make sure neither *I don't know* nor *I don't care* get anywhere near live cameras.

Most cable shows conduct pre-interviews. Typically, the show's producer will call and toss out the same questions the host asks later.

This is part educational exercise, in which the producer picks the guest's brain in search of nuggets the show might want to explore. It's also audition, designed to weed out inept performers. If you stammer in the face of a surprise question, you'll be told at the last minute you've been bumped due to "time constraints" or some other transparent excuse.

The primary motive for the pre-interview, though, is to make sure guests stay in character. In both sports and news media, the biggest crime is to break type.

The usual setup of almost any live-variety news show is a host who intros an issue, flanked by a *pro* guest and an *anti* guest. The segment producer wants to ensure lively crosstalk, so the "pre-interview" is designed to make sure you'll say exactly what the producer expects you to say.

They usually don't need to ask. If Chris Matthews has proudly liberal Joan Walsh on to talk affirmative action with Pat Buchanan, he knows he can sleepwalk through that player-piano setup: Walsh is automatically going to find a way to argue for affirmative action and denounce white privilege, and Buchanan is going to hit back by bleating about reverse racism.

But stations still usually make sure there's no off-the-reservation opinion on the horizon. If you're brought on to play the Democrat, they make sure in advance you'll stay in that lane. If you're brought on to argue the red side, same thing.

These days, however, actual interplay between disagreeing guests is rare. Like sports channels, news outlets increasingly are more like cheering sections than debate forums. You get your side from your channel, while the other side gets its news on another channel.

It's not uncommon now for a channel like CNN to have a host surrounded by three or four guests, all offering different takes on the terribleness of Donald Trump.

Meanwhile, Fox remains as it's been for decades, a place where conservatives tune in to see on-air figures collectively own the libs. Don't be surprised to see Tomi Lahren surrounded by like-minded yahoos, all yammering about the terrors of Antifa.

If the first rule of Fight Club is no talking about Fight Club, the first rule of political debate shows is no reminding audiences they're watching political debate shows.

You can't get on a talk show and point out that the news subject of the hour probably wouldn't ever come up in your day-to-day life, without the prompting of someone in the press. You can't say, "Actually, you wouldn't know Antifa from antifreeze if you didn't watch this station."

Nobody on any channel ever tells you to take a deep breath and relax. On the contrary, the whole aesthetic of modern news is to make you feel a constantly rising tension, a fear you're missing out.

Unlike sports, the news isn't a game. It's genuinely important (although I would argue the networks rarely show the most important issues to audiences, opting for the easiest/most inflammatory instead). The deceptions lay in the notion that there's anything the ordinary person can do about the reams of troubling information we throw at you.

There's more hunger and misery and cheating and corruption and prejudice and unfairness in the world than any one person could even begin to make sense of, let alone do anything about. Yet we bombard you with headlines all day long, and increasingly present the news as a sports-like zero-sum battle between two sides, in which every day can only end with heartbreak or triumph for your belief system.

In sports it's a major taboo for a broadcaster to admit that the outcome of any sporting event shouldn't be in the top 50 concerns for any sane human being, or point out that just because teams from two cities are playing each other, doesn't mean people from those places should dislike one another.

"I felt like asking those guys from Chicago, what if your team was playing Sacramento in a final?" says Toettcher. "Are you going to start hating Sacramento?"

Political news media is similar. It's a variety show designed to freak you out, and as a ratings strategy we've made not freaking out taboo. Any guest who'd be likely to tell you to calm down or spend more time with your kids won't make it past the pre-interview.

We get people so invested in news stories that they're unable to cope when headlines spit out the wrong way. People fall to pieces over news stories, often ahead of their real-world problems. We want you more invested in Terri Schiavo or Brett Kavanaugh than your own family relationships. It's madness, and we'd never treat you this way—if it weren't the best way for us to make money.

13. TURN IT OFF

One Monday in the fall of 1972, oddly enough on September 11, CBS anchorman Walter Cronkite decided to end his nightly broadcast with bad news.

"Professor Hubert Lamb says a new Ice Age is creeping over the northern hemisphere," Cronkite began.

It could have been a joke, or serious. Nothing in his delivery gave any hint. Cronkite's face was an advanced messaging machine, a broadcasting Ferrari.

He went on: "It won't be as bad as the last Ice Age 60,000 years ago when New York, Cincinnati and St. Louis were under five thousand feet of ice. Presumably, no traffic moved, and school was let out for the day."

He paused. Again, not a single revealing tic or twitch in that face.

"And that's the way it is, Monday, September 11th, 1972."

I was just old enough to groan over the hoopla when Walter Cronkite said *And that's the way it is* for the last time on March 6, 1981.

Okay, I get it, I thought. This was a national ritual, and Walter had been with Americans for so many crucial moments in their history, from the death of John F. Kennedy to the moon landing.

But who cared about *And that's the way it is*? Was that supposed to be deep? Even as an eleven year-old, the fawning over the iconic signoff seemed phony, an example of the constant self-congratulation in which TV personalities—anchors, particularly—so often indulge.

My father, a TV man himself, was amusingly dismissive of what he called "the anchor-heads." He was a *reporter*, mind you, not a mere news reader, and he was constantly in trouble with bosses for a sarcastic attitude toward the Ron Burgundies his stations sometimes trotted out as headliners.

I worshipped my old man and inherited some of this. So I considered *And that's the way it is* to be overrated anchor-schtick.

With the benefit of age and industry experience, I now see things very differently. In the context of the medium, Cronkite's signature was powerful stuff.

Cronkite was telling viewers that they could now safely go back to their lives. It was a promise: click off, and the world will hold together, at least until the next day at the same time.

"And that's the way it is" was an expression of confidence, a contract between broadcaster and audience: "I trust you to come back tomorrow. Enjoy the next 23 hours without worry."

This was a message not about the content of the newscast, but about the viewer's relationship to television and the news itself. It was rhetorical punctuation, a period at the end of the sentence.

Of course, Cronkite's routine was clever marketing as well. People grew accustomed to the tradition of sitting around the television hearing old Walter tell it like it is. The signoff was part of the Pavlovian reward. It drew viewers back.

But it had another meaning. In that era, there were actually people who read newspapers from beginning to end. As one former newspaper chain owner put it, this was a time when people could say, "I read the news," and mean "all of it."

The concept of news having an ending still existed.

There was a lot that was wrong and deceptive about the era of news Cronkite dominated. News watchers were presented with a highly limited and simplistic vision of the world, presented almost entirely by white dudes. Coverage downplayed or omitted countless injustices, both at home and abroad. Many of those deceptions were chronicled in *Manufacturing Consent*.

But since the seventies and eighties, we've moved into an entirely new realm of messaging. The subtext is dramatically different from what it was in Cronkite's day.

Most news consumers haven't noticed the change, or are too young to know. But it's an awesome difference, and a terrifying one, if you know what to look for.

***

You can tell a lot about a country by how boring its media is.

If you turn on the TV and immediately feel like going to sleep, it generally means the political class feels secure.

In the Soviet Union of the seventies, a person with the misfortune to turn on the television might be treated to pulse-pounding content like *Rural Hour*—or a tourism show like *Explorer's Club*, which showed Soviet citizens the amazing destinations they could legally visit, like Kiev, or Kiev.

It's no accident that with the arrival of *perestroika* in the eighties came a new form of TV, which for the first time acted like it had to compete for your attention. Soviet programmers brought in bawdy soap operas to dub from Latin America, and just before the collapse of the USSR, introduced an emotive, brightly lit *Wheel of Fortune* spinoff that's on air to this day.

The audience, no longer fully captive, had to be grabbed.

America, much further along in its development, has sprinted far past that point. We are light years beyond having to hustle to grab audiences, and are deep into a phenomenon that is closer to induced addiction or cult worship than mere marketing.

Turn on the TV in today's America and it's a shock to the senses. You can feel the producers in the background panicking at the thought of your thumb on the remote.

Content is designed not just to be lurid and sensational, but immediately disquieting from a psychological standpoint. You're meant to see something in the first flash that upsets you to the point of needing to hang in at least until mental balance is restored.

This is the genius of the "crawl" or "chryon" in modern cable news, that giant banner sweeping across the screen that tells you what the anchor-head plans on saying.

Great examples are ALT-RIGHT FOUNDER QUESTIONS IF JEWS ARE PEOPLE or PELOSI CRITICIZED FOR "FIVE WHITE GUYS" JOKE.

In the former case you'll stick with Jake Tapper for a few more minutes to make sure he tells off that alt-right upstart (whose message he's deliberately put on national television for millions to hear).

In the latter case, if you're watching Fox, you probably are a white guy, so you have to keep the program on to find out why the House minority leader is joking about you.

There's nothing new about yellow headlines. They've been with us since at least the turn of the twentieth century, when Joseph Pulitzer's *New York World* battled William Randolph Hearst's *New York Morning Journal* for circulation.

Famed headers like WOMAN JUMPS FROM BROOKLYN BRIDGE, SURVIVES MAD LEAP or HEADLESS BODY IN TOPLESS BAR[1] operated on the same premise that causes highway rubbernecking, i.e. the inability to turn one's head from something gross or horrible.

There was desperation behind those headlines, but it was just commercial, one newspaper not wanting to lose to another. We still have that same dynamic on cable and in the blogosphere, vastly accelerated if anything. The competition for eyeballs is more furious than ever.

But there's an even deeper added dimension. We don't just want your eyes on us at all times. We want your attention away from something else.

Tone is the first thing you should think about when you turn on a TV news show or click on a news story. The emotional desperation in the attitude of modern news content is striking. There is no Walter Cronkite smiling and telling you it's safe to turn the news off now.

On the contrary, the between-the-lines message of most news isn't just WORRY WORRY WORRY but STAY STAY STAY! Anchors often cast scolding, imploring glares at the screen, all but telling viewers they'll be betraying humanity if they switch off.

Cable stations don't promise "ends" to the news. There is no mental finish line. They pass off one show to another, and these segues have become formalized, even popular. The standard is probably Rachel Maddow's "handoff" to Lawrence O'Donnell, where the two MSNBC anchors gently banter to blur a five minute line between shows.

On the surface it's all jovial and jokey, but it's a million miles from the "Goodnight, and until tomorrow, fuck the Ice Age" message of Cronkite.

A Maddow–O'Donnell handoff is always drearily about anti-Republican solidarity, just as a Tucker Carlson–Sean Hannity baton-pass, while less formalized,

---

1 My father claims to have seen a headline in his youth that read, "Headless, Handless Body Believed Homicide," but we've never been able to track it down.

never leaves the anti-Democrat theme for a second. We are always at war with each other. It never stops, not for one second.

This is a profound expression of political instability at the top of our society.

There is a terror of letting audiences think for themselves that we've never seen before. There's no, "Go back home tonight, rest, and think it over."

Even from show to show the viewer is asked to remain glued to the conflict at all times. In print media your eyes scroll down to similarly themed stories, stringing you from one outrage to another. Keep clicking, keep delving deeper into the argument, make it more and more your identity.

We don't want you signing off until tomorrow because we don't want you to even understand that you have an inner dialogue separate from the news experience. Click on, watch, read, tweet, argue, come back, click again, repeat, do it over and over, rubbing the nerve ends away just a little bit each time. With each engagement, you're signing over more and more of your intellectual autonomy.

You'll soon become dependent on the cycle, to the point where you'll lose the ability to dispute what you're being told, because disputing would mean diluting the bond with your favored news sources. Once you reach this point, you've entered the realm of belief, as opposed to conclusion.

This without a doubt is a form of religious worship. It's what was being parodied in the movie *Network*, in which an anchorman who loses his mind and begins telling the truth on air is swallowed up and turned into the biggest hit show in the country.

That film was a parable about how TV can commoditize and ritualize anything, from profane truth to madness. Mass media makes the act of watching more important than the words. It can take rage and defiance, and in a snap turn it into obedience and submission. Listening in anger to your favorite political program, you will act like a person who is shaking a fist at power, when in fact you've been neutralized as an independent threat, reduced to a prop in a show.

Like all religions, the arc of devotion can be bent with time. When belief flags, the tenets of the faith will become more and more extreme, the manipulations more aggressive, the promises more explicit.

A religion becomes a cult when it doesn't allow the testing of its premises. Cronkite's "See you tomorrow!" model, encouraging you to return to mental autonomy, disappears. Mentally, they don't want you ever leaving the compound now. No interacting with suppressive persons!

Social media has wildly enhanced the illusion that there's no life outside news. Once upon a time, you didn't know who reporters were once they put the microphone down. You rarely knew what they stood for, whether they were jokesters or bullies, conservative demagogues or mellow hippies.

Now reporters never go home. They are on social media day and night. They share everything, from pictures of their cats to takes on the North Korean nuclear crisis. Unfortunately, because pushing any of the various taboos—*I don't care* or *I don't know* or *I hate both parties*—can have career-altering consequences, they don't show truly different sides to themselves. Most of these social media accounts simply become personalized extensions of their politicized public personalities.

So Jake Tapper can spend half his day retweeting about how kids should play with dogs more, and the other half sending messages about how Trump should end the shutdown. Following, you never go home to non-political space: you're always on the compound.

News consumers on both sides today behave like cultists, self-isolating intellectually, kept that way with a steady diet of terrifying stories about fellow citizens. Red-staters are told liberals are terror-sympathizers, desperate, out of white guilt, to eviscerate American culture from within.

Blue-staters are peppered daily with stories of fellow travelers and traitors in their midst, an incredible example being NBC's effort to paint presidential candidate Tulsi Gabbard as a tool of the Kremlin on the day she announced her run.

Most intelligent people in the Gabbard case could see that Beltway hacks were piling on a politician for taking a heretical stance against a foreign military deployment. Still, the underlying message was important: Russian influence is everywhere, and anyone, even a member of congress, might be a witting or unwitting agent. Be vigilant! Suspect everyone, except us! We're the only people you know are unaffected.

This deeply paranoid view of the human experience, telling all America it lives on a violent invisible influence battlefield, is the opposite of what the news used to be. The news was once a placid ritual designed to amp *down* the viewer's political reflex.

The church of the press was a sleepy place then. In the seventies and eighties, in fact, news was infamous for its non-confrontational nature and vapidity. This was the joke of *Anchorman*, that the biggest story in human history was a panda birth.

News companies then were trying to train audiences to be docile and unconcerned.

A local news affiliate would pack its lineup with cat-in-tree segments, and the weather slots got longer and longer throughout the decades. A local reporter once joked to me that the highest paid news-gatherer in every city would soon be a helicopter. Aerial shots of the local skyline were more important than fifty, a hundred exposés.

Within a decade or so after Watergate, audiences had been trained not to want to watch disturbing news. They were soon more interested in the weather.

Today it's the opposite. We are trying to keep your brain locked in conflict, not just for the grubby commercial reason that it keeps people tuned in, but because it prevents them from thinking about other things. But what?

***

Herman and Chomsky in *Manufacturing Consent* identified "five filters," through which they said mass media operates. They were *Ownership, Advertising, Sourcing, Flak,* and an *Organizing Religion.*

Their basic idea: news media is a synthesis of elite concerns. It has to serve the ends of media owners by making a profit, or enhancing the prestige of a larger profit-making network. It also has to coincide with values of advertisers, strengthen the relationships between top news agencies and high-level government sources, and serve the propaganda aims of those sources, often by organizing the population against a common enemy.

The news at its core is still a vehicle for advancing elite interests. Most of the filters still hold. But the model has been disrupted in one key way. As Chomsky notes, the idea of anti-communism as an organizing religion has gone bust.

We've tried out other common enemies. Islamic terrorists were serviceable for a while. Occasionally a dictator like Slobodan Milošević will get some air time in this role. Russia is back for a second run lately, minus the socialist black hat.

None of these antagonists are close enough to home for modern audiences. This is why the biggest change to Chomsky's model is the discovery of a far superior "common enemy" in modern media: each other. So long as we remain a bitterly divided two-party state, we'll never want for TV villains. Who we hate just depends on what channel we watch.

The Soviet Union let us all down by collapsing under the weight of its sociopathic leadership and systemic corruption, removing both itself and global communism as a functional adversary.

The divided nature of our media acts in part to prevent us from seeing similar cracks widen in our own empire.

Once, cats in trees, *Dynasty,* and cool vids on MTV were enough to distract people from broad institutional problems.

Today people are struggling and have lost so much trust in institutions that the only way to keep eyes away from the rot is by throwing the hardest propaganda fastballs. We can't allow attention to flag for even a moment because the evidence of political incompetence and corruption is so rampant and undeniable.

For most nonwhite *and* white citizens, health care services are a catastrophe. There are entire congressional districts without a functioning maternity ward. Stories of couples having to drive a hundred miles at high speed to have their babies delivered are no longer uncommon.

We suffer from profound and worsening inequality in income and criminal justice outcomes, a complete lack of job security for most, crumbling infrastructure (aggravated by extraordinary inefficiency and waste in government), an epidemic of anti-competitive practice and rent-seeking among the biggest companies, and devastating environmental threats on multiple fronts, from overfished oceans to a toxic "garbage patch" twice the size of Texas floating in the Pacific.

These and a hundred other problems are common to the entire global population, not just Republicans or Democrats in the United States.

Fixing these problems would be hard for our leaders. It's much easier to stall by keeping people obsessed with intramural/provincial arguments.

As a bonus, this has been an extraordinarily profitable media strategy. In 2018, most all the big media companies, despite (or perhaps because of) marked declines in journalistic performance, made buck. The *New York Times* made a second-quarter profit of $24 million, which as any newspaper person will tell you is good for, well, a newspaper.

CBS made a third-quarter profit of $1.24 billion, even after President Les Moonves—the guy who made trouble by admitting Trump was bad for America but good for the "bottom line"—was forced to resign in a #MeToo scandal. At the end of 2018, MSNBC sat in the ratings pole position ahead of Fox for the first time in eighteen years, even as Fox cable itself had record revenues of $1.51 billion.

This is the only strategy left that makes money, and serves the right political purposes. In order to satisfy everyone up top with a say in the matter—from advertisers, to Internet distributors, to politicians who drive news, to political donors—this has to be the outcome. Anything but the most intense kind of reality-show civil war would leave Americans free to stare their real problems in the face.

This ruse is inverse Chomsky. If we once manufactured the consent of the population for everything from the Vietnam War to the bombing of Kosovo to the occupation of Iraq, we're now manufacturing *discontent*. It's the only way to prevent a popular uprising.

It can't hold. As we saw with the election of Trump and with the Bernie Sanders campaign (and with countless protest movements around the world, from Catalonia to the *Gilets Jaunes*), voters are not completely stupid. They know enough to be angry. Commercial news media has tried frantically to come up with enough red capes to keep us charging forward, but they're running out of gimmicks.

It will be hard to keep concealed for long the obvious fact that turning off the news results in an instantly positive psychological change for most people. If you want to be happier, if you want to live in a world that may be thick with problems but is at least a sunnier place where people are more decent to one another and more willing to cooperate and show kindness, just turn off the tube.

If you must be a news consumer, be aware of all the pressures laid out in this book. Remember the complex economics at work every time you click on a story or turn on the TV.

From the moment your eyes move to the screen, one company is selling you a consumer product, which you're paying for by being subject to advertising, or through a subscription. Meanwhile, another company is selling *you* to another set of buyers. Your attention is one product, the data about your surfing behavior is another, and so on.

The news, the actual information in the middle, is almost incidental to these transactions. What matters is the amount of time you spend engaged. This is why you should always be suspicious of emergencies, indeed of anyone who tells you to worry about things you can't control.

Think about how Walter Cronkite told you to blow off an Ice Age and smiled as he signed off until tomorrow.

Then think about how Rachel Maddow, just after the 2019 New Year, hypothesized in the middle of a nationwide cold front that the Russians could turn off your heat at any moment. This McCarthyite scare campaign was instantly ratified by the American government's fact-checking arm, *Polygraph,* a division of Radio Free Europe/Radio Liberty. This was a classic example of how political and commercial incentives can align seamlessly.

No parent who goes to bed at night looking at their children nestled under covers can afford not to think about the possibility of the heat being switched off—and not just in your house, but throughout the whole region! What would you do, if there were no warm places to bring your children? Your elderly parents?

This is news that demands the retention of space in your head post-broadcast. It's the opposite of Cronkite's chummy "See you tomorrow." It's fear, loathing, and disquieting outrage they insist you are patriotically required to retain.

These are tactics that betray desperation, an empty hand. We've seen it before. When George W. Bush wanted to invade Iraq, his White House had to go so far down the road of upsetting the American public that it's comic to remember.

Even much-trusted Colin Powell was forced to agree with Bush that Saddam Hussein had drones that, "if transported," could be used to spray poison or "biological agents" on the American heartland. How exactly was Saddam going to do this transporting? On his aircraft carriers? We reported this as serious news. But they weren't really worried about Iraqi drones. They were worried people wouldn't be scared enough to support the war!

That was just a temporary mania, drummed up for the very narrow purpose of getting the population a) backing a pointless invasion, and b) helping the Republicans win a couple of elections, beginning with the 2002 midterms.

This current craze is far more intense, bipartisan, and open-ended. It's not designed to be a temporarily blinding fervor. This is panic you're told not to excise from your life, ever, or else...

Or else what? We don't articulate that, for a very good reason.

Of all the taboos and deceptions in media, this is the one we lie about most. The thing we're most afraid to discuss has to do with precisely that question of what happens if you should stop following the news.

The answer, of course, is nothing. Not only can you live without us, you probably should, most of the time anyway.

And that's the way it is.

14. THE SCARLET LETTER CLUB

In March of 2003, the United States invaded Iraq, beginning an essentially open-ended military occupation of the Middle East, as well as bringing sweeping changes to our relationship to civil liberties and international law.

We now have combat operations in at least seven countries in the region, and regimes of torture, "rendition," indefinite detention, assassination and mass surveillance are all legacies of that one fateful decision.

The war also ushered in a radical change in the role of the media.

Most Americans remember the Iraq episode as a disaster for the press because of an infamous, industry-wide error, having to do with whether or not Iraq possessed weapons of mass destruction.

As detailed below, that wasn't exactly the story. It was far more complicated than that.

Actually, most things are. This is an important theme, seldom remarked upon.

On the one hand, audiences are trained to be obedient, loyal, and to accept a simplified partisan view of the world.

But we will often grab those same mentally weakened audiences and pull them deep underwater, into the depths of stories that quickly become so complicated only the most obsessive news junkie could possibly hope to follow them. The exercise becomes intellectually exhausting for the ordinary person, something both government officials and media executives count on.

Iraq was one of the first stories of this type: we overwhelmed audiences with details and technical gibberish and charts and maps and chemical terminology, and essentially forced consumers to take things on faith after a while. As one of the British officials involved in planning this war noted (in a memo that came out years later), some of the details dumped on the public wouldn't "hoodwink a real expert." But that wasn't the person they needed to fool.

They needed to get exhausted, confused, frustrated audiences, heads all mixed up with fear and anger and a determination to act after 9/11, to buy a case for war that at best was designed to hold up to only temporary scrutiny.

This technique of wearing out viewers with details had come into play somewhat before, with stories like Whitewater and Monicagate, but Iraq was a real milestone. It set the stage for future stories that urged audiences to accept complex sets of plots and subplots on faith.

Another main lesson of Iraq was that media figures who get things wrong do not experience professional consequences. Instead, they remain in place or are promoted, in case they're needed to make a "mistake" again.

We're meant to have forgotten, but journalists who bungled stories like the 2008 financial crisis, the rise of Donald Trump, the Venezuela mess, and even #Russiagate were first actors in the WMD affair.

In the popular imagination, the case for invading Iraq was driven by Republicans and one over-caffeinated *New York Times* writer, Judith Miller. But the blue-state *intelligentsia*, especially the Upper West Side/Georgetown sect of northeast corridor pundits, who are mostly still in place, also hyped Bush's war.

Richard Cohen of the *Washington Post* said "only a fool—or possibly a Frenchman" could reject the WMD case. #Resistance hero David Remnick of the *New Yorker* chipped in for invasion with "Making the Case."

Jonathan Chait of *New York*, a human wrongness barometer if there ever was one, supported the invasion in '03, then wrote a snippy column ten years later warning that "sweeping out... the existing thought, and existing thinkers" who'd erred on Iraq (read: him) would be a "myopic" response.

New York Times columnist Thomas Friedman was wrong about Operation Iraqi Freedom turning around in the "next six months" fourteen consecutive times, famously telling America's enemies they could "Suck on this." Current *Atlantic* editor Jeffrey Goldberg won an Overseas Press Club award for speculating about Saddam Hussein's "possible ties to al-Qaeda."

David Brooks is an on-again-off-again Republican, a famed mangler of words, the author of a book about the superior consumer taste of the American rich, and a self-described teacher of "humility" at Yale. When he was with the *Weekly Standard* in the Iraq years, he had a boner for war and dumped on "peaceniks."

"Nobody from the peace camp will stand up and say that Saddam Hussein is not a fundamental threat to the world," he exclaimed, double negatives be damned. Later, when he joined the lineup of hawk-editorialists then populating the *New York Times* opinion page, he said the same things, only more confusingly and wrapped in more nervous hedges.

Washington Post opinion page editor Fred Hiatt, who'd go on to be named the "fifth most influential liberal in America" by the *Daily Beast,* ran twenty-seven house editorials in favor of the Iraq War. These featured classics like, "It is hard to imagine how anyone could doubt that Iraq possesses weapons of mass destruction" ("Irrefutable," Feb. 6, 2003).

MSNBC did its part by removing antiwar Phil Donahue and Jesse Ventura from its lineup, CNN flooded the airwaves with generals and ex-Pentagon stoolies, and broadcast outlets ABC, CBS, NBC, and PBS stacked the deck even worse: in a two-week period before the invasion, the networks had just one American guest out of 267 who questioned the war, according to Fairness and Accuracy in Reporting.

The first rule of modern commercial media is you're allowed to screw up, in concert. So there was no reckoning for the WMD mess. The chief offenders kept perches or failed up.

As time passed, these media figures used an array of tricks to massage the scale of error out of public memory. Aspects of the WMD affair aren't even seen as mistakes in hindsight, because the propaganda campaign was so far-reaching it made them invisible.

They altered public attitudes about everything from war to civil liberties to self-determination to countless other issues, creating an intellectual context for the "War on Terror" that remained mostly unchallenged even after the "error" was acknowledged.

With cosmetic touches, all was forgotten. Goldberg, for instance, won a National Magazine Award for speculating about a a Saddam-Hezbollah union that might "fire missiles at Israel" to provoke a "conventional, or even nuclear, response." His bio today just says he won for "coverage of Islamic terrorism."

Part of the concealing legend is the idea that the journalistic mistake was limited to believing the Bush administration's claims about the threat Saddam Hussein posed. But the screw-up wasn't just about WMDs.

Over a period of years, reporters and pundits were asked to accept a whole range of ideas and concepts, many absurd: that the war would be over in months, that we'd be greeted with flowers as liberators, that sectarian conflict was unlikely because differences between Shia and Sunni Muslims were exaggerated or nonexistent, and so on.

Evidence was always over the next hill. It was a pioneering effort in a kind of journalistic Ponzi scheme, in which news organizations justified banner headlines in the present by writing checks against a balance of future revelations.

There's an obvious current parallel with #Russiagate, whose early headlines were driven similarly by unnamed sources promising an ascending schedule of future bombshells.

A lot of people will balk at the comparison, which is fine. If you like, forget #Russiagate.

But it's worth going back to remember exactly what many of today's leading voices got away with not so long ago. It's been forgotten just how gargantuan the propagandistic pileup was.

***

Less than a month after the Twin Towers fell on September 11, 2001, American forces went to the Middle East in search of Osama bin Laden and al-Qaeda. We invaded Afghanistan on October 7, and many Americans assumed that would be the end of it.

Not so. Shortly after, we got hints about a next step.

John McCain appeared on the *David Letterman Show* less than two weeks into the Afghan operation, on October 18, 2001. In between laughs, he said "the next phase" of war would be Iraq.

He hinted Iraq was responsible for a recent series of anthrax attacks, a story that itself was on its way to becoming a historic journalistic blunder, as reporters and pundits like Nicholas Kristof would mistakenly pin those attacks on a scientist named Steven Hatfill. At the time, however, McCain insinuated the anthrax "may—and I emphasize may—have come from Iraq."

Soon after that, on January 29, 2002, George W. Bush delivered his famed "Axis of Evil" speech, which named Iraq part of a troika of unconquered nation-states who could "attack our allies or attempt to blackmail the United States." Bush added, "the price of indifference could be catastrophic."

Within a few months of that speech, invasion of Iraq was an open secret. This was a key period for the press, because everyone knew we were going, but the official reason had not yet been articulated fully. This might have been a good time to go digging in search of a reason.

Instead, reporters somehow failed to notice that key elements of the argument for invasion had been made public long before 9/11, by intellectuals with close ties to Bush.

Prominent neoconservatives in the mid-nineties publicly floated the idea of "regime change" in Iraq. "Saddam Hussein must go," wrote Bill Kristol and Robert Kagan in a *New York Times* editorial, "Bombing Iraq isn't enough," way back in January of *1998*.

If you're wondering how we ended up invading one of the few Middle Eastern countries with no connection to 9/11, this was how. Invading wasn't a response to the collapse of the Twin Towers, or an effort to keep safe from the spread of WMDs in the terror age. It was step one in an ambitious new foreign policy vision articulated before most people even heard the name "Osama bin Laden."

Conservatives, said the authors, shouldn't be intimidated into thinking it was politically necessary to cash in on the then-popular "peace dividend." America should reject "unshouldering the vast responsibilities the United States acquired at the end of the Second World War." They should also resist the urge to "concentrate... energies at home," as both Democrats like Bill Clinton and, to an even greater degree, "America first" nationalists like Pat Buchanan were proposing back then.

Most are unaware that neoconservatives were disappointed Democrats, who defected to Republicanism over LBJ's social programs and George McGovern's antiwar stance. Other liberals originally coined the term "neoconservative" as an insult; they meant it to mean the right wing of the Democratic Party. Many of these ex-Dems had a (very narrow) affinity for the thinking of Lev Trotsky, mainly being fans of his ambitious internationalism. The seeds of this could be found in the new policy Kristol and Kagan proposed, which was called "benevolent hegemony."

The United States, Kristol argued, should seek to be "a leader with preponderant influence and authority over all others in its domain." With the Soviets gone from the scene, the argument went, our "domain" should now be planet Earth. Securing "authority" meant pursuing policies "ultimately intended to bring about a change of regime" in countries like "Iran, Cuba, and China." (China!)

America should apply a "continuing exertion of American influence" around the world, rejecting what Kagan and Kristol called "Armand Hammerism," i.e. attempting to build relationships with non-satellite nations based on pragmatism.

Bush speechwriter David Frum was one of the people charged with coming up with the sales pitch for this charming new policy.

When he sat down to write the "Axis of Evil" speech, Frum looked back to World War II. He decided America's enemies were so crazy with hatred, they could not be counted on to behave rationally, even if threatened with destruction. "If deterrence worked," he noted, "there would never be a Pearl Harbor."

Therefore, Iraq was not just about convincing America that Saddam Hussein had links to 9/11, or had WMDs. It was about convincing Americans "containment" was no longer a viable policy anywhere.

Although we'd successfully contained a more powerful Soviet enemy, Americans needed to be talked out of the idea that small, weak, "rogue" regimes should be allowed to exist at all. Long-term, we should have plans for "change of regime" in all such places, China included.

When we deride journalists as stenographers, it's not about them repeating the words of powerful officials. The real crime is absorbing the ideas of powerful people (often crafted by groups of officials in a dreary corporate process) and repeating them as if they're your own personal thoughts.

From beginning to end, the WMD editorialists parroted the language of others. In this sense neocons like Kristol, Kagan, and Frum were less objectionable messengers, because they at least wrote their own material. The northeast corridor pundits, on the other hand, were infected with intellectual echolalia.

Remnick, who'd never argued for pre-emptive war in the past, suddenly told us "a return to a hollow pursuit of containment will be the most dangerous option of all." Fred Hiatt warned "not poking the hornet's nest" was a "strategy of accommodation, half-measures and wishful thinking."

Thomas Friedman's infamous "Chicken a l'Iraq" editorial insisted America couldn't risk containment and had to be willing to be as unpredictable as rogue enemies—that in a game of *realpolitik* chicken, we had to throw out our steering wheel and be "ready to invade Iraq tomorrow, alone."

It's easy to imagine one blockheaded Judith Miller believing killer weapons were over every hill. Far more amazing was everyone from Remnick to Hiatt to Friedman to Cohen and Chait embracing the revolutionary idea that containment was a failure and overnight supporting a fundamentally opposite policy, "benevolent hegemony." This was a real-life version of "Oceania is at war with Eastasia. Oceania has always been at war with Eastasia."

Moreover they didn't just repeat the concept in broad strokes. They repeated all the talking points that had been cooked up by officials specifically with the aim of deceiving the press.

We know this because there was a British inquiry led by Sir John Chilcot into the reasons for the British-American invasion. The so-called "Chilcot Report" made public a tranche of communiqués between British and American officials, showing how the war case was built brick by brick, over a period of about six months between March and September of 2002.

The report got relatively little press in an America consumed with an election season. It was deeply embarrassing stuff for the British and American presses.

In 2009, former British Prime Minister Tony Blair admitted he would have backed an invasion of Iraq even if there had been no WMD issue.

"I mean obviously," he said, "you would have had to use and deploy different arguments."

The Chilcot report, and the Downing Street memos released in 2005, outlined exactly what arguments Blair's government did "deploy."

The Blair-Bush interactions of that time roughly approximated the range of political debate we heard between Republicans and mainstream Democrats before the war. Republicans were unashamed of a real reason for war called "regime change." Democrats, and Blair, were fine with "regime change," but needed a different public reason.

The Brits from the start were wary of the Bush administration. British foreign office political director Peter Ricketts wrote a memo early in 2002 that said,

"U.S. scrambling to establish a link between Iraq and al-Qaida is so far frankly unconvincing... For Iraq, 'regime change' does not stack up. It sounds like a grudge between Bush and Saddam."

Sadly for Britain and for us, Blair was determined to maintain the "special relationship," and endorsed "regime change" in private.

On March 14 of 2002, Blair's foreign policy advisor David Manning had dinner with Condoleezza Rice, and afterward wrote a memo to Blair. "I said that you would not budge in your support for regime change," he wrote. "But you had to manage a press, a Parliament and a public opinion that was very different."

Thus the public case for war was mostly an effort to create political cover for the British.

The Bush administration at first didn't want the UN involved; the British said they couldn't support the invasion without the fig leaf. So they got to work on a new argument based on Saddam Hussein's defiance of UN inspections, and his possession of weapons of mass destruction.

To that end, the Brits cooked up a series of intelligence "dossiers" purporting to outline the Iraqi threat. Early drafts outlined the weapons possessed by Iraq but also by Libya, North Korea, and Iran. Foreign Secretary Jack Straw, upon reading an early draft in March of 2002, blanched.

"Good, but should not Iraq be *first* and also have more text?" he wrote. "The paper has to show why there is an exceptional threat from Iraq. It does not quite do this yet."

They went back to the drawing board and made the report Iraq-ier. Sir John Scarlett, chairman of Britain's Joint Intelligence Committee, wrote the following by way of suggestion on March 15 (emphasis mine):

> The new draft highlights...violation of SCRs [UN Security Council Resolutions]; **use of CW [Chemical Warfare] agents against own people**). You may still wish to consider whether more impact could be achieved if the paper **only covered Iraq**. This would **have the benefit of obscuring the fact that in terms of WMD, Iraq is not that exceptional.**

Tim Dowse, head of counter-proliferation at the Foreign and Commonwealth Office (FCO), wrote a memo full of suggestions for how to get around what he called "the presentational difficulty" of the war case:

If it appears we do have to change our public line, I wonder if we might finesse the presentational difficulty by changing the terms? Instead of talking about tonnes of precursor chemicals (which don't mean much to the man in the street anyway), could we focus on munitions and refer to 'precursor chemicals sufficient to produce x thousand SCUD warheads/ aerial bombs/122mm rockets filled with mustard gas/the deadly nerve agents tabun/sarin/VX...

Dowse added:

I realise that this would not in the end hoodwink a real expert... But the task... would be impossible for a layman. And the result would, I think, have more impact on the target audience.

All of this history is necessary to explain the depth of the reporting failure. Journalists and pundits, before they even got to the question of whether or not Iraq actually had WMDs, had to swallow every one of these clumsy deceptions.

It was a huge gamble for Bush and Blair to imagine that not one news outlet would sniff out that the real reason for war was a goofball global domination plan cooked up in public years before, by overgrown *Risk* players like Kristol and Kagan.

We now know officials were pessimistic this patchwork effort at hiding "regime change" would fly with the public, and especially the media. An assistant to Blair spokesman Alistair Campbell named Phillip Bassett wrote on September 11, 2002: "Think we're in trouble with this."

Bassett among other things worried the dossier had been over-prepared and journalists would catch its excess of rhetorical flourishes.

"Think it needs to be written in officialese, lots of it is too journalistic as it now stands," he wrote. "Some of it (e.g. the opening chapter as a biog of Saddam!) reading like *Sunday Times.*"

Officials began to discuss aiming their report and their rhetoric at the ordinary person, bypassing meddlesome journalists who might ask too many questions. Some worried their intelligence dossier needed to be "more exciting," while others thought neither the public nor the press would buy the "slightly iffy claims about big buildings."

They discussed refraining from pre-publication communications with the press altogether. They were afraid even off the record communications would fuel expectations that we "come up with the goods."

Foreign Office communications chief John Williams was the biggest doubter. He thought the dossier was "unlikely to be enough... There is no 'killer fact... that proves Saddam must be taken on now."

Williams suggested he and his colleagues "reinforce the broad case, so that it strikes a chord with more and more people, as opposed to journalists." He added:

> Our target is not the argumentative interviewer or opinionated column-
> ist, but the kind of people to whom ministerial interviewers are a back-
> ground hum on the car or kitchen radio...

Williams and the others shouldn't have worried. If anything, the opposite proved true. Huge portions of the public reacted with skepticism, while journalists mostly ate the bait.

The Brits released their intelligence findings via a pair of dossiers, one in September of 2002 and another in February of 2003. In response, somewhere between six and thirty million people worldwide were unconvinced enough to march in the streets in protest on February 15, 2003 (I was one).

Journalists meanwhile repeated official language down to the last details.

The British and American authors of the intelligence dossiers "sexed" up their language, afraid reporters would trip on the hedges. One official wrote to Sir Scarlett, saying, "You will clearly need to judge the extent to which you need to hedge your judgments with, for example, 'it is almost certain' and other caveats."

The press ended up doing the same stripping on its own. Within months after the release of the first British dossier, words like "alleged" and "potential" began to vanish from all the national news reports, even though nothing had changed factually. This was especially true after the New Year, when invasion began to look inevitable.

"Today Mr. Bush left it to his spokesman to answer critics who asked what precise threat Iraq and its weapons of mass destruction pose to America," said David Gregory on NBC in late January of 2003, in a typical report a few months before invasion.

Even questions came in the form of statements. "The CIA is being urged to make public more of its intelligence about Iraq's weapons of mass destruction," noted would-be skeptic Dan Rather on January 6, 2003.

Even before they got to the issue of whether or not Iraq had WMDs, reporters bought the Frankenstein's monster of a rationale that had been fabricated across months by British and American propagandists: that Saddam was a unique and "exceptional" evil, that containment wouldn't hold, that the credibility of international law wouldn't survive without invasion, etc.

Had the British-American intelligence collective worked in a lab to create the perfect war salesman, they couldn't have improved upon Jeffrey Goldberg.

Then writing in *Slate* and the *New Yorker*, Goldberg hit nearly all desired themes. Remember the suggestion that the government sources stress "precursor chemicals sufficient to produce x thousand SCUD warheads"?

In *Slate* on October 3, 2002, just a few weeks after the British released their first dossier to reporters, Goldberg quoted a former weapons inspector discussing the Iraqis' potential use of alfatoxin, which Goldberg said "causes liver cancer... particularly well in children." Goldberg added he'd been told Iraqis "had loaded aflatoxin into two warheads capable of being fitted onto Scud missiles..."

Goldberg hammered the "exceptional" theme. He quoted an ad taken out in the *New York Times* by antiwar activists. The ad had to be bought, because it asked the question *Times* reporters wouldn't: "Of all the repugnant dictatorships, why this one?"

Goldberg answered, becoming among the first to stress the "Saddam Hussein is both Hitler and Satan" theme:

Saddam Hussein is a figure of singular repugnance, and singular danger... No one else comes close... to matching his extraordinary and variegated record of malevolence...

Goldberg talked of visiting Kurdistan and meeting "barren and cancer-ridden women," and added:

Saddam Hussein is uniquely evil, the only ruler in power today—and the first one since Hitler—to commit chemical genocide...

Brooks hissed at the peace activists who refused to face the dangers inherent if "Saddam is permitted to remain in power in Baghdad, working away on his biological, chemical, and nuclear weapons programs, still tyrannizing his own people..." He added years later that his thinking at the time was, "If you could go back in time and strangle Hitler in his crib, would you do it?"

George Will derided critics of the invasion as being like "Lord Haw Haw," a character who'd broadcast Hitlerian propaganda to Britain during World War II. He said UN secretary Kofi Annan was Saddam's "servant" and doing a "Neville Chamberlain impersonation." He added Democrat House members who'd supported inspections, Jim McDermott and David Bonior, were two "specimens" of the sort of "useful idiots" (sound familiar?) who'd denied "the existence of Lenin's police-state terror."

Mussolini, Hitler, Lenin—how about Stalin? "He's in league with a Stalin in terms of internal repression," chimed in Jonathan Chait, making what was then considered the "Liberal case" for war.

Remnick also stressed Saddam's "use of chemical weapons on neighbors and his own citizens," then went further back in history in search of a tyrannical comparison. This technique often comes up, by the way, when a dictator gets in America's way. The ruler in question is often described as a deluded fantasist, determined to undermine the benevolent Western order in search of past nationalist glory. He is an Ozymandias, indifferent to the accumulating sands of progress. From Remnick's "case":

> We are reminded, too, of Saddam's vision of himself as the modern Saladin, the modern Nebuchadnezzar II, who (after massacring the Kurds, invading Kuwait, and attacking the marsh Arabs of the south) vows to "liberate" Jerusalem, vanquish the United States, and rule over a united Arab world...

Think about all of this from the perspective of those British intelligence chiefs like Scarlett. They must have been blown away by their good fortune.

Had these intelligence officers surveyed each pundit individually ahead of time, they might have guessed they'd get George Will going the Hitler route.

But Remnick? Chait? Goldberg? Even the token "dissenter" on the invasion front in the *Times,* Kristof, conceded Saddam was "as nasty as Hitler," but less capable of invading neighbors. Nobody questioned the key propaganda objective, getting people to accept the idea of Hussein as an "exceptional" evil.

On their own, without prompting, American journalists went beyond what the intelligence chiefs hoped, even piling abuse upon the French, whose Security Council opposition imperiled the backroom deal cooked up by the British and Americans.

Friedman ranted that France should be "voted off the island," while others blasted critics of the war as being in league with France, or tabbed them with the dreaded moniker "useful idiots" (everyone from Jonah Goldberg to Robert Pollack to Brian Blomquist in the *New York Post* went there).

Meanwhile, there was exactly one major American news organization that didn't buy the British-American war story: the Knight-Ridder newspaper chain. Their Washington bureau chief, John Walcott, offered a simple explanation:

> Our readers aren't here in Washington. They aren't up in New York. They aren't the people who send other people's kids to war. They're the people who get sent to war and we felt an obligation to them.

The northeast corridor pundits with whom Wolcott contrasted himself spoke later of different pressures. Chait was a particularly amazing case.

Even at the time, Chait spoke of having an initial reaction that the war case was idiotic. "Originally," he said in October of 2002, "I thought, 'These justifications make no sense whatsoever.'"

But "then I thought about it," and decided liberal principles "didn't get in the way" of a case for war. He ultimately explained that while he did publicly support the war, he "had a lot of unpublished thoughts," only peer pressure was a problem. "I wasn't afraid to alienate my colleagues, editors, and employer," he wrote, "but I didn't go out of my way to do it, either."

NPR's Brooke Gladstone of *On the Media*, a person I typically like and respect very much, offered a startling defense of the press. She blamed politicians:

> Usually the press is able to question the government, if Congress is questioning the government. But if Congress keeps quiet, the media have no protective cover... They felt the anguish of their audience and the sensitivity of their advertisers to criticizing the government directly. They wished they had Congress to do it for them.

In addition to being incorrect (there were members of Congress who opposed the war), this amazing take explains a lot about how the commercial press views itself. We're meant to be outside the tent, a "fourth estate" acting as a check on others in power. We should be professional jerks who examine every press release the way accountants look at numbers, i.e. as if each villainous digit potentially conceals lies.

Instead, there's a fear of losing one's place. Reporters in large commercial organizations make mistakes as a group because they do everything as a group: they're always amplifying each others' messages, which means a tacit agreement to trust others in a wide social group that includes high-level sources, advertisers, and other influential players.

If any one of these people had included as a possible variable the notion that intelligence chiefs were lying to them, the paucity of the case for war would have come into focus rather quickly, as it did for the millions of people around the world who protested.

And why not? Officials have been lying their faces off to the press for a century. From World War I–era tales of striking union workers being German agents, to the "missile gap" that wasn't (the "gap" was leaked to the press before the Soviets had even one operational ICBM) to the various Gulf of Tonkin deceptions, to the smearing of people like Martin Luther King Jr., it's a wonder newspapers listen to security sources at all.

In the Reagan years National Security Advisor John Poindexter spread false stories about Libyan terrorist plots to the *Wall Street Journal* and other papers, and the tales were only retracted because Bob Woodward found out and ran a story in 1986 revealing the scheme. Yet even Woodward wasn't terribly suspicious of initial Iraq War claims, explaining later that he succumbed to "groupthink." He added, "I blame myself mightily for not pushing harder."

After we invaded, and the WMD hunt turned out to be an oopsie, nearly all of these professional chin-scratchers found ways to address their error. Most confessions followed a script: I was young (Ezra Klein literally said, "I was young and dumb"), I believed the intel, and on the narrow point of WMDs being in Iraq, I screwed up.

None walked back the rest of the propaganda, which is why even as the case for invading Iraq fell apart, our presence in the Mideast expanded. While Judith

Miller became a national punchline, the "continuing exertion of American influence" became conventional wisdom.

Defense budgets exploded. NATO expanded. The concept of a "peace dividend" faded to the point where few remember it. We built and now maintain a vast global archipelago of secret prisons, routinely cross borders using drones in violation of international law, and today have military bases in eighty countries, to support active combat operations in at least seven nations (most Americans don't even know which ones).

The WMD episode is remembered as a grotesque journalistic failure, one that led to disastrous war that spawned ISIS. But nobody's sorry about the revolutionary new policies that error willed into being. They are specifically not regretful about helping create a continually expanding Fortress America with bases everywhere that topples regimes left and right, with or without congressional or UN approval.

They're sorry about Iraq, maybe, but as Chait now says, "Libya was not Iraq." He also said this years ago to the "liberal anti-interventionists," in explaining why "I have not embraced their worldview."

You might get a reporter to apologize for getting a fact wrong, if you hassle him or her enough over a period of many years. But they never apologize for the subtext in which their errors came wrapped. The usual play is an "I was right even though I was wrong" retrospective, often involving not-inconsiderable revisionist history.

Fred Hiatt's *Post* had the stones five years after the Iraq invasion to congratulate itself for having once pooh-poohed Bush's "Mission Accomplished" stunt. He left out that a) the *Post* never backed away from its support for the invasion, and b) the paper didn't even get through a week before it was back writing of Bush's critics: "Their real gripe with Mr. Bush is that he looked great; the president pulled off his 'Top Gun' act as much as Michael Dukakis flubbed his spin in a tank."

They all did some version of this. David Remnick blanched at the idea that the *New Yorker* beat the war drum, calling it "ridiculous." He admitted that yes, "as an individual" he'd argued for war, but his writer Rick Hertzberg had been skeptical in his pages, and really, as far as the WMD question went, "nobody got that story completely right."

The idea that "nobody got that story completely right" is a worse legend than the idea that Saddam had weapons. Nobody got that right? Millions and millions got it right.

There were no protesters in Washington or London or Rome who were on the streets because they were sure Saddam had no weapons. They were there because they knew the whole WMD issue was at best a bullshit excuse for a wrong war that had some other, darker, still-unreleased explanation the incompetent press wasn't seeking out. Only the reporters themselves were dumb enough, or dishonest enough, to pretend that narrow factual question was important.

***

At the end of Franz Kafka's *The Trial,* two men knock on the door of the hero, Joseph K. They are dressed "in frock coats, pale and fat, wearing top hats that looked like they could not be taken off their heads." They are K.'s assassins, come to execute him for the never-articulated crime that triggered his never-explained trial. The men don't look fearsome, though. K. seems to recognize them as third-rate theater performers.

"Some ancient, unimportant actors, that's what they've sent for me," he thinks. "They want to sort me out as cheaply as they can."

K. laughs at the absurdity of his demise as they drag him away, but at the end of the chapter the men in top hats really do kill him, driving knives into his heart. In Kafka's world, the hand of fate is both terrible and ridiculous. He seems to say, you cannot have one without the other. Cruelty and monstrousness inherently come cloaked in absurdity, which makes sense, because without conscience or decency, the human animal is just an ape in a hat.

The aim of the British-American war was deathly serious. It would eventually cost well over a hundred thousand lives and trillions of dollars. But the case was made with laughable sloppiness. When fate knocked on the door of the American press, its slip was showing.

For example, the British released a second intelligence dossier in February of 2002, just before the invasion. This second work, known today in Britain as the "dodgy dossier," was so fake, the bureaucrats who put their name on it didn't even write it.

Parts of it had been plagiarized wholesale from a student thesis written thirteen years earlier, by an assistant professor at California State University named Ibrahim Al-Marashi. This "dodgy dossier" was edited to sound more authoritative. Quotes by former UN weapons inspector Scott Ritter to the effect that Hussein had abandoned his WMD program were removed.

The punchline is that the plagiarism job was uncovered before the invasion. By February 7, 2003, a month before attack, Tony Blair's government was under fire. The "dodgy" dossier, supposedly a high-level intelligence analysis written by MI6, was actually put together by "mid-level officials" from... Blair's communications department!

When the expert authors turned out not to be intelligence analysts but mid-level press officers, this was an admission that the messaging operation's real target was not Saddam Hussein but the media itself. That this crude cut-and-paste job was not even undertaken by the office's best people should have told reporters something else, something profoundly insulting they should have taken personally. But they didn't.

The war-makers left another clue lying out in the open, through a process muckraker Seymour Hersh outlined called "The Stovepipe." The idea of "stovepiping" involved top officials obtaining access to raw intelligence data submerged in bureaucracies, and withdrawing it before the various compliance officers could get hands on it. "Their position," wrote Hersh, "is that the professional bureaucracy is deliberately and maliciously keeping information from them."

The "stovepiping" technique gave people like Dick Cheney access to nuggets like the idea Saddam had been purchasing aluminum tubes, without having to hear the objections of bureaucratic naysayers about whether or not that meant anything nefarious (or whether the information was even true).

In this way, information somehow made it past internal controls to *New York Times* reporters Michael Gordon and Judith Miller, one of whom is still in the business, one of whom is not. On September 7, 2002, they wrote a crucial article, "U.S. Says Hussein Intensifies Quest for A-Bomb Parts," that declared, "Iraq has stepped up its quest for nuclear weapons."

Cheney infamously went on *Meet the Press* that same day and cited the article, saying, "it was public knowledge" Hussein was "trying to build a bomb."

This kind of thing went on repeatedly during the Iraq debacle. The press was used as a laundry machine, tossing dirty information made "reputable" by attaching it to names of prestigious news agencies. This trick, delivering information as unnamed sources and then later referring to reports as having been independently confirmed, made reporters part of the con. The game should have been clear then. What possible excuse could the *New York Times* have for continuing to take the war seriously?

An additional trick was using foreign allies as primary sources of intelligence analysis: information developed abroad sounds authoritative, but can also be disavowed easily if need be. A foreign ally might be more willing to "sex up" intelligence, especially if the target audience is someone else's media, with whom those agencies have no relationship. This is a critical angle non-journalists probably don't get as easily—it's harder for officials to lie to the local press, since they'll have to keep talking to them in the future. If a key fact or two can be fobbed off on a foreigner flown in for a few days, so much the better.

This is one reason to always have ears up when you start hearing bits and pieces of important intelligence cases happen to have been uncovered within the borders of America's closest intelligence allies, particularly England, Australia, the other "Five Eyes" nations, and key NATO members.

When officials use the press to launder information either offered off the record or developed by foreigners, what they're telling you is they want *you* to put *your name* on assertions they won't touch themselves.

It takes a special kind of sucker to want to be that person, but this, frankly, is why pundits and editors who make such screw-ups keep their jobs or get promoted. They're not being paid to avoid factual errors. They're being paid to push underlying narratives, and eat any errors that happen to be discovered along the way.

The Scarlet Letter Club who pushed the Iraq debacle proved they could be relied upon to ignore inconsistencies and trumpet desired themes. They proved they wouldn't consider the possibility they were being lied to.

If told an enemy was the worst dictator ever, they would write acres of text confirming it (even if it meant contradicting earlier claims they'd made that some other dictator was worse). If fed information that didn't pan out or had to be retracted, they wouldn't react with anger but would keep publishing more stuff from the same sources.

They proved they would not look back in time, to see if there were glaring clues for the context of current stories, like the Kristol-Kagan editorials about "regime change." This would pop up in the financial crisis story, with reporters who failed to notice four year-old public warnings from the FBI about an epidemic of "liar's loans."

Finally, the WMD crew additionally proved that on their own volition, they would deride people who disagreed with prevailing narratives as traitors. This, too, would happen over and over again.

The WMD case is unique because thanks to the accident of the Chilcot report and a few other inquiries, we know the extent of official deceptions while those who did the deceiving still happen to be working. Normally the ugly truth comes out a generation later, when all are long dead.

In this case they're still mostly all around, and it's worth asking: have they made the same kinds of mistakes since?

15. WHY RUSSIAGATE IS THIS GENERATION'S WMD

Nobody wants to hear this, but news that Special Prosecutor Robert Mueller is headed home without issuing new charges is a death blow for the reputation of the American news media.

As has long been rumored, the former FBI chief's independent probe will result in multiple indictments and convictions, but no "presidency-wrecking" conspiracy charges, or anything that would meet the layman's definition of "collusion" with Russia.

With the caveat that even this news might somehow turn out to be botched, the key detail in the many stories about the end of the Mueller investigation was best expressed by the *New York Times*:

> A senior Justice Department official said that Mr. Mueller would not recommend new indictments.

Attorney General William Barr sent a letter to congress summarizing Mueller's conclusions. The money line quoted the Mueller report:

> [T]he investigation did not establish that members of the Trump Campaign conspired or coordinated with the Russian government in its election interference activities.

Over the weekend, the *Times* tried to soften the emotional blow for the millions of Americans trained in these years to place their hopes for the overturn of the Trump presidency in Mueller. As with most press coverage, there was little pretense that the Mueller probe was supposed to be a neutral fact-finding mission, as apposed to religious allegory, with Mueller cast as the hero sent to slay the monster.

The Special Prosecutor literally became a religious figure during the last few years, with votive candles sold in his image and *Saturday Night Live* cast members singing "All I Want for Christmas Is You" to him featuring the rhymey line: "Mueller please come through, because the only option is a coup."

The *Times* story tried to preserve Santa Mueller's reputation, noting Trump's attorney general William Barr's reaction was an "endorsement" of the fineness of Mueller's work:

> In an apparent endorsement of an investigation that Mr. Trump has relentlessly attacked as a "witch hunt," Mr. Barr said Justice Department officials never had to intervene to keep Mr. Mueller from taking an inappropriate or unwarranted step.

Mueller, in other words, never stepped out of the bounds of his job description. But could the same be said for the news media?

For those anxious to keep the dream alive, the *Times* published its usual graphic of Trump-Russia "contacts," inviting readers to keep making connections. But in a separate piece by Peter Baker, the paper noted the Mueller news had dire consequences for the press:

> It will be a reckoning for President Trump, to be sure, but also for Robert S. Mueller III, the special counsel, for Congress, for Democrats, for Republicans, for the news media and, yes, for the system as a whole...

This is a damning page-one admission by the *Times*. Despite the connect-the-dots graphic in its other story, and despite the astonishing, emotion-laden editorial the paper also ran suggesting "We don't need to read the Mueller report" because we *know* Trump is guilty, Baker at least began the work of preparing *Times* readers for a hard question: "Have journalists connected too many dots that do not really add up?"

The paper was signaling it understood there would now be questions about whether or not news outlets like itself made galactic errors by betting heavily on a new, politicized approach, trying to be true to "history's judgment" on top of the hard-enough job of just being true. Worse, in a brutal irony everyone should have seen coming, the press has now handed Trump the mother of campaign issues heading into 2020.

Nothing Trump is accused of from now on by the press will be believed by huge chunks of the population, a group that (perhaps thanks to this story) is now larger than his original base. As Baker notes, a full 50.3 percent of respondents in a poll conducted this month said they agree with Trump that the Mueller probe is a "witch hunt."

Stories have been coming out for some time now hinting that Mueller's final report might leave audiences "disappointed," as if a president not being a foreign spy could somehow be bad news.

Openly using such language has, all along, been an indictment. Imagine how tone-deaf you'd have to be to not realize it makes you look bad when news does not match audience expectations you raised. To be unaware of this is mind-boggling, the journalistic equivalent of walking outside without pants.

There will be people protesting: the Mueller report doesn't prove anything! What about the thirty-seven indictments? The convictions? The Trump Tower revelations? The lies! The meeting with Don, Jr.? The *financial matters*! There's an ongoing grand jury investigation, and possible sealed indictments, and the House will still investigate, and...

Stop. Just stop. Any journalist who goes there is making it worse.

For years, every pundit and Democratic pol in Washington hyped every new Russia headline like the Watergate break-in. Now, even Nancy Pelosi has said impeachment is out, unless something "so compelling and overwhelming and bipartisan" against Trump is uncovered it would be worth their political trouble to prosecute.

The biggest thing this affair has uncovered so far is Donald Trump paying off a porn star. That's a hell of a long way from what this business was supposedly about at the beginning, and shame on any reporter who tries to pretend this isn't so.

The story hyped from the start was espionage: a secret relationship between the Trump campaign and Russian spooks who'd helped him win the election.

The betrayal narrative was not reported as metaphor. It was not "Trump likes the Russians so much, he might as well be a spy for them." It was literal spying, treason, and election-fixing—crimes so severe, former NSA employee John Schindler told reporters, Trump "will die in jail."

In the early months of this scandal, the *New York Times* said Trump's campaign had "repeated contacts" with Russian intelligence; the *Wall Street Journal* told us our spy agencies were withholding intelligence from the new president out of fear he was compromised; news leaked out that our spy chiefs had even told other countries like Israel not to share their intel with us because the Russians might have "leverages of pressure" on Trump.

CNN told us Trump officials had been in "constant contact" with "Russians known to U.S. intelligence," and the former director of the CIA, who'd helped kick-start the investigation that led to Mueller's probe, said the president was guilty of "high crimes and misdemeanors," committing acts "nothing short of treasonous."

Hillary Clinton insisted Russians "could not have known how to weaponize" political ads unless they'd been "guided" by Americans. Asked if she meant Trump, she said, "It's pretty hard not to." Harry Reid similarly said he had "no doubt" that the Trump campaign was "in on the deal" to help Russians with the leak.

None of this has been retracted. To be clear, if Trump were being blackmailed by Russian agencies like the FSB or the GRU, if he had any kind of relationship with Russian intelligence, that would soar over the "overwhelming and bipartisan" standard, and Nancy Pelosi would be damning torpedoes for impeachment right now.

There was never a real gray area here. Either Trump is a compromised foreign agent, or he isn't. If he isn't, news outlets once again swallowed a massive disinformation campaign, only this error is many orders of magnitude more stupid than any in the recent past, WMD included. Honest reporters like ABC's Terry Moran understand: Mueller coming back empty-handed on collusion means a "reckoning for the media."

Of course, there won't be such a reckoning. (There never is). But there should be. We broke every written and unwritten rule in pursuit of this story, starting with the prohibition on reporting things we can't confirm.

***

#Russiagate debuted as a media phenomenon in mid-summer, 2016. The roots of the actual story, i.e. when the multinational investigation began, go back much further, to the previous year at least. Oddly, that origin tale has not been nailed down yet, and blue-state audiences don't seem terribly interested in it, either.

By June and July of 2016, bits of the dossier compiled by former British spy Christopher Steele, which had been funded by the Democratic National Committee through the law firm Perkins Coie (which in turn hired the opposition research firm Fusion GPS), were already in the ether.

The Steele report occupies the same role in #Russiagate as the tales spun by Ahmed Chalabi occupied in the WMD screwup. Once again, a narrative became turbo-charged when Officials With Motives pulled the press corps by its nose into a swamp of unconfirmable private assertions.

Some early stories, like a July 4, 2016 piece by Franklin Foer in *Slate* called "Putin's Puppet," outlined future Steele themes in "circumstantial" form. But the actual dossier, while it influenced a number of pre-election Trump-Russia news stories (notably one by Michael Isiskoff of *Yahoo!* that would be used in a FISA warrant application), didn't make it into print for a while.

Though it was shopped to at least nine news organizations during the summer and fall of 2016, no one bit, for the good reason that news organizations couldn't verify its "revelations."

The Steele claims were explosive if true. The ex-spy reported Trump aide Carter Page had been offered fees on a big new slice of the oil giant Rosneft if he could help get sanctions against Russia lifted. He also said Trump lawyer Michael Cohen went to Prague for "secret discussions with Kremlin representatives and associated operators/hackers."

Most famously, he wrote the Kremlin had *kompromat* of Trump "deriling" [sic] a bed once used by Barack and Michelle Obama by "employing a number of prostitutes to perform a 'golden showers' (urination) show."

This was too good of a story not to do. By hook or crook, it had to come out. The first salvo was by David Corn of *Mother Jones* on October 31, 2016: "A Veteran Spy Has Given the FBI Information Alleging a Russian Operation to Cultivate Donald Trump."

The piece didn't have pee, Prague, or Page in it, but it did say Russian intelligence had material that could "blackmail" Trump. It was technically kosher to print because Corn wasn't publishing the allegations themselves, merely that the FBI had taken possession of them.

A bigger pretext was needed to get the other details out. This took place just after the election, when four intelligence officials presented copies of the dossier to both President-Elect Trump and outgoing president Obama.

From his own memos, we know FBI director James Comey, ostensibly evincing concern for Trump's welfare, told the new president he was just warning him about what was out there, as possible blackmail material:

> I wasn't saying [the Steele report] was true, only that I wanted him to know both that it had been reported and that the reports were in many hands. I said media like CNN had them and were looking for a news hook. I said it was important that we not give them the excuse to write that the FBI has the material or [redacted] and that we were keeping it very close-hold [sic].

Comey's generous warning to Trump about not providing a "news hook," along with a promise to keep it all "close-held," took place on January 6, 2017. Within four days, basically the entire Washington news media somehow knew all about this top-secret meeting and had the very hook they needed to go public. Nobody in the mainstream press thought this was weird or warranted comment.

Even Donald Trump was probably smart enough to catch the hint when, of all outlets, it was CNN that first broke the story of "Classified documents presented last week to Trump" on January 10.

At the same time, *Buzzfeed* made the historic decision to publish the entire Steele dossier, bringing years of pee into our lives. This move birthed the Russiagate phenomenon as a never-ending, minute-to-minute factor in American news coverage.

Comey was right. We couldn't have reported this story without a "hook." Therefore the reports surrounding Steele technically weren't about the allegations themselves, but rather the journey of those allegations, from one set of official hands to another. Handing the report to Trump created a perfect pretext.

This trick has been used before, both in Washington and on Wall Street, to publicize unconfirmed private research. A short seller might hire a consulting firm to prepare a report on a company he or she has bet against. When the report is completed, the investor then tries to get the SEC or the FBI to take possession. If they do, news leaks the company is "under investigation," the stock dives, and everyone wins.

This same trick is found in politics. A similar trajectory drove negative headlines in the scandal surrounding New Jersey's Democratic senator Bob Menendez, who was said to be under investigation by the FBI for underage sex crimes (although some were skeptical). The initial story didn't hold up, but led to other investigations.

Same with the so-called "Arkansas project," in which millions of Republican-friendly private research dollars produced enough noise about the Whitewater scandal to create years of headlines about the Clintons. Swiftboating was another example. Private oppo isn't inherently bad. In fact, it has led to some incredible scoops, including Enron. But reporters usually know to be skeptical of private info, and figure the motives of its patrons into the story.

The sequence of events in that second week of January 2017 will now need to be heavily re-examined. We now know, from his own testimony, that former Director of National Intelligence James Clapper had some kind of role in helping CNN do its report, presumably by confirming part of the story, perhaps through an intermediary or two (there is some controversy over whom exactly was contacted, and when).

Why would real security officials litigate this grave matter through the media? Why were the world's most powerful investigative agencies acting as though they were trying to move a stock, pushing a private, unverified report that even *Buzzfeed* could see had factual issues? It made no sense at the time, and makes less now.

In January of 2017, Steele's pile of allegations became public, read by millions. "It is not just unconfirmed," *Buzzfeed* admitted. "It includes some clear errors."

Buzzfeed's decision exploded traditional journalistic standards against knowingly publishing material whose veracity you doubt. Although a few media ethicists wondered at it, this seemed not to bother the rank-and-file in the business. *Buzzfeed* chief Ben Smith is still proud of his decision today. I think this was because many reporters believed the report was true.

When I read the report, I was in shock. I thought it read like fourth-rate suspense fiction (I should know: I write fourth-rate suspense fiction). Moreover it seemed edited both for public consumption and to please Steele's DNC patrons.

Steele wrote of Russians having a file of "compromising information" on Hillary Clinton, only this file supposedly lacked "details/evidence of unorthodox or embarrassing behavior" or "embarrassing conduct."

We were meant to believe the Russians, across decades of dirt-digging, had an empty *kompromat* file on Hillary Clinton, to say nothing of human tabloid headline Bill Clinton? This point was made more than once in the reports, as if being emphasized for the reading public.

There were other curious lines, including the bit about Russians having "moles" in the DNC, plus some linguistic details that made me wonder at the nationality of the report author.

Still, who knew? It could be true. But even the most cursory review showed the report had issues and would need a lot of confirming. This made it more amazing that the ranking Democrat on the House Intelligence Committee, Adam Schiff, held hearings on March 20, 2017, that blithely read out Steele report details as if they were fact. From Schiff's opening statement:

> According to Christopher Steele, a former British intelligence officer who is reportedly held in high regard by U.S. Intelligence, Russian sources tell him that Page has also had a secret meeting with Igor Sechin (SEH-CHIN), CEO of Russian gas giant Rosneft... Page is offered brokerage fees by Sechin on a deal involving a 19 percent share of the company.

I was stunned watching this. It's generally understood that members of Congress, like reporters, make an effort to vet at least their prepared remarks before making them public.

But here was Schiff, telling the world Trump aide Carter Page had been offered huge fees on a 19 percent stake in Rosneft—a company with a $63 *billion* market capitalization—in a secret meeting with a Russian oligarch who was also said to be "a KGB agent and close friend of Putin's."

(Schiff meant "FSB agent." The inability of #Russiagaters to remember Russia is not the Soviet Union became increasingly maddening over time. Donna Brazile still hasn't deleted her tweet about how "The Communists are now dictating the terms of the debate.")

Schiff's speech raised questions. Do we no longer have to worry about getting accusations right if the subject is tied to Russiagate? What if Page hadn't done any of these things? To date, he hasn't been charged with anything. Shouldn't a member of Congress worry about this?

A few weeks after that hearing, Steele gave testimony in a British lawsuit filed by one of the Russian companies mentioned in his reports. In a written submission, Steele said his information was "raw" and "needed to be analyzed and further investigated/verified." He also wrote that (at least as pertained to the memo in that case) he had not written his report "with the intention that it be republished to the world at large."

That itself was a curious statement, given that Steele reportedly spoke with multiple reporters in the fall of 2016, but this was his legal position. This story about Steele's British court statements did not make it into the news much in the United States, apart from a few bits in conservative outlets like the *Washington Times*.

I contacted Schiff's office to ask the congressman if he knew about Steele's admission that his report needed verifying, and if that changed his view of it at all. The response (emphasis mine):

> The dossier compiled by former British intelligence officer Christopher Steele and which was leaked publicly several months ago contains information that may be pertinent to our investigation. This is true regardless of whether it was ever intended for public dissemination. Accordingly, the Committee **hopes to speak with Mr. Steele** in order to **help substantiate or refute** each of the allegations contained in the dossier.

Schiff had not spoken to Steele before the hearing, and read out the allegations knowing they were unsubstantiated.

The Steele report was the Magna Carta of #Russiagate. It provided the implied context for thousands of news stories to come, yet no journalist was ever able to confirm its most salacious allegations: the five-year cultivation plan, the blackmail, the bribe from Sechin, the Prague trip, the pee romp, etc. In metaphorical terms, we were unable to independently produce Steele's results in the lab. Failure to reckon with this corrupted the narrative from the start.

For years, every hint the dossier might be true became a banner headline, while every time doubt was cast on Steele's revelations, the press was quiet. *Washington Post* reporter Greg Miller had a team looking for evidence

Cohen had been in Prague. Reporters, Miller said, "literally spent weeks and months trying to run down" the Cohen story.

"We sent reporters through every hotel in Prague... all over the place, just to try to figure out if he was ever there," he said, "and came away empty."

This was heads-I-win, tails-you-lose reporting. One assumes if Miller's crew found Cohen's name in a hotel ledger, it would have been on page 1 of the *Post*. The converse didn't get a mention in Miller's own paper. He only told the story during a discussion aired by C-SPAN about a new book he'd published. Only the *Daily Caller* and a few conservative blogs picked it up.

It was the same when Bob Woodward said, "I did not find [espionage or collusion]... Of course I looked for it, looked for it hard."

The celebrated Watergate muckraker—who once said he'd succumbed to "groupthink" in the WMD episode and added, "I blame myself mightily for not pushing harder"—didn't push very hard here, either. News that he'd tried and failed to find collusion didn't get into his own paper. It only came out when Woodward was promoting his book *Fear* in a discussion with conservative host Hugh Hewitt.

When Michael Cohen testified before congress and denied under oath ever being in Prague, it was the same. Few commercial news outlets bothered to take note of the implications this had for their previous reports. Would a man clinging to a plea deal lie to Congress on national television about this issue?

There was a CNN story, but the rest of the coverage was all in conservative outlets—the *National Review*, Fox, the *Daily Caller*. The *Washington Post's* response was to run an editorial sneering at "How conservative media downplayed Michael Cohen's testimony."

Perhaps worst of all was the episode involving *Yahoo!* reporter Michael Isikoff. He had already been part of one strange tale: the FBI double-dipping when it sought a FISA warrant to conduct secret surveillance of Carter Page, the would-be mastermind who was supposed to have brokered a deal with oligarch Sechin.

In its FISA application, the FBI included both the unconfirmed Steele report and Isikoff's September 23, 2016, *Yahoo!* story, "U.S. intel officials probe ties between Trump adviser and Kremlin." The Isikoff story, which claimed Page had met with "high ranking sanctioned officials" in Russia, had relied upon Steele as an unnamed source.

But there was virtually no non-conservative press about this problem apart from a *Washington Post* story pooh-poohing the issue. (Every news story that casts any doubt on the collusion issue seems to meet with an instantaneous "fact check" in the *Post*.) The *Post* insisted the FISA issue wasn't serious among other things because Steele was not the "foundation" of Isikoff's piece.

Isikoff was perhaps the reporter most familiar with Steele. He and Corn of *Mother Jones*, who also dealt with the ex-spy, wrote a bestselling book that relied upon theories from Steele, *Russian Roulette*, including a rumination on the "pee" episode. Yet Isikoff in late 2018 suddenly said he believed the Steele report would turn out to be "mostly false."

Once again, this only came out via a podcast, John Ziegler's "Free Speech Broadcasting" show. Here's a transcript of the relevant section:

> **Isikoff:** When you actually get into the details of the Steele dossier, the specific allegations, you know, we have not seen the evidence to support them. And in fact there is good grounds to think some of the more sensational allegations will never be proven, and are likely false.
> **Ziegler:** That's...
> **Isikoff:** I think it's a mixed record at best at this point, things could change, Mueller may yet produce evidence that changes this calculation. But based on the public record at this point I have to say that most of the specific allegations have not been borne out.
> **Ziegler:** That's interesting to hear you say that, Michael because as I'm sure you know, your book was kind of used to validate the pee tape, for lack of a better term.
> **Isikoff:** Yeah. I think we had some evidence in there of an event that may have inspired the pee tape and that was the visit that Trump made with a number of characters who later showed up in Moscow, specifically Emin Agalarov and Rob Goldstone to this raunchy Las Vegas nightclub where one of the regular acts was a skit called "Hot for Teacher" in which dancers posing as college co-ed's urinated—or simulated urinating on their professor. Which struck me as an odd coincidence at best. I think, you know, it is not implausible that event may have inspired...
> **Ziegler:** An urban legend?
> **Isikoff:** ...allegations that appeared in the Steele dossier.

Isikoff delivered this story with a laughing tone. He seamlessly transitioned to what he then called the "real" point, i.e. "the irony is Steele may be right, but it wasn't the Kremlin that had sexual *kompromat* on Donald Trump, it was the *National Enquirer.*"

Recapping: the reporter who introduced Steele to the world (his September 23, 2016 story was the first to reference him as a source), who wrote a book that even he concedes was seen as "validating" the pee tape story, suddenly backtracks and says the whole thing may have been based on a Las Vegas strip act, but it doesn't matter because Stormy Daniels, etc.

Another story of this type involved a court case in which Webzilla and parent company XBT sued Steele and Buzzfeed over the mention of their firm in one of the memos. It came out in court testimony that Steele had culled information about XBT/Webzilla from a 2009 post on CNN's "iReports" page.

When asked if he understood that these posts came from random users and not CNN journalists who'd been fact-checked, Steele replied, "I do not."

There were so many profiles of Steele as an "astoundingly diligent" spymaster straight out of LeCarré: he was routinely described as a LeCarréian grinder, similar in appearance and manner to the legendary George Smiley. He was a man in the shadows whose bookish intensity was belied by his "average," "neutral," "quiet," demeanor, being "more low-key than Smiley." One would think it might have rated a mention that the new "Smiley" was cutting and pasting text like a community college freshman. But the story barely made news.

This has been a consistent pattern throughout #Russiagate. Step one: salacious headline. Step two, days or weeks later: news emerges the story is shakier than first believed. Step three (in the best case) involves the story being walked back or retracted by the same publication.

That's been rare. More often, when explosive #Russiagate headlines go sideways, the original outlets simply ignore the new development, leaving the "retraction" process to conservative outlets that don't reach the original audiences.

This is a major structural flaw of the new fully divided media landscape in which Republican media covers Democratic corruption and Democratic media covers Republican corruption. If neither "side" feels the need to disclose its own errors and inconsistencies, mistakes accumulate quickly.

This has been the main reportorial difference between Russiagate and the WMD affair. Despite David Remnick's post-invasion protestations that "nobody got [WMD] completely right," the Iraq War was launched against the objections of the 6 million or more people who did get it right, and protested on the streets. There was open skepticism of Bush claims dotting the press landscape from the start, with people like Jack Shafer tearing apart every Judith Miller story in print. Most reporters are Democrats and the people hawking the WMD story were mostly Republicans, so there was at least some political space for protest.

#Russiagate happened in an opposite context. If the story fell apart it would benefit Donald Trump politically, a fact that made a number of reporters queasy about coming forward. #Russiagate became synonymous with #Resistance, which made public skepticism a complicated proposition.

Early in the scandal, I appeared on *To the Point,* a California-based public radio show hosted by Warren Olney, with Corn of *Mother Jones.* I knew David a little and had been friendly with him. He once hosted a book event for me in Washington. In the program, however, the subject of getting facts right came up and Corn said this was not a time for reporters to be picking nits:

> So Democrats getting overeager, over-enthusiastic, stating things that may not be [unintelligible] true...? Well, tell me a political issue where that doesn't happen. I think that's looking at the wrong end of the telescope.

I wrote him later and suggested that since we're in the press, and not really about anything except avoiding "things that may not be true," maybe we had different responsibilities than "Democrats"? He wrote back:

"Feel free to police the Trump opposition. But on the list of shit that needs to be covered these days, that's just not high on my personal list."

Other reporters spoke of an internal struggle. When the Mueller indictment of the Internet Research Agency was met with exultation in the media, *New Yorker* writer Adrian Chen, who broke the original IRA story, was hesitant to come forward with some mild qualms about the way the story was being reported:

"Either I could stay silent and allow the conversation to be dominated by those pumping up the Russian threat," he said, "or I could risk giving fodder to Trump and his allies."

After writing, "Confessions of a Russiagate Skeptic," poor Blake Hounsell of *Politico* took such a beating on social media, he ended up denouncing himself a year later.

"What I meant to write is, I *wasn't* skeptical," he said.

Years ago, in the midst of the WMD affair, *Times* public editor Daniel Okrent noted the paper's standard had moved from "Don't get it first, get it right" to "Get it first and get it right." From there, Okrent wrote, "the next devolution was an obvious one."

We're at that next devolution: first and wrong. The Russiagate era has so degraded journalism that even once "reputable" outlets are now only about as right as politicians, which is to say barely ever, and then only by accident.

Early on, I was so amazed by the sheer quantity of Russia "bombshells" being disavowed, I started to keep a list. It's well above fifty stories now. As has been noted by Glenn Greenwald of *The Intercept* and others, if the mistakes were random, you'd expect them in both directions, but Russiagate errors uniformly go the same way.

In some cases the stories are only partly wrong, as in the case of the famed "17 intelligence agencies said Russia was behind the hacking" story (it was actually four: the Director of National Intelligence "hand-picking" a team from the FBI, CIA, and NSA).

In other cases the stories were blunt false starts, resulting in ugly sets of matching headlines:

"Russian operation hacked a Vermont utility"
Washington Post, December 31, 2016.

"Russian government hackers do not appear to have targeted Vermont utility"
Washington Post, Jan. 2, 2017.

"Trump Campaign Aides had repeated contacts with Russian Intelligence," published by the *Times* on Valentine's Day, 2017, was an important, narrative-driving "bombshell" that looked dicey from the start. The piece didn't say whether the contact was witting or unwitting, whether the discussions were about business or politics, or what the contacts supposedly were at all.

Normally a reporter would want to know what the deal is before he or she runs a story accusing people of having dealings with foreign spies. "Witting" or "Unwitting" ought to be a huge distinction, for instance. Soon after, it came out that people like former CIA chief John Brennan don't think this is the case. "Frequently, people who are on a treasonous path do not know they're on a treasonous path," he said, speaking of Trump's circle.

This seemed a dangerous argument, the kind of thing that led to trouble in the McCarthy years. But let's say the contacts were serious. From a reporting point of view, you'd still need to know exactly what the nature of such contacts were before you run that story, because the headline implication is grave. Moreover you'd need to know it well enough to report it, i.e. it's not sufficient to be told a convincing story off-the-record, you need to be able to share a substantial amount with readers so that they can characterize the news themselves.

Later, Comey blew up the "contacts" story, saying, "in the main, it was not true."

As was the case with the "17 agencies" error, which only got fixed when Clapper testified in congress and was forced to make the correction under oath, the "repeated contacts" story was only disputed when Comey testified in Congress, this time before the Senate Intelligence Committee. How many other errors of this type are waiting to be disclosed?

Even the mistakes caught were astounding. On December 1, 2017, ABC reporter Brian Ross claimed Trump "as a candidate" instructed Michael Flynn to contact Russia. The news caused the Dow to plummet 350 points. The story was retracted almost immediately and Ross was suspended.

Bloomberg reported Mueller subpoenaed Trump's Deutsche Bank accounts; the subpoenas turned out to be of other individuals' records. *Fortune* said C-SPAN was hacked after Russia Today programming briefly interrupted coverage of a Maxine Waters floor address. The *New York Times* also ran the story, and it's still up, despite C-SPAN insisting its own "internal routing error" likely caused the feed to appear in place of its own broadcast.

CNN has its own separate sub-list of wrecks. Three of the network's journalists resigned after a story purporting to tie Trump advisor Anthony Scaramucci to a Russian investment fund was retracted. Four more CNN reporters (Gloria Borger, Eric Lichtblau, Jake Tapper and Brian Rokus) were bylined in a story that claimed Comey was expected to refute Trump's claims he was told he wasn't the target of an investigation. Comey blew that one up, too.

In another CNN scoop gone awry, "Email pointed Trump campaign to WikiLeaks documents," the network's reporters were off by ten days in a "bombshell" that supposedly proved the Trump campaign had foreknowledge of Wikileaks dumps. "It's, uh, perhaps not as significant as what we know now," offered CNN's Manu Raju in a painful on-air retraction.

The worst stories were the ones never corrected. A particularly bad example is "After Florida School Shooting, Russian 'Bot' Army Pounced," from the *New York Times* on February 18, 2018. The piece claimed Russians were trying to divide Americans on social media after a mass shooting using Twitter hashtags like #guncontrolnow, #gunreformnow and #Parklandshooting.

The *Times* ran this quote high up:

> "This is pretty typical for them, to hop on breaking news like this," said Jonathon Morgan, chief executive of New Knowledge, a company that tracks online disinformation campaigns. "The bots focus on anything that is divisive for Americans. Almost systematically."

About a year after this story came out, *Times* reporters Scott Shane and Ann Blinder reported that the same outfit, New Knowledge, and in particular that same Jonathon Morgan, had participated in a cockamamie scheme to fake Russian troll activity in an Alabama Senate race. The idea was to try to convince voters Russia preferred the Republican.

The *Times* quoted a New Knowledge internal report about the idiotic Alabama scheme:

> We orchestrated an elaborate 'false flag' operation that planted the idea that the Moore campaign was amplified on social media by a Russian botnet...

The Parkland story was iffy enough when it came out, as Twitter disputed it, and another of the main sources for the initial report, former intelligence official Clint Watts, subsequently said he was "not convinced" regarding the whole "bot thing."

But when one of your top sources turns out to have faked exactly the kind of activity described in your article, you should at least take the quote out, or put an update online. No luck: the story remains up on the *Times* site, without disclaimers.

Russiagate institutionalized one of the worst ethical loopholes in journalism, which used to be limited mainly to local crime reporting. It's always been a problem that we publish mugshots and names of people merely arrested but not yet found guilty.

With Russiagate the national press abandoned any pretense that there's a difference between indictment and conviction. The most disturbing story involved Maria Butina. Here authorities and the press shared responsibility. Thanks to an indictment that initially said the Russian traded sex for favors, the *Times* and other outlets flooded the news cycle with breathless stories about a redheaded slut-temptress come to undermine democracy, a "real-life Red Sparrow," as ABC put it.

But a judge threw out the sex charge after "five minutes" when it turned out to be based on a single joke text to a friend who had taken Butina's car for inspection.

It's pretty hard to undo the public perception you're a prostitute once it's been in a headline, and, worse, the headlines are still out there. You can still find stories like "Maria Butina, Suspected Secret Agent, Used Sex in Covert Plan" online in the *New York Times*.

Here a reporter might protest: how would I know? Prosecutors said she traded sex for money. Why shouldn't I believe them?

How about because, authorities have been lying their faces off to reporters since before electricity! It doesn't take much investigation to realize the main institutional sources in the Russiagate mess—the security services, mainly—have extensive records of deceiving the media.

As previously mentioned, Reagan's National Security Advisor John Poindexter used the press, including the *Wall Street Journal*, to spread false stories about Libya. And in the Bush years, Dick Cheney et al. were selling manure by the truckload about various connections between Iraq and al-Qaeda, infamously including a story that bomber Mohammed Atta met with Iraqi intelligence officials in Prague.

The *New York Times* ran a story that Atta was in Prague in late October of 2001, even giving a date of the meeting with Iraqis, April 8, or "just five months before the terrorist attacks." The Prague story was another example of a tale that seemed shaky because American officials were putting the sourcing first on foreign intelligence, then on reporters themselves. Cheney cited the Prague report in subsequent TV appearances, one of many instances of feeding reporters tidbits and then selling reports as independent confirmation.

It wasn't until three years later, in 2004, that *Times* reporter James Risen definitively killed the Atta-in-Prague canard (why is it always Prague?) in a story entitled "No evidence of meeting with Iraqi." By then, of course, it was too late. The *Times* also held a major dissenting piece by Risen about the WMD case, "C.I.A. Aides Feel Pressure in Preparing Iraqi Reports," until days after war started. This is what happens when you start thumbing the scale.

This failure to demand specifics has been epidemic in Russiagate, even when good reporters have been involved. One of the biggest "revelations" of this era involved a story that was broken first by a terrible reporter (the *Guardian*'s Luke Harding) and followed up by a good one (Jane Mayer of the *New Yorker*). The key detail involved the elusive origin story of Russiagate.

Mayer's piece, the March 12, 2018 "Christopher Steele, the Man Behind The Trump Dossier" in the *New Yorker*, impacted the public mainly by seeming to bolster the credentials of the dossier author. But it contained an explosive nugget far down. Mayer reported Robert Hannigan, then-head of the GCHQ (the British analog to the NSA) intercepted a "stream of illicit communications" between "Trump's team and Moscow" at some point prior to August 2016. Hannigan flew to the U.S. and briefed CIA director John Brennan about these communications. Brennan later testified that this inspired the original FBI investigation.

When I read that, a million questions came to mind, but first: what did "illicit" mean?

If something "illicit" had been captured by GCHQ, and this led to the FBI investigation (one of several conflicting public explanations for the start of the FBI probe, incidentally), this would go a long way toward clearing up the nature of the collusion charge. If they had something, why couldn't they tell us what it was? Why didn't we deserve to know?

I asked the *Guardian*: "Was any attempt made to find out what those communications were? How was the existence of these communications confirmed? Did anyone from the *Guardian* see or hear these intercepts, or transcripts?"

Their one-sentence reply:

The Guardian has strict and rigorous procedures when dealing with source material.

That's the kind of answer you'd expect from a transnational bank, or the army, not a newspaper.

I asked Mayer the same questions. She was more forthright, noting that the story had originally been broken by Harding, whose own report said "the precise nature of these exchanges has not been made public."

She added that "afterwards I independently confirmed aspects of [Harding's piece] with several well-informed sources," and "spent months on the Steele story [and] traveled to the UK twice for it." But, she wrote, "the Russiagate story, like all reporting on sensitive national security issues, is difficult."

I can only infer that she couldn't find out what "illicit" meant despite proper effort. The detail was published anyway. It may not have seemed like a big deal, but I think it was.

To be clear, I don't necessarily disbelieve the idea that there were "illicit" contacts between Trump and Russians in early 2015 or before. But if there were such contacts, I can't think of any legitimate reason why their nature should be withheld from the public.

If authorities can share reasons for concern with foreign countries like Israel, why should American voters not be so entitled? Moreover the idea that we need to keep things secret to protect sources and methods and "tradecraft" (half the press corps became expert in goofy spy language over the last few years, using terms like "SIGINT" like they've known them their whole lives), why are we leaking news of our ability to hear Russian officials cheering Trump's win?

Failure to ask follow-up questions happened constantly with this story. One of the first reports that went sideways involved a similar dynamic: the contention that some leaked DNC emails were forgeries.

MSNBC's "intelligence commentator" Malcolm Nance, perhaps the most enthusiastic source of questionable #Russiagate news this side of Twitter conspiracist Louise Mensch, tweeted on October 11, 2016: "#PodestaEmails are already proving to be riddled with obvious forgeries & #blackpropaganda not even professionally done."

As noted in *The Intercept* and elsewhere, this was re-reported by the likes of David Frum (a key member of the club that has now contributed to both the

WMD and Russiagate panics) and MSNBC host Joy Reid. The reports didn't stop until roughly October of 2016, among other things because the Clinton campaign kept suggesting to reporters the emails were fake. This could have been stopped sooner if examples of a forgery had been demanded from the Clinton campaign earlier.

Another painful practice that became common was failing to confront your own sources when news dispositive to what they've told you pops up. The omnipresent Clapper told Chuck Todd on March 5, 2017, without equivocation, that there had been no FISA application involving Trump or his campaign. "I can deny it," he said.

It soon after came out this wasn't true. The FBI had a FISA warrant on Carter Page. This was not a small misstatement by Clapper, because his appearance came a day after Trump claimed in a tweet he'd had his "wires tapped." Trump was widely ridiculed for this claim, perhaps appropriately so, but in addition to the Page news, it later came out there had been a FISA warrant of Paul Manafort as well, during which time Trump may have been the subject of "incidental" surveillance.

Whether or not this was meaningful, or whether these warrants were justified, are separate questions. The important thing is, Clapper either lied to Todd, or else he somehow didn't know the FBI had obtained these warrants. The latter seems absurd and unlikely. Either way, Todd ought to been peeved and demanded an explanation. Instead, he had Clapper back on again within months and gave him the usual softball routine, never confronting him about the issue.

Reporters repeatedly got burned and didn't squawk about it. Where are the outraged stories about all the scads of anonymous "people familiar with the matter" who put reporters in awkward spots in the last years? Why isn't McClatchy demanding the heads of whatever "four people with knowledge" convinced them to double down on the Cohen-in-Prague story?

Why isn't every reporter who used "New Knowledge" as a source about salacious Russian troll stories out for their heads (or the heads of the congressional sources who passed this stuff on), after reports they faked Russian trolling? How is it possible NBC and other outlets continued to use New Knowledge as a source in stories identifying antiwar Democrat Tulsi Gabbard as a Russian-backed candidate?

How do the *Guardian*'s editors not already have Harding's head in a vice for hanging them out to dry on the most dubious un-retracted story in modern history—the tale that the most watched human on earth, Julian Assange, had somehow been visited in the Ecuadorian embassy by Paul Manafort without leaving any record? I'd be dragging Harding's "well placed source" into the office and beating him with a hose until he handed them something that would pass for corroborating evidence.

The lack of blowback over episodes in which reporters were put in compromised public situations speaks to the overly cozy relationships outlets had with official sources. Too often, it felt like a team effort, where reporters seemed to think it was their duty to take the weight if sources pushed them to overreach. They had absolutely no sense of institutional self-esteem about this.

Being on any team is a bad look for the press, but the press being on team FBI/CIA is an atrocity, Trump or no Trump. Why bother having a press corps at all if you're going to go that route?

This posture has all been couched as anti-Trump solidarity, but really, did former CIA chief John Brennan—the same Brennan who should himself have faced charges for lying to Congress about hacking the computers of Senate staff—need the press to whine on his behalf when Trump yanked his security clearance? Did we need the press to hum Aretha Franklin tunes, as ABC did, and chide Trump for lacking R-E-S-P-E-C-T for the CIA? We don't have better things to do than that "work"?

This catalogue of factual errors and slavish stenography will stand out when future analysts look back at why the "MSM" became a joke during this period, but they were only a symptom of a larger problem. The bigger issue was a radical change in approach.

A lot of #Russiagate coverage became straight-up conspiracy theory, what Baker politely called "connecting the dots." This was allowed because the press committed to a collusion narrative from the start, giving everyone cover to indulge in behaviors that would never be permitted in normal times.

Such was the case with Jonathan Chait's #Russiagate opus, "PRUMP TUTIN: Will Trump be Meeting With his Counterpart—or his Handler?" The story was also pitched as "What If Trump Has Been a Russian Asset Since 1987?" which recalls the joke from *The Wire*: "Yo, Herc, what if your mother and father never met?" *What if* isn't a good place to be in this business.

This cover story (!) in *New York* magazine was released in advance of a planned "face-to-face" summit between Trump and Putin, and posited Trump had been under Russian control for decades. Chait noted Trump visited the Soviet Union in 1987 and came back "fired up with political ambition." He offered the possibility that this was a coincidence, but added: "Indeed, it seems slightly insane to contemplate the possibility that a secret relation-ship between Trump and Russia dates back this far. But it can't be dismissed completely."

I searched the Chait article up and down for reporting that would justify the suggestion Trump had been a Russian agent dating back to the late eighties, when, not that it matters, Russia was a different country called the Soviet Union.

Only two facts in the piece could conceivably have been used to support the thesis: Trump met with a visiting Soviet official in 1986, and visited the Soviet Union in 1987. That's it. That's your cover story.

Worse, Chait's theory was first espoused in Lyndon LaRouche's "Elephants and Donkeys" newsletter in 1987, under a headline, "Do Russians have a Trump card?" This is barrel-scraping writ large.

It's a mania. Putin is literally in our underpants. Maybe, if we're lucky, *New York* might someday admit its report claiming Russians set up an anti-masturbation hotline to trap and blackmail random Americans is suspicious, not just because it seems absurd on its face, but because its source is the same "New Knowledge" group that admitted to faking Russian influence operations in Alabama.

But what retraction is possible for the *Washington Post* headline, "How will Democrats cope if Putin starts playing dirty tricks for Bernie Sanders (again)?" How to reverse Rachel Maddow's spiel about Russia perhaps shutting down heat across America during a cold wave? There's no correction for McCarthyism and fearmongering.

This ultimately will be the endgame of the Russia charade. They will almost certainly never find anything like the wild charges and Manchurian Candidate theories elucidated in the Steele report. But the years of panic over the events of 2016 will lead to radical changes in everything from press regulation to foreign policy, just as the WMD canard led to torture, warrantless surveillance, rendition, drone assassination, secret budgets and open-ended, undeclared wars from

Somalia to Niger to Syria. The screw-ups will be forgotten, but accelerated vigilance will remain.

It's hard to know what policy changes are appropriate because the reporting on everything involving the Russian threat over the last two to three years has been so unreliable.

I didn't really address the case that Russia hacked the DNC, content to stipulate it for now. I was told early on that this piece of the story seemed "solid," but even that assertion has remained un-bolstered since then, still based on an "assessment" by those same intelligence services that always had issues, including the use of things like RT's "anti-American" coverage of fracking as part of its case. The government didn't even examine the DNC's server[1], the kind of detail that used to make reporters nervous.

We won't know how much of any of this to take seriously until the press gets out of bed with the security services and looks at this whole series of events all over again with fresh eyes, as journalists, not political actors. Which means being open to asking what went wrong with this story, in addition to focusing so much energy on Trump and Russia.

The WMD mess had massive real-world negative impact, leading to over a hundred thousand deaths and trillions in lost taxpayer dollars. Unless Russiagate leads to a nuclear conflict, we're unlikely to ever see that level of consequence.

Still, Russiagate has led to unprecedented cooperation between the government and Internet platforms like Facebook, Twitter, and Google, all of which are censoring pages on the left, right, and in between in the name of preventing the "sowing of discord." The story also had a profound impact on the situation in places like Syria, where Russian and American troops have sat across the Euphrates River from one another, two amped-up nuclear powers at a crossroads.

As a purely journalistic failure, however, WMD was a pimple compared to Russiagate. The sheer scale of the errors and exaggerations this time around dwarfs the last mess. Worse, it's led to most journalists accepting a radical change

---

1 James Comey's testimony: "Although we got access to the forensics from the pros that they hired, which again—best practice to get access to the machines themselves, but my folks tell me was an appropriate substitute."

in mission. We've become sides-choosers, obliterating the concept of the press as an independent institution whose primary role is sorting fact and fiction.

We had the sense to eventually look inward a little in the WMD affair, which is the only reason we escaped that episode with any audience left. Is the press capable of that kind of self-awareness now? WMD damaged our reputation. If we don't turn things around, this story will destroy it.

APPENDIX 1: WHY RACHEL MADDOW IS ON THE COVER OF THIS BOOK

First, a note in defense of iconic MSNBC host Rachel Maddow:

On the evening of Friday, March 22, 2019, when word leaked out that Special Counsel Robert Mueller had wrapped up his investigation and was heading home without recommending new charges, the eyes of the collective journalism world darted in Maddow's direction.

A massive machinery of ass-covering began whirring. Maddow was the industry name most intimately connected with collusion. She was practically the Madame DeFarge of Russiagate. In 2017 and 2018, *The Rachel Maddow Show* transformed into the *Trump is a Russian Agent* show, in which each night a new piece of the conspiracy would be stitched into view for audiences. This put her in some career jeopardy if Trump turned out not to be quite so guilty.

It had been a wire-to-wire routine. When Trump was inaugurated, she quipped, "We're about to find out if the new president of our country is going to do what Russia wants." She and fellow MSNBC host Lawrence O'Donnell wondered aloud if Trump attacked Syria in early 2017 as part of a Putin-orchestrated plan to make him look less Putin-dependent.

She described the Trump presidency as a "continuing operation" of Russian influence. She suggested Trump appointments were done at Russian behest, and dished innuendo freely, saying, for instance, that Trump was "curiously well-versed" in Russian talking points. Most infamously, during a national cold front in early 2019, she asked her audience, if "Russia killed the power in Fargo today," then "What would you and your family do?"

It worked, financially most of all. The Russia story helped make Rachel Maddow the number one cable news host in the country in 2017, smashing her Obama-era ratings. Her ascent continued through early 2019, when she eclipsed three million viewers for the first time, an astonishing number for a former little-known host of *Air America* radio.

Those ratings turned into record profits for MSNBC, making her a rarity within a news business that traditionally struggles on the cash front: a bankable star.

When the Mueller finding of no conspiracy or coordination came back, the leading hotshots in the industry made an instant calculation: Maddow's two years of conspiratorial rants probably could not be defended. Almost immediately, in the peculiar way my colleagues in the press have when it comes to facing adversity with a sense of bravery and togetherness, they decided to toss her overboard.

The letter by Attorney General William Barr quoting the Mueller report on collusion came out on a Sunday, March 24. By the next morning, Monday, March 25, the new conventional wisdom was that *if* mistakes were made, it was the fault of cable news, a small inconsequential island of suckage in a vast sea of responsible journalism. The turnover was so fast, editorials against her must have begun being written more or less at the moment the Barr letter landed.

Some pundits didn't name Maddow by name. But everyone knew who media writer Margaret Sullivan of the *Washington Post* was talking about when she said the Mueller decision wasn't a reflection on "serious" journalists.

If anyone had to wear the black eye, Sullivan wrote, it would be "cable pundits" who "make a living off speculation" and those "ridiculous" explosions made by "tiny cannons on Twitter." *Those* people, Sullivan sneered, "aren't really journalists anyway."

From there, the floodgates opened. "Commentary television is not news," snapped David Cay Johnston of the *New York Times,* himself just days removed from saying on *Democracy Now!* that "I think [Trump] is a Russian agent."

He added: "Rachel Maddow in particular has certainly pushed the Mueller matter," doing so in conjunction with "the facts at the time." However, he said, her work was "driven by the commercial values of television."

"Cable television," wrote Columbia Journalism School Dean Steve Coll in the *New Yorker,* "mixes field reporting and news-making interviews with personal asides from prime-time personalities and roundtables of bombast-mongers."

After Mueller's "March surprise" (which wasn't a surprise to me and a lot of other reporters), Coll added it would be "unrealistic" to expect audiences to make the distinction between "editorializing and reporting."

"Yes, the mainstream press gave too much credence to the Steele dossier and rushed to publish too quickly on seemingly incriminating stories," piled on Ross Douthat at the *New York Times*. "But as long as you got news from somewhere other than Rachel Maddow the case for skepticism was amply available as well."

These people all worked in organizations that either bungled Russia stories as MSNBC did, or shamelessly hyped fears to boost ad sales as MSNBC did, or both.

Douthat's *New York Times* outstripped Rachel's act with its insane infographic series, *Operation Infektion: Russian Disinformation from the Cold War to Kanye*. (Kanye!) Maddow never described Russia, as this *Times* animation piece did, as a virus literally eating us alive at the cellular level. She was never so shameless as to blame Russia for your creeping sensation that the American media is not awesome at its job. From *Infektion:*

"If you don't know who to trust anymore, this might be the thing that's making you feel that way," the *Times* suggested, over graphics of red disease eating your cells. "If you feel exhausted by the news, this could be why."

Absent a crazy new development, Rachel will almost certainly be turned into the Judith Miller of Russiagate, the human symbol of What Went Wrong. Just like Judith Miller, she won't deserve to wander the desert alone.

Future commentators will probably make note of the obvious fact that in both cases outspoken women ended up being the ones herded out of the village by colleagues, forced to wear the yoke of journalistic blame. Make what you will of that, but it's not all on her.

Rachel Maddow is not on the cover of this book because of anything she did by mistake, because Russiagate turned out to be a bad guess.

She's on the cover because of what she did on purpose, with the core concept of both her program and her public image, before the Russia story. She transformed from a sharp-minded, gregarious, small-time radio host to a towering patriotic media cudgel, a depressingly exact mirror of Hannity.

Because I still live in the New York area, because most of my friends vote Democratic, and because I work for a liberal-leaning magazine, I heard much protest and rending of garments when the proposed cover art for *Hate Inc.* was released, showing Rachel Maddow sharing top billing with Sean Hannity.

"How can you even compare Rachel Maddow to Sean Hannity?" people barked. It's preposterous! *Unforgivable!* A cheap hot take!

No, it's not. The two characters do exactly the same work. They make their money using exactly the same commercial formula. And though they emphasize different political ideas, the effect they have on audiences is much the same.

The major difference is one is smarter than the other, which is not actually a mark in Rachel's favor. If anything, it's a check against her. Sean Hannity's one-note brain (seemingly located in his neck) and relentless enthusiasm for high-volume blame-seeking appear genetic, deficits he was born with to help him become a perfect Anger-TV pitchman.

Rachel had to think her way into this job. She's smart enough to know better.

I know this because I've known Rachel for more than a decade, going back to her *Air America* radio days.

We met in the Bush years, at the heat of the march to the Iraq War, when she laughed at the crude appeals to national unity and the fear-based marketing of the invasion. Even years later, she lampooned the idea of intelligence agencies being ordered to "Find the evidence."

The Maddow I knew thought all of this was absurd (perhaps even more absurd than angering). I admired her as someone who was smart, quick, and funny. She has since sacrificed even her sense of humor to MSNBC, letting the network commoditize this side of her to the point of unrecognizability.

Her personal politics, at least from what I remember, are further to the progressive side than the hawkish mainstream Democratic line that makes up the meat of her program today. She's even, to small degrees, expressed her sense of being personally distant from the Democratic party on other formats, like *Late Night with Seth Myers.*

That she is now a flag-waver and the country's strictest partisan blows my mind. It's the stuff of movies, one in particular.

***

A Face in the Crowd, the 1957 film by *On the Waterfront* director Elia Kazan, tells a story of a drunken drifter named Larry Rhodes, discovered by an idealistic reporter. The drifter, played by then-unknown Andy Griffith, has natural charm, wit, and an ability to connect with crowds.

He is eventually given a TV program under the new name of "Lonesome" Rhodes. Griffith uses it to create a homespun, aw-shucks, man-of-the-people act that makes him more powerful than politicians.

The movie was diffidently received in 1957, because it was about the as-yet undiscovered power of television. It was revived and praised by liberal commentators in the late 2000s, given credit for predicting the rise of people like Glenn Beck.

James Wolcott of *Vanity Fair* in 2007 described *A Face in the Crowd* as a movie about a man who becomes the "puppet of a populist scheme orchestrated by corporate overlords, who exploit his likability as a lever of social control."

What the movie described, and what the late-fifties public wasn't yet ready to understand, was the power of media to use non-intellectual cues and personality to deliver votes in great sacks. Politicians may gather big tents of disparate constituencies; media figures deliver *fans*. Their followers' support is more insoluble than that of politicians.

"I'm not just an entertainer," Rhodes roars in the film. "I'm an influencer, a wielder of opinion. A force!"

Kazan and screenwriter Budd Schulberg were most afraid that a Rhodes-like character would be appropriated by upper-class, and probably right-wing, pols. It was a keen parable about the coming American culture war, with Rhodes discovered in the sticks and used to sell the upper-crust politics of a California senator named Worthington Fuller.

Rhodes says things like, "I wish you'd give me the cotton-pickin' truth on how you feel about more and more and more Social Security." At which point we learn from homespun Rhodes that the original Americans only needed an axe and a gun, not no derned pension insurance.

The concept of wedding low-information voters to self-defeating initiatives has been a terror of progressive commentators for years. This is why Rhodes was invariably cited as having predicted the rise of types like Ronald Reagan, George H. W. Bush, Beck, Rush Limbaugh, and Donald Trump.

A Face in the Crowd should have been a warning that any kind of superficial cultural identifiers could be used to sell political lines. It isn't just rubes who can be taken in. The college-and-coffee crowd is just as susceptible to brand-over-thought come-ons, and can even fall for appeals to fear and patriotism. The pitchman will be different, but it will still be a pitch.

"In time of imminent crisis and danger," Rhodes grins in the film, "who could rally the people better than I could?"

It's hard to imagine a character less like Larry Rhodes in real life than Rachel Maddow. But the journey ends up being similar. Just as it did with Rhodes, TV ate the person underneath, and used her superficial qualities to sell a political product.

Unfortunately, today's bestselling product is partisan division.

***

People like Margaret Sullivan are half-right. Cable news hosts aren't "journalists" in the traditional sense. They're not selling news but an entertainment product, one that hooks audiences on rhetorical pace and conspiratorial energy.

The cable host is a ship captain, imploring audiences to pull oars. The aim is to drive narratives ever faster, faster, faster, toward a dot on the horizon that distantly represents undefined political triumph, a promised land for viewers.

The oars all have to be pulling in the same direction for this to work. For this reason, you can't invite dissenting voices on unless they're there to be ritually dismantled. This formula used to be exclusive to Fox, whose anchors until recently were the only practitioners of the genre who were any good at it.

Hannity's schtick epitomizes the formula. *The Sean Hannity Show* is an uncomplicated gruel of resentment, vituperation and doomsaying. The plot never changes:

The Democrats are always up to no good, and Captain Sean is there every night to point you toward the secret truth about the *huge short-sighted political mistake the Democrats just made!* (This is one of his favorite segment themes). He'll show you how the mainstream media elite is laughing at you, and trying to force a Leninist program of wealth redistribution, gun confiscation, forced abortion and anti-Christian cultural hegemony down your throat.

Those same *libruls* want to open the borders and replace you at work with an immigrant, who incidentally will be encouraged to vote at least three times.

Every show is some variation on these themes. He'll have on a series of guests to provide context (read: to agree with him in their own words). A recent list of Hannity guests: Donald Trump, Donald Trump, Jr., Ted Cruz, Rush Limbaugh, Rudy Giuliani, Lindsey Graham, Devin Nunes, Alan Dershowitz, Joe Lieberman, Glenn Beck, etc.

Hannity will occasionally do "balance," and what "balance" looks like on one of these channels is a member of the other party (because no other forms of thought exist). The alien will come on to be grilled and, hopefully, defeated. It should be noted that Fox seems to do this more often than MSNBC these days, not that this is necessarily a good thing.

Tucker Carlson seems to do it more than most, probably because he has the most experience with this format from his *Crossfire* days and is better at it than anyone. Hannity of course did it, too, with *Hannity & Colmes*—although Colmes was an obvious Washington Generals act designed to make Hannity look good, while Carlson occasionally had to break a sweat in his pummelings of faux-liberals like Paul Begala.

But "balance" does happen. Donna Brazile, for instance, actually has a decent relationship with Hannity (I even found an episode where she calls him "Boo"). The dance in those episodes is undisguised, symbiotic PR.

Brazile will come on, win over a small slice of Hannity's audience by conceding that he is technically a human being, then plug something like a book. Hannity meanwhile will make sure audiences don't doubt his bona fides for a second, by relentlessly haranguing her about socialism or the Green New Deal or whatever.

This is a huge tell in modern division-media: when the alien idea is allowed on air, it never gets a polite hearing. It isn't allowed to answer at length. Questions are framed as you hear them from prosecutors confronting a defense witness. An example is Tucker Carlson interviewing California Democrat Adam Schiff about Russian interference.

First, Carlson agreed that hacking emails is bad (prosecutors always introduce inevitable negative evidence first, if they can), then pointed out the leaked DNC emails were real, and asked Schiff why it should be bad for voters to get real information. Schiff began to say something about how it set a bad precedent to allow foreign governments to meddle in our elections, but he didn't answer quickly enough:

> **Schiff:** Because Putin is not our friend. He may think...
> **Carlson:** [interrupting, squinting in frustration] I get it, I get it! Nobody's for hacking. But let me just make one point clear. You don't know that Vladimir Putin was behind those hacks.
> **Schiff:** Well, we do know this, I—
> **Carlson:** But you don't know that. So don't pretend that you do.

Next question! That's how the format works. Carlson is the best at this by far. He makes his "contra" guests look like stammering weenies, never letting them express their points. This actually requires some skill on top of an advanced bullying instinct.

His opponents are always left looking a few steps behind Tucker's Giant Enormous Lie-Smashing Brain, the point of the show. The premise is Tucker delivering on his promise to be the "sworn enemy of lying, pomposity, smugness, and groupthink."

Carlson does this even with guests who are trying, in a way, to seek a kind of accommodation with him (see "The Ten Rules of Hate" section about his unnecessarily nasty interaction with former *Times* public editor Liz Spayd).

This degraded form of "balance" is about as good as it gets on cable. The issue here isn't so much that Tucker Carlson is afraid of other points of view, but that his audiences—after years of watching his shows—will be. Watch cable long enough, and the brain atrophies, and you'll soon find yourself unable to handle unorthodox thoughts.

Modern cable news is a promise to protect the viewer from intellectual challenge. The viewer must never have to question his or her beliefs. The easiest way to accomplish that is by focusing constantly on the failures of others, which is why these shows dwell on the iniquity of the "other side" to the exclusion of all else.

There are no morally neutral concepts. We don't meet the 45 percent of Americans who don't vote and/or don't care about politics. We don't meet people in jails or in rough city neighborhoods who think it's all bunk, that neither party is interested in their problems.

We don't meet people whose thinking confuses caricatures. The Democratic shows won't bring on the Muslim or Asian immigrant restaurant owner who comes with nothing but builds a life here through hard work, and as a result resents welfare and business regulation and taxes. That same person won't appear on the Republican show if he or she is too vociferous about immigrant rights and immigration reform.

Gray areas don't work on these shows. There is *us* and *them* and none of the show can be about questioning *us*. This is why the guest lists are so thick with coiffed professional partisans: either politicians themselves or pundits closely associated with one party or another. They are visions of perfection: perfect hair, facial blemishes makeupped away, with matching certitude in their political positions.

The Rachel Maddow Show in the Trump era assumed this exact *us-and-them* format, down to the last detail. It's been amazing, watching a woman who in life is naturally bright and inquisitive, turned into a vehicle for this kind of extreme anti-intellectual exercise.

She does the exact segments Hannity does, in reverse. Those dumb Republicans *sure have made a terrible political miscalculation this time!* Tune in to find out how the GOP courts disaster, confusion with its rush to implement a tax bill! Or: Trump's emergency declaration could backfire and force Republican cooperation with the Dems! The Republican crusade against Adam Schiff could make them "laughingstocks"!

Republicans, we're told, hate immigrants, are all racist, and most important recently, are complicit in Helping Donald Trump Help Vladimir Putin Attack Our Democracy.

Let's have some guests on to talk about all of this. How about Dan Rather, Ron Wyden, Adam Schiff, Michael McFaul, David Cay Johnston, Robby Mook, Chuck Schumer, Cory Booker, Mazie Hizono, Joy Reid, Chris Coons, Patty Murray, Richard Blumenthal, et cetera, et cetera.

These are all, essentially, professional partisans. They're there because they've been proven dependable when it comes to seeing everything as ultimately the fault of Republicans.

MSNBC has had Republicans and ex-Republicans on in the last few years, mostly apostates or never-Trumpers, on to denounce either Trump or the new breed of deplorable MAGA Republican. Occasionally an "R" will appear for some other reason, perhaps to attest to some other crime against oligarchical decency, like being insufficiently worshipful of John McCain.

But Rachel Maddow tends not to do those interviews. Steve Schmidt, the former campaign adviser to McCain, tends to be a Nicole Wallace guest. Bill Kristol is mostly a Brian Williams guest.

This might have something to do with the fact that she denounced Kristol over Iraq just a few years ago. "You can't have any credibility on National Security issues, and bang the drums that we ought to go into Iraq, and that it would work out, and now bang the drums for any subsequent war," she said, referring to Kristol. "Shame on us for even asking their opinion."

Kristol is now a regular guest on MSNBC. He recently argued (true, not on the network), that regime change in China should be a long-term goal.

Jon Stewart raised the possibility of MSNBC turning into a Democratic Fox a long time ago, when he sat for an at-times uncomfortable interview by Maddow. He pressed her on the question of whether or not "it's all tribal" and repeatedly pressed her on the central point of overlooking the flaws of one "side," or even dividing the world into "sides" at all. The problem with the cable news "conflicto-nator," he said, is "we've all bought into the idea that the conflict in the country is left and right, Republicans and Democrats."

He talked of a larger issue of "corruption vs. non-corruption, extremists vs. non-extremists" and pre-empted criticism that he was saying "you do exactly what Fox does, and you're as bad as Fox," noting that anyone who'd watched his show would recognize the "special place" Fox occupies in the hearts of Stewart's *Daily Show* writers.

But he turned the conversation around at Maddow, and said "false equivalence is something you do as well," adding, "we have a tendency to grant amnesty to people we like, and overly demonize people we don't." He added that cable "amplifies a division that I don't think is the right fight... [because] both sides have their way of shutting down debate."

The Stewart interview from 2010 was a warning about the direction of MSNBC. It was heading toward a Coke-Pepsi/BK-McDonald's-style commercial pairing with Fox. Both were selling a fake binary debate, and using demonization as an audience-binding mechanism. It wasn't rocket science, or hard to spot. But the Maddow audience assumed it was immune to the come-on.

Stewart also warned that cable news was designed to rally audiences after emergencies, but life isn't an emergency. "O.J.'s not going to kill someone every day," he quipped. Maddow also talked about this in other interviews with Stewart, saying people get tired of being whipped into terror after terror. "When you have a self-imposed crisis every few months because it's the only way you know how to govern," she said, "wolf has been cried!"

This was years before the "walls are closing in" era of booming ad sales for a network that would cover the Trump presidency as an ongoing emergency, a literal war, with a pretender on the throne. It was thrilling stuff, but it was based on a relentless campaign of dramatic promises that never came to fruition. Meanwhile, Maddow's show never criticized Democrats for anything, and even clearly bipartisan issues like the passage of a massive defense hike turned into Trump-iniquity stories.

The Rachel Maddow Show now features cheery interviews with people like former CIA chief John Brennan or former Director of National Intelligence James Clapper. Rachel harshly criticized Brennan years ago, before this Trump-era transformation, over issues like torture. Her show's blog also went after Clapper once for lying to Congress (saying they weren't sure "why Republicans are giving him a pass on this"). Now the security chiefs are anti-Trump allies, welcome in the tent.

Beyond the parade of security officials who've become legion in MSNBC's ranks, Rachel's shows are massage sessions with Democratic Party glitterati, who often seem more interested in her than she is in the guest (this *Face in the Crowd* dynamic was often present with Rush Limbaugh, Bill O'Reilly, and Hannity as well). In many cases it's clear the Democrat guest is seeking something like an endorsement from Maddow, the bigger star with the bigger Q rating.

This is where the humor issue comes into play. Most any political guest, particularly one currently running for office, will make a point of pretending to go insane with laughter at a Maddow one-liner early in the segment. Part of the conceit of the show is that Rachel Maddow, when she's not relentlessly conquering Republican evil, nurtures a hobby as the most effortlessly funny person on earth.

The Jimmy Dore Show caught a great example recently. On the day word leaked that Mueller finished his investigation, Senator Amy Klobuchar asked Rachel if she'd caught any trout. Rachel said at the top of the show she'd interrupted a trout-fishing vacation to race to a studio to cover news of the Mueller investigation closing.

The exchange:

> **Maddow:** No—well, you know, I've learned two things in life. Never ever ask a woman if she's pregnant and never ever—
> (*hysterical laughter by Klobuchar*)
> **Maddow:** Never ever ask a person who has just completed a day of fishing if they caught a fish.
> (*more hysterical laughter*)

There's nothing monstrous about this, but it's a dreary audience-binding ritual, much the same as the *New York Times* selling audience solidarity when its post-election headline in November of 2016 read:

DEMOCRATS, STUDENTS, AND FOREIGN ALLIES FACE
THE REALITY OF A TRUMP PRESIDENCY

Again, that headline doesn't so much give you news as it does reinforce your sense of who besides you is reading the newspaper. SENSIBLE PEOPLE LIKE YOU REACT TO TRUMP WIN is how that head will read to future historians.

What makes this a critical part of the Hate media era is that one group is bound most of all by its collective disgust and disdain for the other. Maddow defenders will say she's nowhere near as vicious and deceptive as Hannity and therefore doesn't belong in the same category. But she builds her audience the same way. All the things "we" used to complain about with Fox, now are common on MSNBC.

Fox invented the viewer who assumed everyone who didn't agree with him or her was a Clinton/Obama fan. For years I would be astonished that every Fox-watching conservative who wrote to complain about *X* or *Y* in one of my articles assumed I was on the Obama payroll and would never criticize a Democrat.

When I'd reply that I'd actually written whole books doing just that, they'd typically disappear. Fox had trained them to think that the only kind of people on earth apart from Righteous People Who Agree With Me are Democrats. They hated the idea of new and different personality types more than they hated my reporting.

There will be Democrats who protest: but Republicans are racist! It's right to be organized in solidarity against them! Donald Trump is evil! *Rachel is right!* That's why she doesn't belong in the same discussion as Hannity, a bully who reportedly has a history of saying that homosexuality is practiced by people committing "deviant, twisted acts." She's never done anything like that!

Okay. But are all Republicans alike? Are they caricatures? How many people are defined by something they do once in four years? (Or don't do at all—remember, non-voters are significantly more numerous than either faction.)

Traveling the country covering elections, I met a huge spectrum of people at Republican events. Some threatened me physically. Others I thought were crazy. Others I actually liked, or at least found interesting. In Arizona I ran into a biker gang outside a Trump event—this was after he'd been elected, during a story I was doing for *Rolling Stone* about whether or not Trump was crazy—whose members were blasted out of their minds. One said he'd voted for Trump because "fuck it and fuck them."

"Fuck who exactly?" I asked.

"I don't know. Anyone. You?"

The "fuck it" vote felt like a huge part of Trump's win. Lots of people recognized Trump was a jackass and that's actually why they voted for him. As has been reported many times, people who disliked Trump *and* Clinton were maybe his most important constituency.

These people were so pissed and depressed and angry with everyone—especially phonies on television—that they sent Trump to Washington hoping he would blow it all up, so America could start over. Such people are not going to be receptive to a twenty-four-hour lineup of anti-Trump news because they hate the partisanship more than Trump.

The "Trump: Let's get this shit over with" theory—the idea that America was already a failed state and a vote for Trump would just help us to the inevitable ending faster—was posited on the *Horace and Pete* show during the 2016 election.

It might have made Rachel laugh back in the old days, even if she didn't agree with it. Exploring the nature of that level of political nihilism could have been something she'd have considered interesting once.

An intellectually confident audience should be able to engage these attitudes without instant recrimination, just like they should be able to engage the notion that Democrats and Republicans are actually partners in some important areas. They should be able to take in the hard truth about the ballooning defense budget, giant tax breaks for private equity chiefs, bailouts, handouts to big Pharma, and other problems with bipartisan origins.

But they can't. We've built audiences who can't handle contradictions, oddities, or subtleties. Everything is a clear fight between good and bad sides.

The Rachel Maddow Show and *The Sean Hannity Show* have become *Crossfire* for the new generation. In this updated version of fake political combat sold as theater, the pugilists never meet in the ring.

MSNBC and Fox are two phony-tough bar belligerents who yell and scream taunts from a safe distance, while their "friends" hold them back to make sure no one actually has to win or lose. In the metaphor, viewers are the "friends" who hold their hosts back.

The implied context of both shows is a never-ending culture war. Each cherry-pick that day's news to see, *gotcha*, whose side did better today.

There is no other content. In this sense *The Rachel Maddow Show* is an absolute adherent to the Ten Rules of Hate. The program, coupled with *Hannity*, is America's leading purveyor of the "There are only two ideas" concept, the insane notion that Democrats and Republicans own the only two brands of thought in existence.

This is why the most rigidly enforced rule of all (similar to the op-ed sections of the big daily papers, where you'll find Republican pundits but no socialists, pacifists, anarchists, or any other form of "ist") is the exclusion of other brands of progressivism from the supposedly left-leaning program.

This tunnel-vision strategy is what led to the excesses in Russiagate, when the *Rachel Maddow Show* committed exhaustive resources to a story that went off the rails. Just like Fox, whose founder Roger Ailes bragged about suckering an older audience, MSNBC repeatedly promised an audience whose median viewer is sixty-five that the trauma of Trump's election would soon be relieved, when Mueller led Trump out of the White House in handcuffs.

During this time the network wasn't above fear-mongering, jingoism, xenophobia, and other tactics that used to be an anathema to progressive thinking. We used to think these things the exclusive province of channels like Fox.

The essence of hate is fear. It's the key lesson in *To Kill a Mockingbird*: we fear what we can't see. We tell stories about what's on the other side of the wall. Harper Lee describes how the town of Maycomb despises Boo Radley, spinning legends about Boo coming out at night to kill pets.

Maybe he does, maybe he doesn't. But we can't know unless we knock on his door and ask. Rachel Maddow, like Hannity, has built an audience of non-engagers. It's conscious strategy, the result of years of effort among Democrats to build their own version of the right-wing propaganda machine. This has been a constant obsession of socially liberal media magnates since the Clinton years.

But right-wing propaganda works precisely because it's a total betrayal of how reporting is supposed to work. Journalism gives people the facts no matter where they lead, and operates on the assumption that informed citizens make better decisions.

Fox pioneered the opposite view, that people are too stupid to be trusted with all sides of an argument. They created techniques for factory-style partisan politicization of content, picking and choosing stories to shape viewers into voters.

"We report, you decide," was an industry in-joke. In fact Fox wanted audiences who jumped past thought to emotion, outrage, and loyalty. In sports terms, Fox voters root for the laundry. They resist switching allegiance because they've been trained to reject outside ideas as contaminants.

These are all awful things, and this longtime vision of Democrats who want to ape the Fox model know it on some level. Watch Rachel's own reaction when she reports on another uncomfortable interview she did, with Bernie Sanders in 2016. In that interview, she noted, "He also said the Democratic Party should fund its own version of Fox news!"

At which point she smiled and threw her hands out in dramatic fashion, a gesture of ironic exclamation. The joke was, we already have the Democratic Fox, or, we're trying, anyway.

If you're a Democrat, you naturally think "our" Fox is not such a bad thing as the original. But thinking MSNBC is better than Fox is not the same as thinking Democrats are better than Republicans. The standard for news reporting is different than politics.

One political party may be preferable to another. A news channel, though, can't be a vehicle for a political party and be anything but a bad thing.

A political party cannot spend time dwelling on its own weaknesses and corruption and still hope to succeed. A news organization has to look hard in the mirror to be credible. It has to challenge everything, including its own audience.

Rachel Maddow, small-time radio host, was free to do that. Now that person has been consumed by a billion-dollar brand and the inflexible political platform it sells. What she reads each night is not the news. It's *Stars and Stripes* for a demographic, the same job that made Sean Hannity a star. Only she does it for a different audience, Lonesome Rhodes for the smart set. Even she must realize it can't end well.

APPENDIX 2: AN INTERVIEW WITH NOAM CHOMSKY

Ask the average liberal arts graduate about Dr. Noam Chomsky and one of the first comments is likely to involve his presentation. Despite his status as one of the world's leading experts in linguistics, he has a reputation for being a dull intellectual—someone "known for erudition rather than crowd-grabbing eloquence," as one columnist once put it.

I always thought this was a bit of clever marketing on Chomsky's part. If you read his books closely, there's a conspicuous streak of ironic defiance that runs through his work. It animates his writing and ideas, and catches any reader conditioned to expect a bore by surprise.

He has a deadpan, dry sense of humor. If you asked him to sum up all of human history—and now that I think about it, I should have done this—he would probably say something like, "Unsurprisingly horrible."

In person, Chomsky is affable, funny, and generous. A million things have been written about him and he seems way beyond caring. A few years ago he moved to the University of Arizona in Tucson from his longtime home in Boston, at MIT. When I commented on the heat—I almost collapsed walking from my car to his office—he laughed and said that he actually likes it. Boston in the summer is much worse, he said, and seemed to mean it. He looked like a happy man.

I came to ask about the legacy of *Manufacturing Consent*. How did he think his famous examination of the media has held up over the years? Did he think the famous "propaganda model" still played out in the Internet age? What, if anything, had changed? Why had a non-journalist ventured into this topic? I asked the same question about his co-author, Wharton School professor Ed Herman, who sadly had passed away the previous year.

One of the first things Chomsky mentioned about Herman is that the "propaganda model" was "a little more his than mine," which is why he insisted that the book's byline read Herman/Chomsky, and not Chomsky/Herman. As it turned out, the book had a bit of a strange history, and he seemed to enjoy recounting it. We ended up talking about the future of the news media, and about the immediate political future.

There is a whole literature of reporters running to Chomsky in search of quotes about how this time, things are really bad—and coming away disappointed when Chomsky answers, with a shrug, that, no, things have always been this crazy, just remember X and Y and Z…

This drives reporters nuts.

Chomsky maintains that Trump's daily insanities are a distraction, that the real problems involve his administration's dismantling of regulatory systems, its failure to focus on global warming, and its worsening of the threat of nuclear war. All things that, while historically awful, mostly happen behind closed doors, away from headlines.

Particularly in the Trump era, when there's constant pressure in the media business to scrape up a ten-alarm quote about how whatever lunatic thing Trump did today is the Worst Thing Ever, Chomsky has been, for reporters, a constant source of disappointment.

And the world could use a little more of whatever well of equanimity he's drinking from.

Taibbi: Professor, it's a great honor. Thanks so much for the time.

Chomsky: Thank you.

Taibbi: I want to talk about *Manufacturing Consent,* a book that had a huge influence on reporters like myself.

Chomsky: Sure.

Taibbi: What was the genesis of that project? How did you decide to do a treatment of the media? Neither of you specialized in the subject.

Chomsky: Well, the first book we wrote had a very interesting history. It was called *Counter-Revolutionary Violence.* There was a small, but quite successful, publisher that was publishing this. It was largely doing materials for universities, small monographs and things. One of them was this one we wrote, called *Counter-Revolutionary Violence.* They published 20,000 copies, and started advertising. But it turned out the company was owned by Warner Brothers. And one of the executives in Warner Brothers saw the ads, and didn't like it.

Taibbi: What didn't he like about it?

Chomsky: When he saw the book he practically went through the ceiling. So he asked them to withdraw the book. And they didn't want to do it. They said they would agree to publish a counter-volume if he wanted. No, he didn't want that. Wanted it withdrawn. What he finally did was put the publisher out of business, and destroyed all of their stock.

Taibbi: Goodness.

Chomsky: Including our book, and everything else.

Taibbi: Just to get rid of your book?

Chomsky: Yeah. And I brought it to the attention of some of the main civil libertarians, people like [*Village Voice* columnist] Nat Hentoff, and so on. But they didn't see any problems with American civil liberties. I can understand their point. It's not state censorship.

Taibbi: Right.

Chomsky: You're not supposed to notice that we have private governments that are much more powerful than the state. Anyway, that's not part of the ideology.

So this was okay, technically.

Well, we said, "Alright, that's gone." But we decided to expand it. The next major book we did together was a two-volume *Political Economy of Human Rights*, which came out in 1979. And it was around that time that we started working on looking at how the media handled things. And that led us to finally *Manufacturing Consent*.

Ed, as you may know, was a professor of finance. And his main work, his academic work, was called *Corporate Power, Corporate Control*, which is a standard text on corporate power.

But he's pretty left wing, so it was critical. The part of *Manufacturing Consent* on ownership and control, that's basically his work, the introductory part. Then we kind of shared much of the rest. His style is different from mine. We worked together very well, but in different ways.

Actually we never even met! We met probably two or three times overall. That was pre-Internet, so it was all on paper.

Taibbi: It was all done by correspondence?

Chomsky: Correspondence.

Taibbi: Wow. Like typewritten? Handwritten?

Chomsky: (smiling) Oh, typewritten!

Taibbi: Wow.

Chomsky: If you remember what it was like then—probably you don't.

Taibbi: My generation is probably the last that does.

Chomsky: But the parts that are really carefully organized, all these charts on how many reports there were on one Polish priest—

Taibbi: Versus those in Central America.

Chomsky: Right. If I were doing it, I would have just given some examples. But when he did it, he did all of the statistics, and got the charts correct, and so on.

The main part that I wrote myself was mostly the Indochina part, and the parts on the Freedom House attack on the media.

This is a part that people don't really recognize, that a large part of the book was a *defense* of the media. It was actually a defense of the media from the attacks of organizations like Freedom House.[1]

Taibbi: Right.

Chomsky: But it's kind of interesting that journalists didn't like that defense. And the reason was—part of it first came out in an article of mine in a journal that was short lived, a critical journalism review[2] that was run by Anthony Lukas, kind of a critical journalist, very cool.

I wrote a long article in it about the two-volume Freedom House thing. What we basically argued is that the journalists are doing honest, courageous work that's professional, and serious. And in lot of difficult circumstances, they do a very good job.

But they're all doing it within an ideological framework, which reflects the dominant hegemonic common sense.

1 Freedom House, as described in *Manufacturing Consent*: "Freedom House, which dates back to the early 1940s, has had interlocks with AIM, the World Anticommunist League, Resistance International, and U.S. government bodies such as Radio Free Europe and the CIA, and has long served as a virtual propaganda arm of the government and international right wing."

2 *MORE*, which went out of business in 1978.

Taibbi: Right.

Chomsky: So in fact, they would describe what's happening accurately, and that thing would be described as a mistake, a deviation, inconsistent with our values and our principles and that sort of thing.

Whereas in fact, it's exactly in accord with their principles and values.

The idea that they were not courageous tribunes of the people flaunting doctrine and so on was unpalatable. The idea that, "We're just honest professionals who are captured by an ideological framework that we're even unaware of," is an unacceptable idea. Nobody liked that.

Taibbi: So you got pushback on that immediately from reporters?

Chomsky: Yes. I mean, some did. I had some close friends who thought it was fine, but there was pushback, yes.

Taibbi: The main idea in *Manufacturing Consent* is basically that idea: that it *looks* like we have a vigorous system of independent journalists, but the debate has been artificially narrowed. Was there a moment when you first had that thought? Do you remember?

Chomsky: Probably when I was 10 years old! Actually remember, the work that I had done on my own before this was a critique of the intellectual culture. And my own view, Ed and I slightly differed here, is that the media aren't all that different from the general intellectual culture, the academic culture.

So the effect of the institutions: ownership, advertising, and so on, that's all there. But an overriding effect is just the way the general hegemonic culture works, and you see that in the academic world. You see it in scholarship, and you see it in a very striking way in the media.

But it's much easier to study in the media. Academic scholarship is diffuse. You can't do statistical analysis of how many articles there were on this, and that sort of thing.

So it's kind of focused on the media, and sharpened, then it's influenced, of course, by the filters that we talked about.

But I think riding through it is something that you see through the intellectual culture generally. In fact, the work that I'd done back in the sixties and on, it was mostly about that, continuing to the present. It's mostly about general academic intellectual culture. Which does show up in the media in a very striking form, and that's why we incidentally kept it to the elite media. So we talked about the *New York Times, Washington Post,* CBS. We didn't talk about the tabloids.

Taibbi: But basically you're talking about the same instinct for conformity, the inability to understand that you're working within a predetermined framework.

Chomsky: It was exactly what you said before. It's the assumption that you're being adversarial, independent, questioning everything, and so on.

But it's the same in scholarship. If you tell a scholar, "Look you're just conforming to ideological prejudices," they go crazy. You can see what happened when something really became prominent that questioned the basic ideological framework. Like when Howard Zinn's book...

Taibbi: The *People's History of the United States.*

Chomsky: Right. When that became popular, historians just went berserk. There's a very interesting book that just came out about that, if you want to take a look.

Taibbi: Is there? I didn't know.

Chomsky: It's called *Zinnophobia...* It's a very careful analysis of Oscar Handlin, and all the guys who bitterly attacked the Zinn report.

Taibbi: Well, that gets to one of the other themes of your book: *flak.*

Chomsky: Right. This is it. In the intellectual culture. Of course there's plenty of it.

Taibbi: Have you thought over the years about what parts of the propaganda model have held up more than others? Clearly *flak* is one that has.

Chomsky: Actually there is a second edition, did you see that?

Taibbi: Yes, with the update.

Chomsky: We pointed out there correctly, that one part of the model was much too narrow: the part about anti-communism.

(Editor's note: In Manufacturing Consent, *heavy emphasis is placed on anticommunism as an organizing religion underpinning the media business. Here, Chomsky is talking about how other theologies have entered the scene since 1988.)*

Chomsky: It's got to be broader than that. Anti-communism was a salient illustration of the enemy that you construct to justify everything you're doing. But it could be terrorism, it could be anything.

Taibbi: Populism is another one.

Chomsky: You mean, what's called populism.

Taibbi: Yes.

Chomsky: That term had an honorable history. It was the most democratic movement in American history.

Taibbi: Well they've quickly turned it into a different kind of a word.

Chomsky: Yes. Which happens.

Taibbi: When you published *Manufacturing Consent*, it was at the height of the go-go, *Top Gun*, Reagan eighties. Everybody was feeling very positive and patriotic about America, or at least that was the line.

Chomsky: We were a "City on a hill."

Taibbi: Exactly.

Chomsky: Did you ever go into the origin of city on a hill?

Taibbi: No, I didn't.

Chomsky: It's an interesting case. The term had never really been, barely been used before Reagan. But Reagan picked it up, and did the "Shining city upon a hill" speech.

But if you go back and you read John Winthrop's sermon, he says almost the opposite. When he says we're a city on a hill, what he means is everyone is looking at us, and if we don't live up to the ideals that we profess, we're going to be punished.[3] Of course, in his case, by the Lord. Not by society.

So it's really saying we're exposed, we have to try to live up to these ideals. He didn't say we were doing it, by any means. In fact, he knew we weren't. That was the point.

Taibbi: Instead, they turn it into a catch phrase for exceptionalism.

Chomsky: Yeah. So wonderful, isn't it?

Taibbi: Hilarious.

Chomsky: And of course it all went along with Reagan's nice smile, and all that.

---

3 From Winthrop's sermon: "For we must consider that we shall be as a city upon a hill. The eyes of all people are upon us. So that if we shall deal falsely with our God in this work we have undertaken, and so cause Him to withdraw His present help from us, we shall be made a story and a by-word through the world. We shall open the mouths of enemies to speak evil of the ways of God, and all professors for God's sake. We shall shame the faces of many of God's worthy servants, and cause their prayers to be turned into curses upon us till we be consumed out of the good land whither we are going."

Taibbi: So here you come, in the middle of all that exceptionalism, and you publish *Manufacturing Consent*, which is exactly the opposite. It presents an image of a country that is completely deluded, and bloodthirsty, and it has this terrible history it can't face up to.

Chomsky: We had much more of that in the *Political Economy of Human Rights*, which wasn't about the media. It was partly about the media, but it was mainly about the actions.

That was just an anathema. Nobody could even look at *that*. Which was pretty striking, because the most—well, it was pretty interesting. There was an interesting reaction to those two volumes. If you look at them, we covered a lot of ground, but the focus was on two cases. One of them was East Timor. The other was Cambodia under Pol Pot.

Those are two places, same region of the world, during the same years, both huge massacres. East Timor was probably worse.

There was only one difference between them. In one case, you could blame it on someone else. In the other case, we were doing it.

Taibbi: Right.

Chomsky: And what we pointed out is that in both cases, there's massive lying but in opposite directions. In the Cambodia cases, there were all kinds of claims that there was no basis for. When things were refuted, they got elaborated upon and continued. Any invention is okay.

On the East Timor case, there appeared to be either ignoring, or pure denial. And of course the East Timor case is far more important, because that we could have stopped at any time. Because we were crucially responsible for it.

And in fact that was proven when finally twenty-five years later under a lot of domestic and international pressure, Clinton was pressured to tell the Indonesians to call it off. And he basically told them, "Look, the game's over," and they pulled out a minute later. But it could have been done for twenty-five years.

So the East Timor case was vastly more important. Basically the same story, but lying in opposite directions and phenomenal, actually phenomenal lying in both cases.

Take a look at the reaction to the book. The East Timor thing had never been mentioned. The Cambodia thing, everybody went berserk. They said, we're protecting Pol Pot, we're defending genocide. No. We were simply saying, if American intelligence probably has the story correct, then the stuff that you guys are publishing is crazed lies. It would have impressed Stalin.

So there's a huge literature attacking us, usually me, on Cambodia, and total silence on East Timor.

Taibbi: Because it's so totally indefensible?

Chomsky: Because you can't face it.

In fact, that holds until today. Take a look at Samantha Powers's book, which was very highly praised. Everyone loved it, it's a wonderful book. She's probably perfectly honest, just naïve, but she was castigating the United States—which makes it good because it's kind of critical—castigating it for not dealing properly with *other people's* crimes.

It's such a perfect choice of topic. If a PR person had invented it, they couldn't have made it better. So everyone loved it and it won prizes, and it's wonderful. But there's nothing about any of our crimes. I think she mentions East Timor, and she says, "We made a mistake in East Timor. We looked away."

Looked away? We gave the green light to go ahead, provided the arms, backed them all the time.

(Note: East Timor's Commission for Reception, Truth and Reconciliation in 2006 concluded that America's "political and military support were fundamental to the Indonesian invasion and occupation," which led to the deaths of at least 100,000 people.)

Chomsky: That all happened, but the most you can say is that "we looked away" in East Timor.

Taibbi: There's an analogous situation going on now with Yemen.

Chomsky: Yemen is the same. We're giving them intelligence on where to bomb. We're giving them weapons. But we don't know anything about what's going on. Must be a mistake of some kind!

Taibbi: That's another part of the model that seems to have held up perfectly since 1988: the concept of worthy and unworthy victims.

Chomsky: That's exactly it.

Taibbi: Syria and Yemen are almost perfect analogues to the Cambodia and East Timor examples in your book.

Chomsky: We used that term for East Timor and Cambodia. So the main themes of *Manufacturing Consent* are really there, apart from the institutional structure, you know. But that's a very dramatic example. Because here's two—you know, East Timor probably came as close to real genocide as anything in the post World War II period.

Taibbi: And yet, you won't hear that word '"genocide" or see it anywhere in the popular press really attached to that incident—at least, not insofar as our involvement was concerned.

Chomsky: There are other rather interesting cases. Take Kevin Buckley, the *Newsweek* bureau chief in Saigon. A very good journalist. After the My Lai Massacre, Buckley and an associate of his, Alex Shimkin, did a careful study of what was going on in the Quang Ngai province, where the massacre took place.

And what they discovered was what people in the peace movement already knew, that there was nothing special about My Lai. It was going on all over the place, and furthermore, these massacres were minor. The major massacres were via the saturation bombing.

From guys sitting in air conditioned offices and telling B-52s to bomb everything in sight, you know. Those were the huge massacres. The My Lai, My Khe, the others like it, they were kind of footnotes. *Newsweek* wouldn't publish it, so he gave me the notes, and we basically published his notes, but nobody noticed that, either.

Taibbi: That was in the previous book?

Chomsky: It was in the previous book, in the section on Vietnam. This was right at the time that the Argentine neo-Nazi regime was instituted, strongly supported by the United States. I had material on that, too, and a lot of other things, it covered a lot of ground.

Now, see, Reagan was using—Congress barred direct military aid to Guatemala. So Reagan, what he did, interestingly, was set up an international terror network. But we don't use people like Carlos the Jackal. We use terrorist states.

Taibbi: Right.

Chomsky: So we used Argentina, one of the neo-Nazi regimes. Taiwan. Israel was a big part of it. They provided the arms and the training and the support for the Guatemalan massacres.

Incidentally, people are still fleeing today from the Mayan areas that were subjected to virtual genocide. But they are driven back to the border, of course.

Taibbi: That brings me to another question. One of the main themes of *Manufacturing Consent* was that it was hard for people to recognize propaganda as propaganda, because it was private and there was an absence of direct state censorship.

Chomsky: It's very much like the destruction of the press. It wasn't state censorship, so it's okay.

Incidentally, there's an interesting book that just came out that finally says some of the obvious things about this, by a woman named Elizabeth Anderson. She's a philosopher and an economist. It's called *Private Government*, and her point, which is a major point, is that there is a government, but governments can be repressive. But most of our lives are under private government, which she says are indistinguishable from communist dictatorships.

Any business, for example. If you subject yourself to it, you become essentially a slave of the institution with no rights, give away your liberty, and so on.

The interesting part of her book, which is somewhat new, is she goes through the the seventeenth- and eighteenth-century advocacy of free markets by Adam Smith, Tom Paine, you know, up to Abraham Lincoln, and points out that that was a left wing position.

Because they were advocating free markets, because they wanted to undermine state monopolies and mercantilism, and to allow people to become free, independent artisans not subject to any authority. And they regarded wage labor as equivalent to slavery. The only difference is that it's temporary. You can get out of it.

And when the Industrial Revolution came along, everything changed. You could only survive by being subordinate to a major corporate structure, and wage labor became the norm.

The contemporary libertarians are still citing the the seventeenth- and eighteenth-century condemnations of wage labor and contract as being libertarian, because now it's not government. Everything has inverted totally. It's very much like you were saying before with censorship.

Taibbi: Well, that's interesting, because we're in this unusual place now. The media landscape almost totally exists on a couple of distribution platforms. They're private, technically. Facebook, Google, but there's now a bit of an inter-relationship between those companies and the government. And some places, like

Israel, it's more of a direct relationship. Would that be a change in the model if they were to adopt a more directly censorious role?

Chomsky: Take a look at the Facebook phenomenon. Where are they getting their news from? They don't have reports.

They're just getting it from the *New York Times*, so it's the same sources of information. They're just putting it out in trivialized form, so that people with a ten-year-old mentality can handle it. It's a very dangerous thing. They're not doing any of the things that the media do. They don't frame things. They don't select. They don't send reporters out. They don't investigate, you know, they just collect information and hand it over to kids to look at in ten minutes so you don't believe the newspapers.

Taibbi: After you published *Manufacturing Consent*, there was a major change in the business. I had seen this pretty dramatically because I'd grown up in the media. But suddenly in the late eighties and early nineties, there was a new commercial strategy that Fox employed. It was less about getting the broadest possible audience, but more about capturing a demographic, continuing to feed them news that they agreed with. It was a siloing effect—silos of news, fed separately to each demographic.

Chomsky: That's right, that's new.

Taibbi: And that has been massively accelerated by the Internet, by Facebook, and the platforms.

Chomsky: The other aspect of that, which I think is maybe underestimated, is talk radio, it reaches a huge audience. And I've often thought, I don't know if they've got it around here, but in Boston, I used to listen to it all the time while I was driving. It's totally insane.

Taibbi: It is. But how does that affect the model? Because *Manufacturing Consent* was significantly about organizing *everybody* behind hegemonic imperatives. But we now have a system where the news and its attendant messaging is fractured. Information is distributed differently, to each different silo. And many violently disagree with each other.

Chomsky: Well, you know what's actually happened, I think, is they disagree—but the divisiveness, I think, is somewhat misinterpreted. It's always described as some groups moving left, others moving right. I don't think that's happened. I think both groups have moved to the right. There's a divide, but it's misrepresented.

Take Bernie Sanders. Take a look at his policies. I mean, Eisenhower wouldn't have been surprised by them. No, literally!

Eisenhower's position was that anybody who questioned the New Deal was out of his mind. There was strong support for unions by corporate leaders, in fact, because they kept things organized, and you didn't have strikes and so on.

But, the Sanders proposals are pretty much—you know, they would have been considered maybe mildly liberal in the 1950s. But certainly not radical, not revolutionary. It's just the whole spectrum has moved so far to the right that they *look* extreme.

Taibbi: Does the divisiveness also serve any other propaganda purpose? For instance, having people not realizing shared economic problems?

Chomsky: Definitely, there is an element.

Taibbi: You talk a lot in *Manufacturing Consent* about deceptions that are flagrant, like for instance the story about the supposed Bulgarian plot behind the attempt to kill Pope John Paul II in the Vatican in 1981. I remember you writing that "there was no credible evidence for a Bulgarian connection from the beginning," and yet the whole press corps dove into it. It later came out that there were indications that our government was really working hard to sell a Soviet connection to that incident.

Chomsky: There's a book on that.

Taibbi: Despite episodes like that, we've had so many that were similar. Take the Iraq War: WMD you could have seen through, I thought, from the very beginning.

Chomsky: There are still people who believe there were WMDs.

Taibbi: And of course that story turned out very badly for the media. Do you think all that blatant deception resulted in a situation where people were willing to believe somebody like Trump—

Chomsky: Over the media?

Taibbi: Yes.

Chomsky: Well, I think it's true. Although, honestly, I think one of the unfortunate effects of *Manufacturing Consent* is that a lot of people who've read it say, "Well, we can't trust the media." But that's not exactly what it said. If you want to get information, sure, read the *New York Times*, but read it with your eyes open. With a critical mind. The *Times* is full of facts. You're not going to find the information there on Facebook.

Taibbi: Or 4chan.

Chomsky: Also, don't confine it to the media. There's skepticism now about institutions altogether. In fact, faith in institutions has declined radically, almost all across the board. Like Congress, the support for them is sometimes in the single digits. About 80 percent of the population since the eighties have consistently in polls been saying, the government is run by a few big interests looking out for themselves. Which is...

Taibbi: True. Right?

Chomsky: And I think it's the impact of the whole neoliberal aggression that was major. That began technically with Carter, really picked up with Reagan and Thatcher, across the world. You've had tremendous damage to the general population under the neoliberal, business-first principles. And it's just happened everywhere. Take a look just at wages, I mean, real wages today are lower than in the late seventies. There's been economic growth, but into few pockets. Productivity keeps increasing, but not wages. Up until the mid-seventies, real wages tracked productivity. If you look back, then, there's a split of productivity keeps going up, but wages stagnate or decline. And that's true by every measure you look at.

Taibbi: And naturally, people are upset about that.

Chomsky: They're upset. And the same in Europe, at least the anger, the hatred of institutions, the ugly attitudes emerge to try to blame somebody for what's going on. And you see in the European elections, in every election the centrist parties collapse, and they go to fringes. You see it in Brexit. Brexit is suicidal. But the people are so angry that they just want to get out of it.

Taibbi: During the 2016 election, I remember very vividly the experience of covering Trump and being behind the rope with all the reporters and Trump pointing us out and making us villains. He'd basically say: "There are the elites, they're stenographers for the bad guys." And that was very effective I thought.

Chomsky: Yes, and it's straight out of fascist history. Go after the elites, even while you're being supported by the major elites.

Taibbi: Right.

Chomsky: You ever read Thomas Ferguson? He's a political economist, a very good one. His whole life he's been working on things like the impact of campaign funding on electability. And he did a very careful study of the 2016 election. What turned out was that, in the end, in the last couple of months when it was looking very clearly as if Clinton was going to win, the corporate sector really got pretty upset. And they start pouring money into funding not only for Trump, but heavily into the Senate and the House, because they wanted to make sure the Republicans controlled the House and the Senate.

And if you compare the increase in campaign funding with the shift in attitudes, it's almost perfect. It pushed not only Trump, but also the whole Congress into Republican wins. Just as a reflection of campaign funding.

So the real elites knew where their bread was buttered.

Taibbi: But Trump uses this trick of presenting other people as representatives of the elites.

Chomsky: Standard technique of the fake populists against the elites, while you're actually working for them.

Taibbi: Why do you think the population has become so much more conspiratorially-minded since the publication of *Manufacturing Consent*? Or has it? It seems to me that it has. Could it be that—well, when you wrote *Manufacturing Consent*, there was a commonly accepted set of facts. We had three networks, they mostly reported the same things, now—

Chomsky: Well there were conspiracies. I mean, take a look at the Kennedy conspiracies. That's much earlier. This goes way back in American history when Richard Hofstadter wrote about it fifty years ago. But it's true that it's been inflated recently, and I think it's just a reflection of the very natural anger at institutions altogether, across the board. Maybe the Army sort of escapes, but practically nothing else. And if you can't trust institutions, why can you trust the media?

Taibbi: But that's one of the developments, isn't it? That the media increasingly are viewed as an institution, whereas previously this was not so much the case?

Chomsky: Oh, they are. Because Trump is very effective in terms of eliciting anti-institutional furor against the media, making media the enemy, which is a clever trick. He's a good politician.

Taibbi: A lot of people who are fellow reporters have commented to me over the years—and I agree with them—that *Manufacturing Consent* really captured something about the inner workings of the media business. I think of things that Chris Hedges has talked about, about the dynamics inside media companies: if you're too independently-minded, if you have too obvious a bent toward independent thought, sooner or later, you're going to run into trouble. You won't be promoted, or you'll get wrapped up in some kind of bureaucratic fiasco. Some kind of label will get attached to you, particularly in the giant daily news operations.

Chomsky: They'll say you're too biased, emotional, too involved in things. But you see, it's the same in the academic world. It just might be bigger words over here.

Taibbi: There might just be a hair more intellectual mediocrity in our world than yours, I would think.

Chomsky: Well, I'm not convinced of that.

Taibbi: Obviously, the structure of media now with the Internet-based distribution systems, what do you see as the future there? Will it be easier or harder to "Manufacture Consent" with so much concentration?

Chomsky: The crucial word was *distribution* systems. The Internet doesn't dig up any information. So, the information's coming from the same place it will always come fom. It's the reporters on the ground. Unfortunately, there are fewer of them.

But I think, in a lot of ways, it's hard to measure, but my impression is that the media are probably more free and open than they were in the fifties and sixties. And the reason is that a lot of the younger people, the people who are now in the media, went through the sixties experience, which was very liberatory. It really opened people's minds, so they tend to be more critical and open-minded and so on.

People forget how conformist the media were in the fifties and sixties. It was shocking. When you look back, it's mind-boggling.

In 1961, I think around November, Kennedy authorized the U.S. Air Force to start bombing South Vietnam. They used South Vietnamese markings, but everybody knew what was going on. They were American planes. This is a big thing: starting to bomb the rural population in a foreign country. I think the *New York Times* may have had ten lines on it on a back page.

Nobody knew, nobody paid any attention. I don't think that could happen now. And there are many cases like this.

Taibbi: Do you think that this is a source of concern to the government and large corporate interests, this idea that maybe there is a little bit too much freedom? A little too much independence? Maybe, something needs to be done.

Chomsky: There's a very important book, which came out 1975. It's called the *Crisis of Democracy*. It's the first publication of the Trilateral Commission, which is a group of liberal internationalists from Europe, United States, and Japan, three main centers of capitalist democracy.

What's the "Crisis of Democracy"? The "Crisis of Democracy" is that in the 1960s, all kinds of sectors of the population that are supposed to be passive and apathetic begin to try to enter the political arena to press for their own interests and concerns, and that imposes too much of a burden on the state, which becomes ungovernable. So, what we need is "more moderation in democracy." That's their phrase. People should go back into their corners and leave it to us.

In fact, the American rapporteur Samuel Huntington looked back kind of nostalgically to the Truman years. He says Truman was able to govern the country politically with the aid of just a few Wall Street bankers.

Then we had democracy. But he goes after the media. He says the media have become too adversarial, too independent. We may even have to institute government controls to try to contain them, because of what they're doing.

That's the *liberal* position. The Trilateral Commission also went after what they called the de-legitimation of the universities. They said that the institutions—and this is their phrase—these institutions responsible for the "indoctrination of the young"—are being de-legitimized.

We've got to have more indoctrination. Remember, that's the liberal end of the spectrum. Over to the right wing, you get much harsher things... but that's the intellectual background. We've got to stop "too much democracy," "too much freedom."

The 1960s were always called the "Time of Troubles." That was a time when all this started.

Taibbi: You mention that in the book, that they talked about an "excess of democracy" in terms of the media coverage of Vietnam.

Chomsky: This is the main source of it. When the book came out, I immediately got the MIT library to buy about ten copies, because I figured they were going to put it out of print. *(laughing)*. Which they did. They later printed it again. That's never discussed. I've discussed it a lot.

Taibbi: All of that rhetoric that you're talking about is now resurfacing. We're hearing again about "too much democracy." And there are many discussions about having to rein in the media, really on both sides of the aisle politically.

Chomsky: Yes. It's very much the same.

Taibbi: Well, terrific. Professor, thank you so much.

Chomsky: Thank you.

ACKNOWLEDGMENTS

I'd never have written this book had I not been approached by two enterprising young men, Hamish McKenzie and Chris Best of Substack. Their company has not only given me and other writers a new avenue to independence in an increasingly narrow media landscape, they also allowed me to realize a lifelong dream of writing serialized books.

I'm especially indebted to Hamish, who encouraged the project throughout, promoted it, and even did the boring work of uploading and formatting the chapters, for which I'm grateful.

Colin Robinson, who gave me my start writing books and is the publisher of this one for OR Books, is someone to whom I'm greatly indebted, both personally and professionally. He has helped talk me through some difficult times, and has impacted the world through his books—which often contain his uncredited voice—and through his entrepreneurial wisdom. I use the word entrepreneurial half in jest, to annoy his communist heart.

Obviously there are a great many writers and journalists interviewed in the book to whom I owe a great deal for talking about things that are not always comfortable in this industry. For this I must thank people like Liz Spayd, Thomas Frank, Fred Toettcher, Jane Akre, Nomi Prins, Jeff Cohen, Hunter Pauli, Joan Williams, and many others not quoted by name.

Noam Chomsky, who was generous enough to entertain a re-think of his great book and to grant me time to discuss it, is someone to whom I'm especially grateful. This book, in a way, was also intended as a long thank you to him and to the late Professor Herman, for having written *Manufacturing Consent* in the first place.

I should also thank all the people who've been mentors and teachers in the journalism business. There are so many, from *Rolling Stone's* Jann Wenner, Will Dana, Eric Bates, Jason Fine and Sean Woods to the late Wayne Barrett of the *Village Voice*. One of the great muckrakers in the history of New York, Wayne was my first boss and a friend. I'm glad I got to visit him shortly before his passing and should add, if all journalists have funerals as well attended and heartfelt as his— even his enemies attended in tears—it will mean we're doing something right.

Lastly, however, I want to thank my father, Mike Taibbi. We have had many disagreements over the years and suffered estrangements that lasted years and caused us both considerable pain. I don't think he knows that throughout all of that time, even in the darkest moments, he has always been the ultimate model to me for what a reporter is and should be. I've met most of the biggest names in the business, from the great Seymour Hersh to winners of Oscars and Pulitzers, but none of them hold a candle to my father as a reporter.

I was grateful to have the chance in this book to describe what it was like as a child, experiencing the fascination of watching him work. My father in his time was a famously difficult and combative personality even in public, and if you look you'll find an unfortunate line or two about him (along with quite a few compliments about his work) in various local gossip pages. In Boston he once made the papers, I remember, for refusing to wear socks while he anchored a TV broadcast. Some other items were probably less amusing.

Those who were and are close to him know he was mercurial and magnetic as a younger man, a charmer and joke-teller in one minute, raising a hell of a scene in the next. But as a reporter I never saw him at a loss. To me at least, he seemed completely in control and in his element always, and I wish I'd taken notes watching him over the years, because he was a master of his craft that any young reporter could learn from.

I've already described how he worked the phones. A reporter should love the telephone and my father practically had one glued to his head for decades. He was even better at working scenes in person. Tall, dark, athletic, and engaging, he struck up conversations with everyone and anyone in a heartbeat. To the point of comedy, he was unafraid of barging in and interrupting people.

In a scene my mother and I both remember with a mixture of horror and hilarity, my father once dragged my eight year-old self to the back room of the now-gone Café Pompeii in Boston's North End. This was where the infamous Anguilo family—the top mob crew in New England—used to hang out.

The men back there were chain-smoking and playing some version of *carambole,* a pool game with cigarette butts propped up as obstacles in the middle of the table. My father's pitch was basically, "Hey, my name's Mike. Can my son play?"

The tough guys looked at each other, shrugged, and let me take a few shots. I remember my father talking so fast with a smile that nobody even had time to tell him to shut the fuck up. In hindsight I'm surprised we didn't both end up stuffed in the trunk of a Lincoln. My mother nearly collapsed into her *gelato* in the other room.

This is an extreme example, but the primary skill of any reporter is to break the seal of mistrust with strangers and find common ground. My father's usual method is telling a joke, and while his humor gets mixed reviews—the famed "chef-king of lower Manhattan," Kenny Shopsin, used to give me a discount if I could keep my father from telling a joke to completion—I never once saw it not work, on the level of calming a potential source down and breaking the ice.

It's how he has always been able to go anywhere, from heroin shooting galleries to Afghan villages, and get people to talk to him right away.

Sometimes he would lecture me about the job, and say things like, "The story's the boss." I used to roll my eyes. Now I look back and realize that he really was a purist about the job. He cared deeply about being correct (as opposed to being right), which was one of many things I tried consciously to borrow from him, although in my case it came out more as neurotic terror of being caught in an error.

He would show up at a scene—a fire, a murder, a presidential speech, didn't matter—suss things out, get the right people talking on camera in a snap, and write eight perfect sentences in a matter of minutes. Then he'd read them with perfect diction in a stand-up, zoom back to the station, and sit in the edit room with the techs and cut it up for air on time, every time.

The job at its core is about telling you what, who, when, where, why, and how, as quickly as possible. We are good at this job when we talk to a lot of people, the ones who know, and tell you what they think, not what we think. My father was a master of the people side of this equation, and equally at home with the writing and communication side, where his scripts were and are fast, concise, and evocative.

In the writing of this book I realized often that I was despairing over the devaluing of the job as my father had done it.

There are plenty of people today who do what I do, i.e. write with snark and an eye toward getting a rise out of audiences. But my father's way of doing this job is what's missing. The great misread of 2016 doesn't happen if the bulk of campaign reporters had been as skilled at talking to people from all walks of life as my father.

My old man can't stand Donald Trump, but I guarantee that if you put him in a room with a bunch of Trump voters, within ten minutes he'd have them all telling lawyer jokes or betting on who could throw a football through a tire-swing from twenty yards first. They might not end up agreeing, but he'd hear what they said, directly, and not from some pollster's study.

This is what we lose when we link to things instead of actually communicating with human beings. This job, at its core, should be about talking to people, which no one ever did as well as my first teacher, whom I can never thank enough.